Labour and Employment in a Globalising World

Autonomy, Collectives and Political Dilemmas

P.I.E. Peter Lang

Bruxelles · Bern · Berlin · Frankfurt am Main · New York · Oxford · Wien

Christian AZAÏS (ed.)

Labour and Employment in a Globalising World

Autonomy, Collectives and Political Dilemmas

Acknowledgements to the IRISSO at Paris Dauphine
for their financial support

Éditions scientifiques internationales
Brussels, 2010
1 avenue Maurice, B-1050 Brussels, Belgium
info@peterlang.com; www.peterlang.com

Printed in Germany

ISBN 978-90-5201-658-0
D/2010/5678/65

Library of Congress Cataloging-in-Publication Data
Labour and employment in a globalising world :
autonomy, collectives and political dilemmas / Christian Azaïs (ed.).
p. cm. ISBN 978-90-5201-658-0 1. Labor market. 2. Labor supply.
3. Labor policy. 4. Manpower policy. I. Azaïs, Christian.
HD5706.L2195 2010 331.1--dc22 2010039428

CIP also available from the British Library, GB

Bibliographic information published by "Die Deutsche Nationalbibliothek"
"Die Deutsche Nationalbibliothek" lists this publication in the "Deutsche Nationalbibliografie"; detailed bibliographic data is available on the Internet at <http://dnb.ddb.de>.

Acknowledgements

This book would not have been published without the interest and commitment of many. It is the outcome of four workshops presented at the *International Institute of Sociology 37th World Congress* in Stockholm. It is the product as well of the tenacity of 14 researchers from eight different countries: I would like to thank them for their investment and for joining me in this endeavour.

The project would not have been possible without financing from the IRISSO (Institute of Interdisciplinary Research in Social Sciences-Board) and the support of its two directors, the former director Catherine Bidou and the current one Dominique Damamme, and of Thierry Kirat, as well as the professionalism of Edith Buser, Director of the Office of Research Development at the University of Paris Dauphine. I would particularly like to acknowledge Mariane Georgopoulos, for translating several articles of the book and Donna Kesselman, for her scientific appraisal of the introduction.

I would like to thank Nicolas Chochoy, who contributed the poignant South-North picture from Beijing and Benoît Fleury, with the North-South picture from Paris, both appearing on the cover.

Many thanks to Sandra Kuzniak and Muriel Legardien, from PIE Peter Lang, for their generous time and attention to the crucial technical aspects.

Any remaining flaws, of course, are my own.

Christian Azaïs

Table of Contents

PART III. INDIVIDUAL AUTONOMY *VS.* COLLECTIVE RESPONSIBILITY IN A WORLD OF FLEXIBLE LABOUR

PART III. A. AUTONOMY AT WORK

PART III. B. AUTONOMY AND CAPITALISM

INTRODUCTION

Labour and Employment in a Globalising World

Christian AZAÏS[1]

Recent transformations in work and employment in developed countries may well be reproducing situations once typical of the developing world. Flexibility and corporate decision-making autonomy, recasting of workers' rights and trade union roles are now firmly embedded on public policy agendas. These challenges depend on the ability of social actors to impact labour markets and the scope of their influence. *Labour and Employment in a Globalising World: Autonomy, collectives and political dilemmas* is a collection of essays which explore topical issues regarding work and employment from South to North. The book contextualises South-North comparisons within globalisation and converging patterns as one of its component parts. The postulate poses globalisation as a force of both standardisation and differentiation. Institutional and negotiating models standardise as they accommodate autonomous work tendencies and legal grey zones. The forms they take differ with regards to national and historical particularities.

The South-North political paradigm is innovative and also engenders a paradox: growing disparities and irregularities within labour and employment markets tend, as well, to converge. This does not, however, preclude conflict, for the process of differentiation dominates the one of standardisation, both being characteristic traits of modern day capitalism. The paradigm is political as it impacts the workplace and beyond, society in the broad sense. It is a driving force of globalisation.

This introduction endeavours to illustrate how political globalisation contextualises labour and employment. It is a more realistic depiction than the reductionist economic construct. It then lays out the book's content and initiates a pluridisciplinary debate through the problematical approaches of the authors.

---

[1] This introduction would not be what it is without the remarkable and sharp dedication and generosity of my friend and colleague Donna Kesselman. Let her be sincerely and deeply thanked for the rewriting job. Mariane Georgopoulos translated several articles from French to English. A great *merci* to her.

When Globalisation Sheds Light on Politics

Globalisation is a comprehensive process of multi-level social, economic and political interdependencies. The "local", nonetheless, is of particular relevancy.

Globalisation is said to heighten market competition, as it punctuates the world's economies. Thus Suzanne Berger underscores "the changes in the international economy and in domestic economies that are moving toward creating one world market [...] To make this term [globalisation] a useful one, it needs to be pared down to the core idea, which is the emergence of a single world market for labour, capital, goods and services". And she continues: "a more concrete definition of globalisation, then, is the acceleration of the processes in the international economy and in domestic economies that operate toward unifying world markets" (Berger, 2006: 9). The definition is too static. For Saskia Sassen (2002), globalisation is the equivalent of hyper-mobility: international networks of communication and the elimination of problems inherent in distance and localisations. It's the spatial dimension which is emphasised here. Globalisation does transform the spatial and socio-economic scales of regulation (Swyngedouw, 2000). But this movement does not contradict the local dimension as enterprises continue to depend upon territories and their human capital, they are not mere predators of lower labour costs. The quality of the labour force – its education standards, skills and adaptability –, institutional stability and reactivity are conditions of sustainable economic development.

Globalisation is political as it incites *glocal* interactions and interdependencies. It is neither a 'win-win' nor a 'win-lose' relationship, but impacts the way groups act, interact and assimilate ongoing transformations. Appropriate tools are needed to apprehend its repercussions upon work and employment in their respective national environments.

Globalisation is paradoxical precisely because these phenomena cannot be standardised. Its differentiations are as much contextual as they are analytical because they are perceived from multiple viewpoints. (Assayag, 2005). Global and local are not contradictory, the *glocal* is inherently comprehensive. The *viewpoints* are conditioned by the factors advanced to justify a particular problematical stance. For example, the ideology of neoliberal market regulation reduces all social processes to their economic component and relegates the other dimensions of capitalism – ecology, culture, politics, civil society – to "the sway of the world-market system", whose defining trait is what Ulrich Beck calls "globalism" (Beck, 2000b: 100). According to "globalism", an economy which engulfs all other single societal phenomena modifies one's perception of reality. When praising globalisation, neoliberal economists point to the expansion of world trade and take for granted Montesquieu's statement: "trade smoothes *mora*". They subsequently call for opening up all borders towards inexorable world-market consolidation. Trade is viewed as the ultimate vehicle of world-wide wealth distribution. Whether economics is a justifiably dominant doctrine with regards to market interactions is not at issue here, but that one must not, as Beck reminds us, disregard the other dimensions of capitalism, notably politics, which neoliberal theory tends to take for granted.

Globalisation obliges the researcher to change her/his own naturally bilateral viewpoint as is cogently illustrated by Uzbek's premise, borrowed from Montesquieu's *Les Lettres persanes*, that globalisation is in essential conflict with ethnocentrism. When she studies the young Turkish population in Germany and their behaviour towards religion and dress codes, Valérie Amiraux concludes that they adopt a new "*façon d'être*" – self identity – which is just as *valid* as that of the kemalian period. Her starting point differs from typical Euro-centric thematics (Amiraux, 2002 in Giraud, 2007: 394). The same is true for Jackie Assayag when he examines globalisation and its impact upon India (Assayag, 2005). Both analyses emphasise distinct and interacting logics that cannot be reduced to the economy. They help to comprehend the various dimensions of globalisation, which are inexorably intertwined while not identical, once the thread of politics is pulled.

In this way, David Held *et al.* highlight the distinction between hyperglobalists, transformationalists and sceptics (Held *et al.*, 1999: 10). The former conceive globalisation as the dawn of a new age (Ohmae, 1990), arising from the erosion of national-state potency. The nation-state is a thing of the past, bowing to technology and capitalism as the new driving force of the world market. Today's actuality of systemic crisis and the renewed assertion of sovereign authority reveals the flaws in this view.

Transformationalists argue that interconnectedness has reached heretofore unattained heights. The nation-state's power has declined. Globalisation is a transformative medium of state ascendancy and world politics and thus converges in both integration and fragmentation of intermediate spaces (Held *et al.*, 2000).

By comparison sceptics point to the persistent prevalence of states and markets (Hirst, Thompson, 1999). They acknowledge and promote the dual movement of internationalisation and regionalisation, while disputing the claim that globalisation actually produces any radical change. National predominance and sovereignty prevail.

More recently, in his definition of globalisation, Olivier Giraud enhances the centrality of the nation-state, be it as the prerequisite vehicle for engendering any form of new world organisation or for grasping the meaningful consequences of its decline. In any case globalisation is a challenge the state and the nation must grapple with. As Non-Governmental Organisations (NGO), transnational actors, interrelations, Internet, mafias, etc., increasingly occupy the political sphere they broaden the scope of state jurisdiction and, to the least, concern. Thus, globalisation is complex for it remains the "central producer of politics" (Giraud, 2007), but not the only one: "Globalisation [...] denotes the *processes* through which sovereign national states are criss-crossed and undermined by transnational actors with varying prospects of power, orientations, identities and networks" (Beck, 2000b: 101).

Globalisation can also be discerned through interlocking characteristics at all levels – international, national or regional..., as Giraud observes: "Globalisation is a dynamic more counterposed to the national framework than bound to it" (Giraud, 2005: 113). This view highlights the role of the state as a conveyer of changing power relations, as illustrated by Held *et al.* (1999): "Sandwiched between global forces and local demands, national governments are having to reconsider their roles and functions". Then Giraud explains globalisation's three fundamental impacts: "First, it accentuates the transformative power dynamics of the main political actors in their national setting. It simultaneously bolsters the international diffusion of new ideas, schemes of interaction, frames of reference. Finally, it comforts emerging paradigms of political regulation which embody international collective action"[2] (Giraud, 2005: 106-107). The following contributions express the functioning of the "international diffusion of new ideas" and relevant political regulations with regards to work and employment.

Globalisation correlates at once to a "broadening, deepening and speeding up of world-wide interconnectedness in all aspects of life" (Held *et al.*, 2000). This includes political life in nation-states, turning them into 'decision takers' instead of 'decision makers'. Therefore, globalisation does not simply reflect increasingly transnational economic and non-economic relations. It implies emerging types of structures and coexisting processes (Mayntz, 1998: 8).

Globalisation is also a "process (or set of processes) which embodies a transformation in the spatial organisation of social relations and transactions, generating transcontinental or interregional flows and networks of activity, interaction and power" (Held *et al.*, 1999). According to

---

2 The Swiss case referred to by Giraud in this book illustrates this hypothesis. "En premier lieu, elle renvoie à la transformation des rapports de pouvoir des principaux acteurs intervenant au sein même des systèmes politiques nationaux. (...) la globalisation est également associée au renforcement de la diffusion internationale de nouvelles idées, modèles d'action, cadres de référence. (...) Enfin, la globalisation renvoie à une série de nouvelles régulations politiques qui sont l'expression d'une action collective internationale".

Göran Therborn (2000: 154), globalisation illustrates "tendencies to a world-wide reach, impact, or connectedness of social phenomena or to a world-encompassing awareness among social actors". As the concept thus englobes several processes, Therborn proposes it be used in the plural: *globalisations*.

Defining globalisation as a 'universalising' phenomenon occasions the re-invention of differences (Assayag, 2005: 19-20). In fact, globalisation and the supposed modernity it triggers (Beck, 2000a; Serksnyte, below) are the complex result of multiple and previous interactions. Some of them are obvious; some are obscure or laying in wait. Thus, globalisation is a composite of contradictory processes which proceed in multiple directions and ways (Assayag, 2005: 271).

In this fabric of "increasing diversity" (Assayag, 2005), a multiplicity of problematic anchor points combine to apprehend globalisation as a single process of standardisation and differentiation, the approach adopted in this book. It entails as well a tendency to individuation: the individual is individual thanks to her/his *dialogical* relation to the group (Assayag, 2005: 295), thus expanding upon the economics-based, ideologically reductionist paradigms.

The field of work and employment globalisation impacts the way subjectivities and identities are re-calibrated; how they are part of us, of our certainties and expectations. It is simultaneously creative and destructive, expressed through "accommodations and adaptations, translations and appropriations, and even interbreeding and hybridisations" (Assayag, 2005: 276).

Thus, globalisation reinforces the *glocal* sphere, and herein lies the general statement of this book. Globalisation is at the core of the work and employment debate through its plethora of forms and contractual relations. They are inclined to converge in an overlapping space between developing and developed countries. As an economic, political and social phenomenon our analysis draws upon the relevant interdisciplinary literature, various national case studies and thematic perspectives. Its unity stems from the central function of politics in all these realms.

Our analysis of current trends structures globalisation's impact into three main themes, from macro to micro perspective, each advancing its particular conceptual blueprint. The first outlines what has changed in labour market policies; the second, in labour-management negotiations, the last is more work-centred; focusing upon autonomy at work and the evolutions of the capitalist workplace.

The articles concur in their critical stance towards neo-liberal acceptance of globalisation. Economic and social thought has primarily dealt with four major concerns: "the present form of world economy; the dominant regime of capitalist accumulation; the modes and effectiveness of contemporary economic governance; and the robustness of national economic autonomy and sovereignty" (Held McGrew, 2000: 19). These concerns are applied to work and employment in the articles here. The perspectives they propose from the South as from the North thus provide partial but contextualised visions from wide-ranging disciplinary angles.

This book is not a comparative work *stricto sensu*; term-to-term comparisons tend to compartmentalise social phenomena, with often ethnocentric overtones. Work and employment are the products of societal structuring and can rarely be removed from their original settings without the risk of distorting their substance. When international comparisons are carried out they most often remain embedded within their national labour markets. This partially explains the difficulties encountered in the formulation of European Union employment policies.[3]

The selected authors demonstrate how societies and cultures are impacted by the transformative dynamics of politics. Developing countries appear to be winning the cut-throat "race to the bottom" for lower wages and labour costs. Has globalisation thus altered the content of workers' exploitation? While these and other processes are of global scope, are not they structured by local constraints, such as labour force composition and labour-management institutions?

Globalisation enhances flexibilisation and casualisation in contemporary societies,[4] but also differentiation among groups of workers. The concept of *hybridisation* introduces a spatial dimension which helps us grasp this phenomenon. Typical of post-industrial societies, it is closely linked to the emergence of new forms of work and widening wage scale differentials that result in individualisation. What used to be a characteristic of developing countries is ever more frequently encountered in developed ones.[5] *Hybridisation* reflects the intertwining patterns of

---

[3] The rejection of the European Constitutional Treaty by the French electorate in 2005 is basically due to its 3rd part, dealing with social reforms and neo-liberal policies with regards to labour markets and welfare systems. The lack of political vision has also been attributed to referendum's defeat.

[4] Gray uses the concept of "flexploitation" (Gray, 2004). However, "precarisation" was the term preferred in the call for the 11th Biennial French International Sociology of Work Conference (JIST 2007 London): "Restructuring, precarisation and value".

[5] In France, for instance, the steadiness of the wage distribution has changed in the last years. The wage *per capita* tends to increase, slowly but differently among workers. For example, during the 1998-2005 period, the wage increase rate reached 1% for the P090-P100 deciles and 6.1% for the last 99th one, which corresponds to a 50% variation during the period. The gap between the highest and the lowest wages has come to a peak, which strengthens the thesis of a globalisation sealed with differentiation and flexibilisation, *i.e.* the so-called hybridisation (Azaïs, Carleial, 2010).

individual insertion in the labour market. It encompasses flexibilisation and casualisation and leaves its mark upon employment contracts. As a process, hybridisation illustrates how new work or contractual structures grow out of pre-existing forms and crystallize new categories of individual engagement. More than the simple combination of situations, hybridisation is a social "construction" in a globalising world and intervenes at various levels. It is a dynamic process of continuous adaptation, training and learning, which are proper to globalisation. It is also testimony to the fact that there can be no transposition of so-called models given the prevalence of societal and national conditions and their specificities. It signifies that transformations underway worldwide and encompassing entire economic sectors and territories generate reactions – local and global – and sustain the principle of differentiation as globalisation's core trend. In this sense, hybridisation depicts the diversity of situations workers are engaged in, and can be considered as one of its characteristic traits.

Several previously commonplace assumptions in Europe and other developed countries have since been called into question. One is the consensus around the pertinence of attempting to sustain a wage-earning society, founded upon the longstanding employment relationship, intimately linked to institutionalised social protection. This welfare state, which took years to reach maturity, has been subject to criticism in recent years. Despite predictions to the contrary, however, the welfare state has retained its function as the main social provider despite, as will be shown here, it's accommodation to the far-reaching effects of workfare. Several papers focus on this timely issue, mainly through the lens of activation policies.

This contrasts to the situation of countries in the South. First of all, the emergence of late capitalism (alternately christened as "underdeveloped" or "less developed" or even "developing") prevented labour markets from fully functioning as a social integrator, even when the wage-earning employment relationship had crystallised and become significantly generalised. This structuration, however, was unable to coalesce strong collective forces to protect vast numbers of workers. Mathias's expression "restricted wage-earning relation" (1987) renders such a relationship, as one which embodies a particular content. Consequently, at a time when the welfare state social contract is being brought into question in Northern countries, it is worth questioning whether a comparable process is underway in the South, and thus the applicability of this hypothesis in these countries.

The ubiquity of informal activities suggests that the status of work in countries of the South has not followed an identical trail as in the North. The comparison of these trajectories is a major contribution of our work.

Furthermore, while we have chosen to adopt a simplified South/North distinction, each group of countries is composite so that no overall welfare state concept can apply. No all-encompassing definition can account for the multitude of experience, be it South or North. The contribution of this book and each of its articles highlights singular but converging features of globalisation in the labour market's various realms.

The book is divided into three parts. Each one focuses upon relevant national transformations in globalised labour markets. Can the South help us better apprehend impending transformative trends in the world of labour? To answer this question, the contributions shed light upon critical dimensions of globalisation through the lens of political review.

Structure of the book

Each part invites authors to comment upon timely issue related to work or employment. The contributors come from a variety of countries (Australia, Brazil, Finland, France, Germany and the USA) and academic backgrounds (Economics, Law, Philosophy, Political Science, Psychology and Sociology). Their fields of investigation include the countries mentioned above in addition to Denmark, Italy, Sweden and Switzerland, but not all contributions deal with a particular national case study. Some are more theoretical and transcend a single geographic or spatial sphere. The plurality of approaches is in itself a component of our hypothesis that globalisation is differentiated through its various analytical viewpoints.

Three main interrogations are raised respectively within each of the corresponding parts. The issues, though, are interrelated and differentially linked within a globalising labour market which has no strictly defined South-North border distinctions.

Part 1

The first part, entitled *Legal frameworks: What has changed in labour market policies?* investigates work and employment through institutional approaches to public policy, and more particularly activation policies. The three articles cover five countries – Brazil, Switzerland, Denmark, Finland and Sweden – in the complementary disciplines of economy, politics and law. Their broad-spectrum political approach is essential to understanding how local actors digest global employment trends and help reveal some of the differences they entail for countries be they South or North.

Starting with Brazil, Liana Maria da Frota Carleial, in her contribution, "The Brazilian Labour Market: Structural Features, 'New' Flexibilisation and Recent Performance", studies the constitution of this labour market. The historical overview insists upon how the adoption of a neo-liberal agenda in the early 1990s resulted in fragmentation, deregulation and privatisation. These trends continued during President Lula's first administration when, during its first two years in power (2002-2004), the new left-wing government pursued essentially the same policies as the previous administration.

Carleial traces her argument from the early 20th century to the 1990s, when Brazil introduced its neo-liberal agenda and flexibilisation became the overriding trait of the already casual Brazilian labour market. The labour market reforms introduced during the Cardoso administrations (1994-1997 and 1998-2001) were adopted without having to amend formally existing labour law. To do so, the former government used *ad-hoc* congressional manoeuvres and the growing incidence of common law jurisprudence in favour of labour market flexibilisation. Under popular pressures for democracy neither President Cardoso nor his successor, President Lula, could initiate reforms without first working out consensus among the country's main institutional actors – employer associations, trade unions and, at times, Parliament.[6] The central government thus played its traditional role of arbiter among conflicting social interests.

As for labour market trends in most developing countries, Brazil has been a social laboratory for the flexibility and casualisation which has now attained developed countries. For Carleial their root cause lies in what he terms the incomplete welfare state, thereby establishing a causal relationship with the degree of development.

When examining "The effects of activation measures on disadvantaged jobseekers' rights and obligations in Denmark, Finland and Sweden", Paul Van Aerschot spells out common features in activation policies, for training and other back-to-work programmes for jobseekers typify today's "shift from rights to obligations".

As they are essentially geared to opening labour markets such measures have uncertain results in terms of employment. For van Aerschot, a fine line exists between the sanctions imposed to enforce compulsory participation and the violation of a recipient's elementary worker rights. He proposes instead programmes designed to facilitate labour market entry for people with reduced employability through the creation or subsidising of specifically tailored jobs. Work-orientations should take into account the jobseeker's overall needs, which are not limited to employment and not treat them as mere *clients*. The approach exposes

6 Although President Cardoso's governments (1994-2001) frequently resorted to *Medidas Provisórias* (decree-laws adopted without the vote of the legislative branch).

the gap between current practice and official public policy and provides an interpretation of globalisation in terms of contrasting cultural awareness. It also points to incipient modifications in the very nature of state institutions as in state theory.

Moreover, much as in the Brazilian case, tendencies towards more individualised treatment are manifest. This is to some extent due to employment agency preferences for more individual-centred missions, adapted to jobseeker's particular skills and abilities. For van Aerschot, these reforms have repercussions upon jobseekers' labour market positioning and the personal decisions she or he must take. The shift from a collective rights (or what the author calls "administrative-legal decision-making") to an individual-based approach violates previously existing rights to privacy and equal treatment. Indeed, individualised measures are not always suited to jobseekers' specific needs due to uncertainties derived from broad discretionary measures. Interactions between the jobseeker and frontline decision-maker matter, as does the role of intermediaries and the increased job-market flexibility the measures incur.

In this context, Switzerland is a specific case where federal law is rooted in precedents and enforced at both local (*canton*) and global/national, scales. In "Implementing the new Swiss employment policies in the context of globalisation" Olivier Giraud distinguishes between the *good* cantons, *i.e.*, those implementing orthodox orientations, and the *bad* ones, which do not. The author examines the factors taken into account by cantons in the political choices they make and suggests that each canton enjoys some degree of leeway. The way each canton practically adapts federal employment decisions is a test-case of Swiss federalism and, at the meso level, of the main actors and political decision-makers in the employment arena. A specialist in cross-country studies, Giraud portrays executive federalism in Switzerland, especially the political determinants of transposing Federal Unemployment Insurance Law (LACI) to the canton level. This study depicts interactions between multi-level governance and generalised employment activation policies in Europe, the intricate relationship which articulates employment policy sanction and integration.

This book's first part opts for a macro analysis of labour policy and market structuration that conceives globalisation as a concrete construction. Each article presents, in its own way, the roadmaps countries adopt to navigate within an increasingly flexible world of work. Brazil, where work and employment flexibility have taken on substantial proportions, even for developing countries, is taken as a reference case. The main thesis is that labour market practices in a country like Brazil may be forerunners of mid- or longer term developments in developed countries. In other words, can Southern countries be termed as large-scale "social laboratories" for metamorphoses underway? The authors have adopted several criteria to test this hypothesis, such as the impact of the change of scale in Switzerland: labour policies are primarily driven by the cantons with only minimal Federal intervention, thus punctuating the significance of the local.

Some elements of convergence emerge from the case studies. Neo-liberal agendas are implemented in all countries, though more so in Brazil than in Switzerland, Denmark, Finland or Sweden, and all labour market policies have implemented some form of activation. The state is the key player. Citizens are termed as 'clients', forced to improve their own personal employability in order to obtain social benefits when applying for vocational training. The European Employment Strategy, as put forward by the OMC – Open Method of Co-ordination, includes various mediations opening to alternative processes and result in their uniformisation. This clearly shows that diverse mediations produce different arrangements and therefore that globalisation in employment matters does not obey a unique purpose (Zeitlin and Pochet, 2005).

What distinguishes the three contributions is the particular configuration of the role of the state. The Brazilian state can hardly be compared to its Danish, Finnish, Swiss equivalents, mainly due to their specific historical developments and positioning in international political, economic and social relations.

Methodologically, in their respective approach as to the Brazilian and the Scandinavian cases, the texts by Carleial and van Aerschot are macro-oriented, while Giraud combines macro and meso concerns at both federal and canton levels. He thus paves the way for Part 2. While employment policies are the centre of concern of the first part, the second marks a change of scale, towards the local state and firm levels in Brazil and France. Our focus in this part is labour and management relations. It sets the terms of the debate around today's workplace, which will be developed in the final part.

Part 2

Decentralisation and specialisation of labour and employer associations: emerging negotiation paradigms turns around two main issues: decentralisation and specialisation. One has a spatial dimension while the other, an organisational one. The contributions analyse the way negotiations take place at the micro level, since the adoption of new management principles by firms and, at macro and meso levels, through the implementation of France's recent industrial policy of "poles of competitiveness" (*pôles de compétitivité*). The difference of scale between labour-management interactions, on the one hand, and the mainly top-down governmental approach, on the other, elucidates the impact of state employment policies in a deregulating labour market.

The authors – a sociologist and an economist – outline the political challenges faced by both firms and governments. Paola Cappellin, "Entrepreneur associations and trade unions: towards a merging of the labour policy agenda?", spells out the new dilemma for firms, virtually compelled to integrate financial imperatives when establishing human resources policies. She borrows from Northern American literature when adapting the concept of 'social responsibility' to Brazilian business associations and organisations, and how they internalize these concerns. She then looks at corporate social practices in the state of Rio de Janeiro and how trade unions relate to corporate social responsibility (CSA). While a product of global market competition, the forms of social responsibility vary, especially according to the size of firms. She also portrays CSA as an expression of growing interdependency between corporate and social actors which neither party can afford to avoid. Cappellin situates her argument between employment and labour, thereby announcing the major concerns of part 3 which specifically deals with work issues.

Through his analysis of French industrial policy, Jacques Perrat's piece "Territorialised industrial policies and new spatial divisions of labour: what is at stake for socio-economic actors?", deals with labour market regulation and, in doing so, covers both spatial and organisational spheres. For Perrat there has been a shift from a functional division of labour, typical of the Fordist period, to a mix of horizontal differentiation of localised blocks of skills that have an impact on territorial rating. He is particularly preoccupied with the repercussions this has on workplace conditions. The author then looks at the alternative strategies adopted by trade unions to face these challenges.

Both Cappellin and Perrat emphasise the meso level and the growing interactions between firms and trade unions, just as the key role the latter are playing in the globalising labour market. Their articles bridge the gap between shopfloor and institutional considerations of the evolution of modern-day capitalism. They conclude with the observation that worker autonomy is among its major trends, which transitions us to the book's third and final part.

Part 3

Individual autonomy vs. collective responsibility in a flexible world of work takes on the issue in a strict sense, the core of labour issues studied here. Seven authors address concrete experiences of autonomy at work and place them in the broader context of contemporary capitalism.

The reflexion opposes individual autonomy and collective responsibility and dwells upon the meaning of this autonomy in a flexible world of work. Concepts such as *atomisation* and *controlled* (or *conceded*) *autonomy* are explored. They are illustrated though themes such as "Autonomy at work", on the shopfloor and "Autonomy and capitalism" at more globalising labour market levels. Both offer insights into what is actually changing in the world labour market and how practices in the South are likely markers for future developments in the North. Nevertheless no generalisation can be definitively drawn from the sole example of Brazil.

The cases described in chapter "Autonomy at work", by two sociologists and two economists refer to the United States, France and Italy in the North, and to Brazil in the South. Related articles in the following chapter B, "Autonomy in capitalism", are more general, even if Germany is portrayed as a prominent reference case.

Autonomy at work

In his contribution, "Autonomy, general working capacity and collective action", Patrick Dieuaide explores the deeper meaning of "autonomy". The term is used indiscriminately to refer to what in fact are distinct phenomena: the "worker's own initiative" to act, autonomy defined by the hierarchy (what he calls "managerial injunction"), or the "professional autonomy" of the specialist who "owns" her/his own skills and know-how. In this sense, Dieuaide's piece introduces the discussion pursued by Cinara Rosenfield. Both agree that the polysemy of the word "autonomy" complicates the task of analysing it. Dieuaide defines autonomy less in terms of control or prescription than as workers' appropriation of the conception and execution of their own acts. Autonomy cannot – or can no longer – be perceived merely in terms of leeway, but as a set of 'abilities to act'. In contemporary capitalism, workers are called upon to be wholly – body and soul – devoted to their work. Work as a dynamic and cooperative process incorporates the cognitive sphere. Its governance supposes new rules of management founded upon knowledge as an intermediary objective for the workers themselves and not an *in se* process.

In the same way, based on field research in Brazil and Portugal Cinara Rosenfield argues in "Informational worker autonomy: freedom or control?" that autonomy at work is a composite notion, one which contains both freedom and control. Her meaningful expression of 'conceded autonomy' – *autonomia outorgada* – contends that in Information and Communication Technologies (ICT), and especially in teleworking (among autonomous and wage-earning teleworkers), conditions do not fundamentally differ from the fordist period. In the current well-established information-age, scenarios in Portugal and Brazil are comparable, in spite of the unequal degrees of national development. Rosenfield concludes that deskilled and repetitive work is not the privilege of fordist workers; similarly, work in ICT is not as creative and autonomous as one might assume. In both cases, workers are subordinated, nevertheless information labourers ought to "be at the same time subjects and work in cooperation". As a figure which is imposed, conceded autonomy implies that "the end justifies the means" (Azaïs, 2004). Flexibility, in terms of "time, place, contract, subordination, functional organisation" (Rosenfield), is the guiding principle of telework. Hence she defines it as "an element of the strategic organisational changes that point to new forms of flexible work taken by ICT". The point is not to determine who, between the teleworker and the fordist worker, is the most flexible or autonomous. The answer may be found, beyond the boundaries of economics, within the logic of values and the quest for meaning, given that "conceded autonomy is part of an instrumental logic". Implicitly suggested here is Appay's observation, over a decade ago (1997), which stressed the importance of controlled autonomy in the workplace. The phenomenon does not refer to an individual's particular positioning but refers to the restructurations of labour market organisation, thereby placing the *precarisation* of work at the core of a more comprehensive social reality (Appay, 2005; Azaïs, 2007). The frontier between the subordinated and the autonomous worker is thus not easy to ascertain and contingent.

In "Subordination or autonomy? The hybridisation of the labour market: the Italian case" Christian Azaïs takes a similar approach when attempting to apprehend the distinction between subordination and autonomy. His concept of *hybridisation* illustrates how different kinds of contract constructions intertwine with the shifting nature of work relations. The concept is specifically applied here to the Italian case, and to a particular type of labour contract, the *co.co.co.*, *collaborazione coordinate e continuativa* (coordinated and continuous collaboration). He recalls how the *parasubordinazione*, as referred to in Italian scholarship, denotes a grey zone between subordination and autonomy. It is telling illustration of *hybridisation* and of current labour market evolutions. The diversity of contracts in the Italian experience foreshadow modifications of previously assumed European distinctions between 'remunerated life' and 'non remunerated' life' (Bologna, Fumagalli, 1997). As Azaïs underscores, "reality is more complex than the simple separation between dependent and independent work" (Azaïs, 2004). Indeed, the labour market is comprised of multiple configurations of employment status, the most prominent trait being their diversity and the ever-diminishing lack of job security. What makes the wage-earning relationship a hybrid one is the establishment of informality as an embedded labour market component.

Now that it has reached the very heart of wage-earning employment, informalisation has transformed it into a hybrid relationship. This is the emblematic link with the South.

Laima Serksnyte-Sappington's, "New organisational realities: individualisation and atomisation in the organisations of 'second modernity'" describes how firms have incorporated mutations within their organisational structures. According to Serksnyte, the so-called 'First Modernity' period, during which rationality prevailed, was followed by the "Second Modernity" (Beck, 2000a): the accelerated and flexible techno-scientific development of firms, their ability to appropriate new products and processes, and the shifting human perception towards ever greater task differentiation and training. The changes she points out are not specific to work, but also correspond to overall market adaptations that firms are compelled to undertake. Uncertainty, "dissolving rigid role-based practices and pre-established social and economic expectations" makes the Second Modernity worker "increasingly flexible, fairly autonomous, trainable, multi-tasking, able to cross diverse knowledge sets and embrace risks, while simultaneously coping with change". The author analyses what she terms the *new* Second Modernity period employee. However, while the "new employee" is called upon to make exceptional efforts, firms apparently remain more reluctant to adapt their own practices. They prefer to autonomise employees, thereby erode their collective responsibility, while maintaining a top-down hierarchical organisation, leaving less freedom to and thus depreciating individual initiatives.

Serksnyte's conclusions are not too far from Cappellin's: both insist upon a certain reluctance of firms to keep up with the times and embrace new behaviours, while in the meantime expecting employees to consistently adapt.

This chapter focuses upon current work and labour market experience and their impact upon individuals. The case studies confirm the thesis of labour market hybridisation, the intricacies of working conditions and contracts with regards to corporate practices that announce major metamorphoses of capitalism.

Autonomy and Capitalism

The moot question of *Autonomy and Capitalism* is explored here through a multidisciplinary approach to three contributions, those of a philosopher, of the collaboration among specialists of industrial relations, political economy and sociology, and finally of a psychologist. Their contributions each develop various features of globalisation.

In his "Limits of fulfilment in an age of flexibility: changes in Management semantics and the critique of capitalism", *Christoph Henning probes the lack of proximity of a number of concepts* originating in managerial discourse and which are transposed *ipsis litteris* in the social sciences. This becomes an obstacle for the researcher, whose scientific method must begin with sufficient distance. Henning is concerned about the proliferation of management concepts in the social sciences and their inability to stimulate critical dynamics for they are in essential contradiction with social theory. The only solution is to return to erstwhile concepts – including "social class", "exploitation", "alienation" – in *lieu* of importing ill adapted concepts from other fields, whose logical underpinnings can in no way guarantee the "future of a critical theory". As for autonomy, he argues that "instrumentalised autonomy is not autonomy proper". The language of individual autonomy must therefore be reconstructed without sacrificing its scholarly content, as semantic evolutions do not automatically coincide with actual occurrences in the workplace. Language may also reflect shifts in societal self-perceptions or possibly underlying power structures. In order to avoid the pitfall of being disproportionately economics-orientated its perspective it must be essentially political. In this sense, he enlarges in his piece upon Rosenfield's hypothesis on autonomy in favour of a rigorous conceptualisation of globalising labour patterns.

Interested in the changes in work regulation, David Peetz's and Georgina Murray's piece, "Ideology Down Under and the Shifting Sands of Individualism" applies these arguments to transformations in industrial relations. They see the now common wisdom discourse of individualised behaviour as inherently dismissive of the workers collective culture. This elite ideology is subject to overstatement and does not necessarily have equivalents in popular culture or popular ideology.

Taking the example of the Australian capitalist class, they explain how its main representatives – organisers (employer associations and think-tanks), executives and interlocking directorates – are the key architects of this transformative process. These actors create and propagate individualistic ideology amongst elite groups and within the state. The authors contrast this process to shifts of popular opinion with regards to industrial relations and related issues. They conclude that: "the revolution in workplace regulation is an adaptation to the interference of elite, not popular ideology". They convincingly portray a workplace which remains an arena of social dispute, perceived through the light of antagonistic political interests shed by globalisation.

In the book's last contribution, "Public sectors becoming a flexible labour world: consequences for the employees", Kerstin Wüstner examines the globalised workplace through its consequences upon increasingly flexible structures for public employees. Her findings derive from a survey carried out in a city council in Germany and analysis of private and public sector practices. The specific question is whether job performance of public employees in flexible settings significantly differs from performance of those working in "traditional" public sector environment. Wuestner defines a typology of five prototypical situations which reflect how individuals experience employment: job satisfaction, burnout, distress, autonomy and eustress. Her conclusions on the differences between employees in flexible and "traditional" workplaces shed light upon the pertinent factors and corporate organisational strategies which impact working conditions. The findings can be applied to France and help to understand, for instance, tragic occurrences when white-collar employees were driven to committing suicide. Their act must not be considered an individual but a collective one. It is a reassertion of group responsibility and refutes the claim of increasing workplace autonomy as a unilateral gain which is cherished by workers.

The political dilemmas induced by a globalising world of work is at the heart of our concerns in this collective endeavour. How are social actors engaged in these ongoing transformations? How do legal frameworks adapt through innovative contractual constructions? How should they be re-interpreted in various contexts? How can one formulate a South to North paradigm, given that analytical categories differ or do not cover identical realities from one country to the next? These problematic threads help weave the articles published here into an emerging research agenda.

Our editorial intent enhances the wealth of social science investigation on the global marketplace and the interdisciplinary debate launched here. Each of the contributions responds to forces for change, be they restructuration, deregulation or innovation, in an age of accelerated pace. They impact economies and societies, whatever their degree of alleged maturity. The contributors confirm our basic hypothesis of politics as the variable which articulates a coherent, if not unified, object of comparison. The theoretical framework has yet to be built.

References

Appay, B., "Social *Précarisation* and Controlled Autonomy. Contradictions within the Changing Production Systems", in *Work quo vadis? Re-thinking the question of work.* Holmer and Karlsson. Aldershot, Brookfield USA, Singapore, Sydney: Ashgate, 1997, pp. 319-330.

Appay, B., *La dictature du succès. Le paradoxe de l'autonomie contrôlée et de la précarisation*, Paris, L'Harmattan, Collection Logiques Sociales, 2005.

Assayag, J., *La mondialisation vue d'ailleurs – l'Inde désorientée*, Paris, Seuil, 2005.

Azaïs, Ch., "Transformations du travail: éléments de comparaison France/ Brésil", *Restructurations productives, précarisation, valeurs*, XIe Journées Internationales de Sociologie du Travail, JIST 2007, Londres, 20-22 juin 2007, www.jist2007.org.

Azaïs, Ch., "De-segmentação do mercado de trabalho e autonomia: algumas palavras introdutórias", *Caderno CRH*, Centro de Recursos Humanos, Universidade Federal da Bahia, Salvador (Brazil), Vol. 17, No. 41, Mai-Ago, 2004, pp. 15-24.

Azaïs, Ch. and Carleial, L., "L'hybridation, caractéristique contemporaine des marchés du travail? Analyse à partir des cas français et brésilien", submitted to *Revue Tiers-Monde*.

Bayart, J.-F., *Le gouvernement du monde – Une critique politique de la globalisation*, Paris, Fayard, 2004.

Beck, U., *The Brave New World of Work*, Cambridge, Polity Press, 2000a.

Beck, U., *"What is globalisation?"*, Cambridge/Oxford, Polity Press/Blackwell Publishers, 2000b, pp. 99-103.

Berger, S., *How we Compete: What Companies around the World are Doing to Make it in Today's Global Economy?*, New York, Currency Doubleway, 2006.

Bologna, S. and Fumagalli, A., "Dieci tesi per la definizione di uno statuto del lavoro autonomo", in S. Bologna and A. Fumagalli, *Il lavoro autonomo di seconda generazione. Scenari del postfordismo in Italia*, Milano, Feltrinelli, 1997, pp. 16-23.

Giraud, O., "A globalização vista do Norte e do Sul: quais seus mecanismos sociais?", *Revista do CRH, Globalização e Trabalho*, Salvador, No. 51, 2007, pp. 389-399.

Giraud, O., "Nation et globalisation: mécanismes de constitution des espaces politiques pertinents et comparaisons internationales", in J.-C. Barbier and M.-T. Letablier (dir.) *Politiques sociales – Enjeux méthodologiques et épistémologiques des comparaisons internationales*, Bruxelles, PIE Peter Lang, 2005, pp. 95-115.

Gray, A., *Unsocial Europe: Social Protection or Flexploitation?*, London, Pluto Press, 2004.

Held, D., McGrew, A. (eds.), *The Global Transformations Reader – an Introduction to the Globalisation Debate*, Cambridge, Polity Press, 2000.

Held, D., McGrew, A., Goldblatt, D. and Perraton, J., *Global transformations – Politics, Economics and Culture*, Stanford, Stanford University Press Stanford (CA), 1999.

Hirst, P., Thompson, G., *Globalisation in question*, Cambridge, Polity Press, 2nd ed., 1999.

"Mathias, G., "État et salarisation restreinte au Brésil", *Revue Tiers-Monde*, 110, avril-juin, Paris, IEDES/PUF, 1987, pp. 333-346.

Mayntz, R., "New challenges to governance theory", European University Institute, Jean Monnet Chair Paper RSC No. 98/50, 1998.

Ohmae, K., *The borderless world*, London, Collins, 1990.

Sassen, S., *Global networks, Linked cities*, London, Routledge, 2002.

Swyngedouw, E., "La transformation des échelles spatiales de la régulation: vers une nouvelle articulation", *Géographie, Économie, Société*, 2 (2), 2000, p. 211-244.

Therborn, G., "Globalisations: Dimensions, Historical Waves, Regional Effects, Normative Governance", *International Sociology*, Vol. 15, No. 2, 2000, p. 151-179.

Zeitlin, J. and Pochet, Ph. (eds.), with Magnusson, L., *The Open Method of Co-ordination in Action – the European Employment and Social Inclusion Strategies*, Bruxelles, PIE Peter Lang, 2005.

PART I

INSTITUTIONAL FRAMEWORKS: WHAT HAS CHANGED IN LABOUR MARKET POLICIES?

The Brazilian Labour Market

Structural Features, "New" Flexibilisation and Recent Performance

Liana CARLEIAL

Ph.D. in Economics, full professor at the Federal University of Paraná (Brazil)

Introduction[1]

The Brazilian labour market is founded on a fragile urban industrial base, boosted by the coffee boom of the early 20th century that strengthened the national industry. Hence, since its inception, it has been marked by a spatial concentration in São Paulo, as well as by a division according to ethnicity, region, wage and gender.

The important economic growth experienced by the country between 1950 and 1980 was accompanied by an intense urbanisation spurred by inter-region migratory movements, themselves motivated by the consolidation of industry and by the low standards of living in the countryside.

Thus, in three decades, Brazil created 26 million jobs, urbanized its population and created an important industrial base by combining foreign and national private and public capital. However, the result of this accelerated process (which was not based on a universal access to education and land reform, which would have allowed for income redistribution) is a fragile labour market, where informal workers represent around 40% of those employed and with a wage structure dominated by low salaries.

The crisis surrounding the public sector's ability to finance development, along with the external and internal debt crises in the 1980s, plunged the country's labour market into a deep crisis, worsening the characteristics mentioned above.

1 The author wishes to thank Professor José Dari KREIN from Cesit – Campinas University (Brazil) for the information he provided and which has been referenced accordingly in this article.

In the late 1980s, the country, preparing to adopt a neo-liberal agenda, was treading the path toward free trade, privatisation and market deregulation, including labour. With the administration of Fernando Henrique Cardoso (known as the "FHC era") came the flexibilisation of the labour market, carried out not through amendments to existing labour laws, but rather taking the form of a set of rules introduced through an *ad hoc* manoeuvre and by an increased acceptance of the flexibilisation of the labour market in judicial decisions. This is the object of this article, which will first discuss the structure of the Brazilian Labour Market; second, the crisis in the 1980s; third, the changes in the 1990s responsible for the ongoing flexibilisation, and; finally, lay out more recent trends felt under the Lula government.

The Brazilian Labour Market

Our starting point for understanding the nature of the labour market in Brazil, in all its historical and structural features, focuses on just how a slaveholding economy managed to rise and become a primary-export economy.

Here, the urban labour market is structured around business and financial capital in the exporting cities, plus a thin layer of service providing for the State. Since the specific urban areas that put the exporting regions on the map are few in number and originally poorly interconnected, they bring out a second feature – namely, the regional segmentation of early urban labour markets.

Third, the abolition of slavery drew into the cities a population entirely without schooling and with little chance of finding its way into urban employment, thereby forming the basis of a chronically marginalized population with significant ethnic segmentation, as a result.

Fourth, induced European immigration – especially for coffee plantations in the state of São Paulo – made for the implantation of a labour force, differentiated from the native workers, who did not possess the construction skills so important to that budding industry. So the urban labour market in Brazil was, from its earliest beginnings, divided up on the basis of attributes such as region, trade skills, ethnicity, and wages.

Finally, the development period Brazil went through during the 20th century, albeit important, failed to eliminate these problems. The era brought no great unification, no universal schooling or literacy, no widespread land reform, but rather subjected the country to an enduring dependence on external resources for financing its development.

Thus, Brazil changed from an essentially agricultural country to an urban nation with a complex and diversified industrial structure, in a relatively short period of some forty years. After World War II, industrialisation – which had previously been erratic and very sensitive to the vagaries of its primary exports – developed a much sharper outline. It then grew from a foundation of import-substitution, supported by the three pillars of foreign, Brazilian private and public capital.

This was what moulded the features of Brazilian industrialisation: geographically concentrated, technologically dependent on central Nations, with a strong presence of multinational corporations and weakly geared to the production of capital goods – even though it is the Latin American country with the largest such production.

Employment during the Substitution of Imports

This period changed the face of Brazilian society and its economy, with remarkably high rates of GDP growth. Between 1950 and 1980, when industry was consolidating itself, labour market dynamics responded to the following influences:

- a significant rate of GDP growth, greater than that of the active workforce and indicative of increased work opportunities (see Table 01);
- strong currents of domestic migration, outstripping demand for labour in the largest cities.

A deeper analysis of this period will reveal large shifts in the population participating in the various industries. Brazil, in fact, adheres strictly to what Kuznets advanced: economic development is accompanied by important population and industry sector changes.

In 1950, for example, approximately 60% of the active population worked in agriculture; yet, by 1980, that share had fallen to roughly 30%. Heavy industry, comprising civil construction, manufacturing, and milling, accounted for 14.19% of the active workforce in 1950, and 24.4% in 1980. The service industries, meanwhile, moved from a relative share of 25.91% to 45.7%.

As expected, these shifts also affected product shares for the various sectors. Thus, in 1950, the relative share of Net National Product for agriculture was 15%, while in 1980 it was only 7%. Heavy industries, with a 27.2% share in 1950, rose to 39% in 1980. The service industries, which accounted for 57.07% of Net National Product in 1950, dropped to 53%.

Table 01. Annual GDP and active workforce (PEA) growth rates: Brazil, 1951/1980

Period	Gross Domestic Product (GDP)	Active workforce
1951/60	7.7	1.1
1961/70	6.2	4.5
1971/80	8.6	3.9

Source: IBGE, Census

More accurate observations are required when one analyzes the employment indicators for that period more closely. First, the number of jobs added during those thirty years is truly impressive: according to the Brazilian Geographic and Statistical Institute (IBGE), 26,679,401 jobs were created. That amounts to more jobs than France's active workforce for the 2000s! This, therefore, is a most significant number.

Second, we observe that only 5,250,401 jobs were in manufacturing and milling. Even so, that meant a geometric growth rate of 5% for those working in those industries – greater than the growth rate for all jobs combined, which was only 3.2%. Third, we stress that, in 1980, total employment in manufacturing and milling was only 15.7% of all jobs – the largest such figure attained by Brazilian society (see Table 02).

Industry's shrinking share in terms of its capacity to absorb the workforce is evidence that typifies the Brazilian labour market. We know that in countries now considered developed, industry's share in the workforce is much larger. This has many implications in the makeup of an active workforce (Castel, 1995), in which labour legislation is passed, enforced, and capable of generating a fairly solid bonding of "labour and protection", as encountered in European societies.

As one would expect, steady employment increased with the expansion of industry. In 1950, only 50% of the active workforce was classified as "employees"; 29% was classified as "self-employed", 23% as "employers" and 5% as "unpaid workers". By 1980, 66% of the active workforce qualified as "employees", reducing the number of self-employed workers to only 25%, as shown in the IBGE's Demographic Census reports (Cacciamali, 1988).

One should also bear in mind that, according to Paiva (1984: 13) and Cacciamali (1988) and based on this same database, throughout the period from 1950 to 1980 and even with industrial growth, the informal workforce remained at about 40%, making it a structural feature of the Brazilian labour market.

Criteria used by the author define the formal economy as comprising the active workforce identified as employed in "industry", "commerce", "transportation", "communications", "warehousing", "social work" and "public service".

The informal economy was determined by subtraction and encompasses all other employment situations, except for the active population classified as employers and those working in personal service areas classified as belonging to the service industries. This procedure takes into account the concept that the latter do housework.

We see than that during the period from 1950 to 1980 (the consolidation era for Brazilian industry, and therefore for steady employment and the creation of millions of jobs) this market was visibly heterogeneous, and comprised regularly employed wage-earners duly registered, employees of large companies and government corporations, and an entire spectrum of jobholders covering the underemployed and piecework or casual labourers.

The institutions governing the labour market are thus flimsy and result from granted, rather than demanded, legislation and from the marginal population, which gives rise to a "freeing up" of hiring and firing practices, high turnover, lax worker training, poor qualifications, and low wages (Baltar and Proni, 1996). Linked to these lingering development problems is the Brazilian state's "rump" regulation (Oliveira, 1988). The result is that, side-by-side, we have various labour markets with different regional, wage, legal (with or without signed benefits booklets), and job qualification segmentations.

These historical structural features also made for weak trade union organisation, densely concentrated around the more industrial regions. Indeed, this helps us understand Brazilian civil society's low active involvement. Yet we must consider that, while there has been a persistent drop-off in unionisation in the developed world, things were different in Brazil during the 1980s. Indeed, the 1980s saw the peak of unionisation efforts among government employees, while actions taken by the Industry Chambers (especially in the automobile industry) turned out to be very positive for unionism nationwide. In 1989, a labour union survey carried out by the IBGE showed that Brazil had 17 million union members, which accounted for 28% of the working population. This is no mean figure, even in international terms (Medeiros and Salm, 1994: 60).

Table 02. Some indicators relating to employment in the manufacturing and milling industries: Brazil, 1950-1980

Indicators	1950	1960	1970	1980
(1) Total job holders	17,117,362	22,750,068	29,557,224	43,796,763
(2) Total job holders in secondary sector	2,427,364	2,940,242	5,295,417	10,674,977
(3) Total job holders in manufacturing & milling	1,608,309	1,954,187	3,241,861	6,858,598
(4) = (3) / (2)	66.3%	66.5%	61.2%	64.2%
(5) = (3) / (1)	9.4%	8.6%	11.0%	15.7%
(6) = (2) / (1)	14.2%	12.9%	17.9%	24.4%

Source: IBGE, Census (from Salm *et al.*, 1987).

Finally, we note that:

As a nation, Brazil has never managed to assemble a workforce *à la Castel.*

Brazil has never managed, therefore, to put together an adequate system of protection and social benefits.

Wage labour has never assumed a role as the central aspect of social and economic citizenship.

Self-employment, freelance work, casual labour and odd jobs have always weighed heavily in Brazilian society.

Throughout the entire development of industrial consolidation, steady work (with the chance of advancement) has coexisted side-by-side with the most varied and unsteady types of occupation in the labour market. Here, the changes in overt unemployment have never managed to mirror the magnitude of the labour market's structural crisis.

Brazilian society has thus always coexisted with forms of societal organisation that are surprising to developed nations today – namely, the proliferation of precarious jobs vis-à-vis the share held by steady employment.

To this general picture of a deeply divided labour market and a weak civil society, have been added the adjustments designed to prepare the country for competitive participation in a globalized economy, with emphasis on the productive restructuring of companies and a reduction of trade and investment barriers.

The "Freeing Up" of the Brazilian Labour Market as of the 1990s

As we have seen, industrial development and economic growth from 1950 to 1980 allowed the formation of a significant urban labour market with widespread steady employment for wages.

Yet during the 1980s, with the deepening crises of foreign debt and of the State as producer and employer, the succession of "economic packages" to control inflation and the falling investment rate (from 1974 to 1980 it stood at 24% of GDP, but has remained at about 16% since 1988) cast doubts on the labour market, reducing formal employment and raising the number of freelancers and of employees without signed benefits booklets, until overt unemployment began to emerge as a problem. Associated with this was a "feminisation" of the labour markets, with the female employment rate rising from 33.6% in 1979 to 39.2% in 1990 (Sabóia, 1996).

In a sense, the 1990s corresponded to a loss of control over the nation's future possibilities. Despite all the difficulties and limitations in the "import-substitution" growth model, prior to the 1990s the dynamics of growth were decisively settled by the State and its industrializing efforts. The manufacturing structure became diversified, with emphasis on large government and private corporations, which caused large-scale migrations and Brazil's rapid urbanisation.

What is special, as of the 1990s, can be seen in the globalisation and productive restructuring movements. These occurred within the implementation of a neoconservative matrix with the following characteristics:

- Inflation control
- Lowering of trade barriers to increase competitiveness and privatisation of large government corporations
- Financial and labour market deregulation
- Controls on public spending, reducing the role of the State.

The Federal State, which had been a beacon for previous cycles in the Brazilian economy, has practically disappeared from the scene, making the private sector the prime mover in this new scenario. Thus, we have seen the privatisation of the more important publicly-owned companies. Procedures by large corporations for "outsourcing" production have established subcontractor networks of small- and medium-sized manufacturing units, of which (from a production standpoint) a few have managed to consolidate and qualify in the markets. From a labour market standpoint, they have worked to further destabilize earnings and social benefits.

One can also observe the relocation of companies from region to region. This as yet poorly understood movement in search of cheap labour and frayed unionisation also takes advantage of fiscal contests among the different States competing for shares of new investment.

In addition, we see the effects of exchange-rate pegging in Brazil's overvalued currency, allowing a rapid expansion of imports (particularly of intermediate and capital goods) which has worked to increase imported components in Brazilian manufactures, and further, a rationalisation of manufacturing processes – both of which were detrimental to employment. Clearly, the combination of the above has allowed industrial production to grow without any increase in employment – a scenario of great controversy surrounding industrial productivity trends. As we saw in the previous section, the primary result for the labour markets was the combination of increased casualisation and overt unemployment. The increase in casual labour alone has meant a lowering of Brazilian labour market regulatory benchmarks and has represented the most consistent tendency toward "freeing up" this market.

On the other hand, the economic policies carried out in the 1990s (namely, opening up trade indiscriminately, privatizing public companies and the process of productive downsizing) created the conditions for Direct Foreign Investment (DFI) that had all but disappeared during the crisis of the 1980s. It is also true, however, that the change in the pattern of competition among companies, strongly centred on mergers and acquisitions of companies according to the network firm model, has acted as the process' engine. The graph below shows that the return of DFI does *not* alter the pattern of gross accumulation of capital in Brazil, thereby also not altering the country's productive capacity in a positive manner.

Graph 01. DFI and Gross Formation of Fixed Capital (% of GDP)

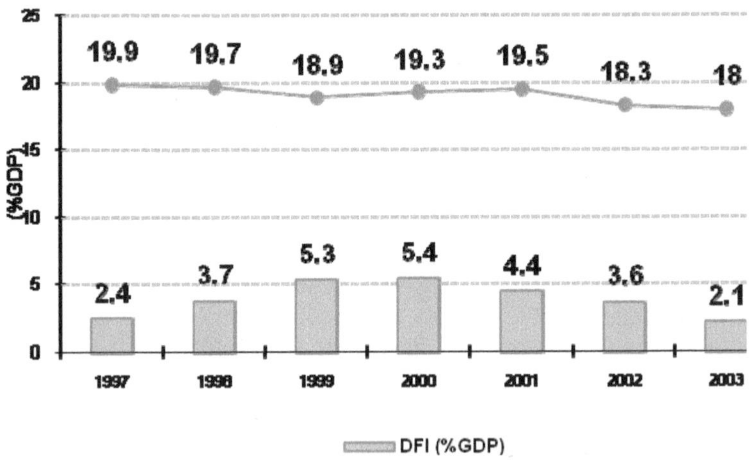

Source: BCB (www.bancocentral.gov.br) and Fundação IBGE (www.ibge.gov.br)

We believe that the decisions on economic policies in the 1990s (such as liberalizing trade, privatizing state companies, the acquisition and/or merging of national companies by multinational groups organized as network firms) has transferred to such groups important decisions on production, technological standards, worker qualification, etc. This has redefined Brazil's underdevelopment, which is now globalized. This redefinition requires that industrial policies create tools so that their actions go beyond the scope of production; in turn, this demands the creation of a sphere for negotiation between the government and multinationals to ensure the opportunities for bringing into the country, on a case-by-case basis, stages of project conception and development in important industrial sectors, which will allow an expansion of the productive structure, the resizing of the participation of national capital in relevant production chains, technological learning, the creation of more qualified positions and the generation of positive effects on the nature of Brazil's participation on international trade.

The Lula Administration, in power since January 2003 after carrying over 53 million votes of Brazilian citizens (the result of a struggle of almost 25 years which gathered social movements and a major share of the civil society), has chosen to ignore the agenda by which it was elected and to intensify the so-called neo-liberal reforms started by previous governments. Its macroeconomic policies, based on the combination of a growing primary surplus, high interest rates, floating exchange rates and the free mobility of capital, have proved to be unable to steer the country towards economic growth and development.

The Brazilian economy's growth rate over the last 20 years of the past century stood, on average, at 2.0% per annum, well below that of the developmental phase between 1950 and 1980. In the period since the application of neo-liberal policies, beginning in 1994, growth has faced a "stop-and-go" phenomenon that reveals its incapability to maintain a growth rate compatible with the needs of the labour market in Brazil.

Thus, informality has spread in Brazil (as well as in Latin America as a whole), as a consequence of the neo-liberal structural adjustment programmes implemented in the region under the auspices of the International Monetary Fund. That is the reason, according to the 1992 National Sampling Household Survey (PNAD-IBGE), that 51.9% of those employed worked in the informal market, measured by the participation of workers without a benefits booklet signed by the employer and autonomous workers. In the last decade, i.e. 1992/2002, this percentage has risen to 52.6%, or 36.3 million among the 69.1 million people employed. It is also worth mentioning that, over this same decade and from a spatial point of view, this phenomenon has gained strength in the metropolitan areas throughout Brazil and, if broken down by sector, among industrial workers.

Based on administrative records from RAIS (the Annual Report of Social Information), Costanzi (2004) has shown that the total number of those employed with a signed benefits booklet rose at a faster pace than the GDP growth rate for a period of seven years, *i.e.* since 1998, and that informal labour in the metropolitan areas stopped rising as of 1999. Thus, in 2003, when the economy stagnated, the number of formal jobs rose by 3%, in 2002, when GDP rose by 1.93%, formal jobs grew 5.5%, while for the previous years the results were the following: 2001: 1.31% and 3.66%; 2000: 4.36% and 4.94% respectively.

Graph 02. People employed by position occupied (1999-2003)

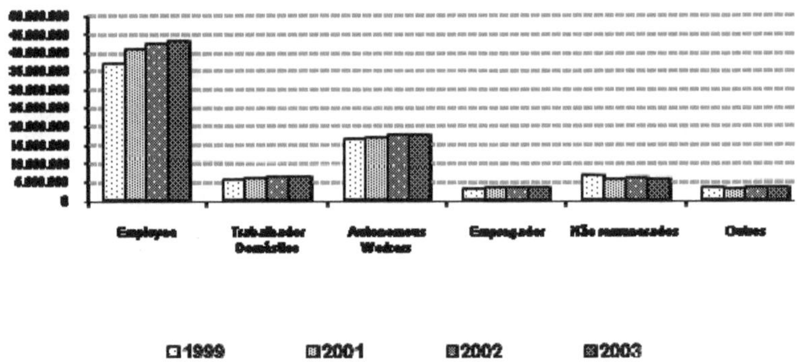

Source: IBGE – PNAD 2003

However, it is important to bear in mind that the trend that is pushing the labour force toward wage-earning jobs continues to be observed in a significant manner. According to PNAD-IBGE, between 1999 and 2003, the number of people employed in wage-earning jobs rose from 37,681,753 to 43,089,178, representing an increase of 14%. A wage-earning job is certainly the prevailing manner of entering the labour market. When the participation of autonomous workers is considered for the same period, the growth of their numbers was very small, passing from 17,003,134 to 17,709,344. It must be noted that the nature of the contract changes, but wage-earning jobs are the prevailing form of occupation (see Graph 02).

We can also observe that in a country with a structural concentration of income (Gini index of 0.559), an average open unemployment rate of 10.9%, in 2004, measured in six of the largest metropolitan areas of Brazil, the nature of the economic policy has caused the continuous decrease of the average real wage of those employed, as shown in Graph 3.

Graph 03. Average Monthly Income for Labour – Persons of over 10 years of age (R$)

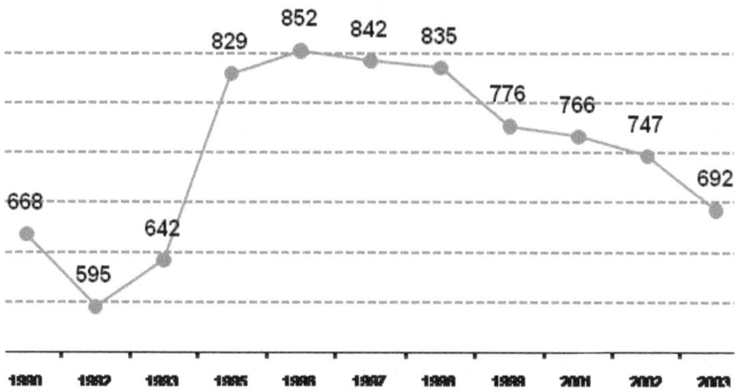

Source: Fundação IBGE – Pesquisa Nacional por Amostra de Domicílio (http://www.ibge.gov.br).

Therefore, in a globalized world dominated by the movement of capital from the productive to the financial sphere, wage and employment levels have become adjustable variants. Also, as Chesnais (1997) accurately pointed out, there is an attempt to bring to the labour market the same contractual reversibility found in the financial market. At the same time, we witness a huge income transfer via financial and technological products and services markets to investors-stakeholders within one society and between developing and developed countries; we also observe a fierce competition among the social systems of different countries as well as work protection systems. It is within this spirit that we wish to debate the Brazilian labour reform.

Elements for the Debate on Brazilian Labour Reform

Hiring a worker with the employer's signature in his benefits booklet defines the employer-employee relationship in an important way. The benefits booklet is specific to Brazil, and originated during the Getúlio Vargas administration. It drew a line between workers having some protection and all other workers in Brazil. To have a job with a signed benefits booklet has several implications, and provides access to important labour rights. A job with an employer-signed benefits booklet means:

- Social recognition of one's role as a worker
- The right to a 44-hour week
- Paid weekends and public holidays
- Annual paid holidays
- Paid retirement, provided the worker meets job tenure and social security payment requirements
- Tenure-based severance indemnity fund
- Access to the tenure-based severance indemnity fund, once certain requirements are met, such as minimum job tenure with an employer-signed benefits booklet.
- One-third of a monthly wage as additional vacation pay
- Indemnification, if fired without cause
- Employer-provided transportation and meal vouchers
- Sick pay
- Christmas bonus of one month's wages.

In addition to these clear entitlements and benefits, registered workers can also obtain indirect benefits – for example, greater chances of in-house training, or extra foreign language courses.

In Brazil, workers with signed benefits booklets are governed by the Consolidated Labour Laws (CLT). Although it is obvious that it is employment itself, rather than possession of the benefits booklet, that defines the workers and confers appropriate rights, in practice the law is only observed for those who have employer-signed benefits booklets.

Since the 1980s, however, the number of workers thus qualified has fallen significantly. This was a result of a slower economic growth rate, the Brazilian economy's greater internationalisation and the government crisis. If casual labour was already an undeniable reality during the 1990s, "it is because of the economic opening initiated in 1990 (and exacerbated since 1994) that there was a migration of industrial workers to the service industry", declared Paulo Paiva, who was labour minister at the time. With that, "there occurred a greater casualisation of the market".

Nevertheless, Brazil's re-democratisation during that same decade nurtured the social and union movements. Both made significant gains with the ratification of a new federal Constitution (1988), which considerably broadened social and labour rights.

During the 1990s, especially after the Real Plan, international competitiveness and market share pressures (associated with glutted labour markets) fostered the belief that the labour market needed to be deregulated so as to reduce labour costs, favour increased corporate competitiveness, and even serve as a strategy for creating jobs. Therefore, an additional concerted effort occurred toward what is considered "freeing-up" the Brazilian labour market. All of this ran counter to the expectations which had seen the light during the previous decade.

The changes already in place can be broken down as follows:

Measures designed directly to reduce the State's interventionist role in the labour market.

Measures aimed at "freeing up" work shifts

Measures that necessarily expanded the State's regulatory framework during the 1990s to include, for example, the significant increase in casual workers (as we saw in the previous section of this article).

Within the first grouping, we may include the decision to de-index wages, thereby precluding automatic wage indexing implemented by the Brazilian government since 1995. The resulting abolition of wage-adjustment mechanisms gave workers and employers the right to negotiate adjustments within each professional or economic category (Krein and Oliveira 1999: 641). At the same time, mediation among all parties was encouraged. Provided there is agreement, however, the parties may proceed freely or with the help of the Labour Ministry.

Complementary to this was a provisional measure (MP 794/1994) regulating profit-sharing plans (PLR). Negotiations were thus fragmented down to the level of each company, which facilitated wage differentiation and individual wage setting, tying worker remuneration to personal and company performance. By the same token, companies are allowed to find ways to transfer resources to workers without incurring vacation or holiday bonus pay, and without wage-indexing clauses in the labour contract.

The set of measures aimed at "freeing-up" work shifts can be summed up in two primary innovations: (a) the regulation of part-time labour agreements; and, (b) a comp time "hours bank" (*banco de horas*).

According to Orgis (2000: 44), the first of these was not new, for it has always been possible to hire workers for smaller shifts at proportional wages. This is hard to put into practice due to the low wages paid in Brazil, which lead the worker to seek a full-time job. A provisional measure (MP1709/1998) was drafted to encourage this practice. Through its workings, the Brazilian government allows a scaling of vacation time proportional to actual job shifts. According to legal experts, this violates the Constitutional principle of equal pay.

The second measure, the comp time "hour bank", was instituted through Law 9601/1998. This law authorizes the compensation of hours worked in a 120-day timeframe, without overtime pay (for hours worked beyond the legal workday, provided they do not exceed the 10-hour per day limit). Before this law was passed, this possibility was restricted to a one-week period.

Simultaneously, Provisional Measure 1709/1998 allows this compensation to take place over a period of up to a year. Current practice requires that this instrument be provided for in collective bargaining agreements. It also requires that, within one year, the number of hours worked in a week be set at 44, and provides for payment of all overtime hours worked, if within a one-year period these hours have not been duly compensated for.

Our analysis in this section is by no means exhaustive, for its purpose is simply to outline the current trend towards "freeing-up" labour legislation in Brazil. In this regard, we should also mention that there is a very widely accepted interpretation that there has been a sort of loosening of labour legislation enforcement, which tends to facilitate ignoring the law. In some cases, for example, the labour inspector just notifies the company of the irregularity noted, but without imposing a fine, the notification of the offence then being submitted for approval by the Regional Labour Delegate. This has made the Ministry of Labour's inspection procedures more flexible as regards practices that fail to respect the clauses of the collective labour contract. Indeed, the prevailing attitude is heavily charged in favour of fostering negotiations, a situation that no doubt favours the nullification of current legislation.

As a last resort, there is talk in Brazil of adding versatility to article 618 of the Consolidated Labour Laws, which would place any and all labour rights on the negotiating table between labour and capital. There are significant risks, therefore, of loss of labour rights and usurpation of what minimal social protection exists.

To conclude, we shall briefly examine the trend toward changing the State's activities in protecting Brazil's labour market. The three preceding sections sought to identify historical and structural difficulties in the makeup of the Brazilian labour market and the aggravation of these difficulties over the past ten years – this, in addition to the near impossibility of putting together an active workforce in Brazil (Carleial, 1997).

We now have an urgent task at hand: to reconstruct distribution mechanisms for the entire population, not just the wage-earning worker – and certainly not restricted entirely to workers with employer-signed benefits booklets. We need legal mechanisms to protect the casual labourer, subcontractors, and the self-employed.

The Brazilian government made some progress in that direction during the past decade, in the sense that it instituted a "public system for employment, labour and income" that seeks to plot an alternative path in which the understanding of what constitutes "employment" goes beyond the case of the worker with a signed benefits booklet. In practice, however, it has restricted itself to broader-scope training programmes and workforce preparation, which is, at the same time, closer to each regional and local reality. To this end, its activities have been decentralized through partnerships with various levels of government and with teaching and training institutions throughout Brazil.

Even if this activity is but a beginning toward a better understanding of what constitutes employment in Brazil, the challenge is still how to place on the statute books the protection needed by these various configurations that undertake the work in today's Brazil.

References

Baltar, P.E.A. and Proni, M.W., "Sobre o regime de trabalho no Brasil: Rotatividade da mão de obra, emprego formal e estrutura salarial", in Oliveira, C.A.B.; Mattoso, J.E.L.(Orgs), *Crise e Trabalho no Brasil: Modernidade ou Volta ao Passado?*, Campinas, Editora Pagina Aberta, 1996, pp. 109-150.

Cacciamali, M.C., *Mudanças estruturais no produto e emprego no Brasil 1950-80,* Teaching certificate thesis (mimeo). São Paulo, USP, 1988, 280 p.

Carleial, L., "Trabalho em tempos de novas tecnologias: Velhos e novos desafios", in *Proposta* 26, No. 72 (March/May), Rio de Janeiro, 1997, pp. 14-22.

Castel, R., *Les Métamorphoses de la Question Sociale: une Chronique du Salariat*, Paris, Fayard, 1995, 350 p.

Chesnais, F., *La Mondialisation du Capital.* Paris, Syros, 1997, 328 p.

Constanzi, R. N., "Evolução do Emprego Formal no Brasil (1985-2003) e Implicações para as Políticas de Geração de Emprego e Renda", in *Texto para Discussão* No. 1039, Rio de Janeiro: IPEA.2004, 32 p.

Krein, J.D. and Oliveira, M.A., "Mudanças institucionais e relações de trabalho: As iniciativas do governo FHC no período 1995-98", in *ANAIS*, 6mo Encontro Nacional de Estudos do trabalho, Vol. 1, Belo Horizonte, ABET/UFMG, 1999, pp. 639-672.

Medeiros, C.A. and Salm, C., "O mercado de trabalho em debate", in *Novos Estudos Cebrap*, No. 39, São Paulo, Cebrap, 1994, pp. 49-66.

Ministério da Fazenda, *A economia Brasileira: O desafio da estabilidade e do crescimento sustentado*, 1997. Online: www.fazenda.gov.br.

Oliveira, F., *Inovações em políticas econômico-sociais: O caso do Brasil*, Research paper (mimeo), São Paulo, Cebrap, 1988, 45 p.

Orgis, G., *Flexibilização e redução da jornada de trabalho: Uma análise do caso Brasileiro à luz da experiência francesa*, Curitiba, UFPR/Labour Economics (mimeo), 2000, 120 p.

Sabóia, J., *Mercado de trabalho no Brasil: Evolução e tendências recentes*, (mimeo), Rio de Janeiro, Universidade Federal do Rio de Janeiro, 1996, 31 p.

Salm, C. *et al.*, *Mercado de trabalho no Brasil: Estrutura e conjuntura*, Research paper, Rio de Janeiro, MTb/UFRJ, 1987, 150 p.

The Effects of Activation Measures on Disadvantaged Jobseekers' Rights and Obligations in Denmark, Finland and Sweden

Paul VAN AERSCHOT

Senior Lecturer, University of Helsinki

At the end of the 20th century, labour market legislation in Denmark, Finland and Sweden underwent multiple changes. Though the timetable and content of these reforms differed in each country, the main features of the new policies are similar. One of these features is a greater emphasis on the active role of the unemployed jobseeker, whose obligation to participate in training and other activation programmes has been systematically increased. Another characteristic is the adoption of a more individual approach to employment services. Employment agencies increasingly focus on individualised projects that take into account the jobseeker's particular skills and abilities.

The purpose of this article is to analyse the effect of these reforms on the unemployed jobseeker's position and on the decision-making concerning each individual case. Administrative-legal decision-making often leaves much room for discretion. The individualisation of the measures used to further the jobseeker's employment leads to specific, or even to tailor-made, applications based on extensive discretionary powers. This involves an altered conception, and possibly a weakening, of the legal principle of equality. The increased powers of the officials should be counterbalanced by the effective implementation of existing legal provisions protecting the client's rights.

During the past few years, active labour market policies and the extension of activation measures to social benefits recipients other than jobseekers have changed the position of the unemployed in the Nordic countries. "Position" means here the set of rights and obligations attached to a person's status when claiming certain social benefits. The main objectives of the new policies have been to make recipients enter or re-enter the open labour market and to prepare them to do so by improving their employability. Subsidiary goals concern improving their living conditions and preventing exclusion by engaging them in work-oriented activities.

The activation approach includes a shift in working methods, involving an individualised approach to cases. This comprises mapping out the recipient's skills, qualifications and work experience, but also determining those of his characteristics which might be useful on the labour market or, on the contrary, unfavourable to his progress. To a certain extent, the approach replaces traditional social work with labour counselling, so as to turn the passive recipients of social benefits into jobseekers actively applying themselves to improving their situation. The clients' active engagement is linked to (or even constitutes a condition for) the entitlement to the social benefits they claim. Within the framework of activation policies there is a move towards convergence through, on the one hand, the assimilation of social benefits beneficiaries into the domain of the labour market and, on the other, the enhanced personalisation of job seeking and employment-oriented activities. In the three Nordic countries in question, recipients of social assistance and beneficiaries of unemployment benefits traditionally belonged to two different groups. Each of these had its own status and was essentially served by its own organisation (primarily either employment agencies or local social services). The new policies tend to blur the boundaries between these two categories and, to some extent, even to merge them into one.

The new dominant perception of beneficiaries can be described as a prototype of the client, who presents the following features:

– the client is at least potentially employable and is a jobseeker;

– she/he is able to develop her/his potential by participating in the work-oriented activities arranged or approved by the authorities;

– her/his case is dealt with on an individual basis;

– she/he is capable of deliberating over her/his moves and of negotiating on an equal footing with the frontline decision-maker involved. However, in the case of disagreement, she/he is under the obligation to comply with the officials' directions.

These policies also stem from the premises that the free labour market can accommodate all jobseekers who have adapted to its demands and that jobseekers can choose between different self-development alternatives.

Depending on their status, skills and capabilities, this "labour market construction" of clients affects them in different ways. For example, formerly "typical" claimants of unemployment benefits are now subjected to closer scrutiny, are required to provide more detailed information about themselves and to adhere to the directions given to them more strictly. Similarly, recipients of social assistance are obliged to participate in various activation measures and to submit to the demands inherent to their new status as active jobseekers including, among others, an assessment of their capacities and limitations and compiling a CV. Dealing with the needs of this group, previously covered by social work, is now subordinated to work-oriented activities.

In the three Nordic countries involved, activation policies have been developed in a different manner and according to a different timeframe. In Denmark and Sweden, there are, broadly speaking, two categories of unemployed jobseekers. One category consists of those fulfilling the rather strict conditions required to qualify for earnings-related unemployment benefits based on membership in an unemployment insurance fund (e.g. Arbejdsdirektoratet 2006; Hytti, 2002: 335-336). It has been a long-standing practice supported by legislation that these jobseekers have to participate in labour-market programmes. The other category is composed of people not meeting these conditions, who have to resort to social assistance. These recipients have increasingly been subjected to activation measures. In addition to this twofold classification, jobseekers in Finland may belong to a third group comprising people receiving a low level, flat rate unemployment allowance (e.g. *Vår sociala trygghet*, 2005: 188-193). Their activation obligations are similar to those of recipients of earnings-related unemployment benefits.

In this article, I shall focus mainly on the implications of activation programmes for jobseekers with a weak position in the labour market. A weak position means that they have considerable difficulties in obtaining gainful employment. These disadvantaged jobseekers may receive social assistance or unemployment benefits. They are targeted by special activation programmes or may participate in active labour market policy measures together with jobseekers in a better position. My purpose is to identify certain factors affecting the implementation of activation provisions which may threaten the rights of these recipients in particular. Naturally, the rights of other beneficiaries may also be endangered by the same elements, but they are less dependent on the discretion of officials and better able to defend themselves or to otherwise cope with their situation (on the effects of activation on jobseekers in different positions, see Malmberg-Heimonen, 2005: 53).

Problems of Implementation

Activation is regulated by specific legislation, but the implementation of the legal norms concerned is, to a great extent, determined by the way frontline decision-makers adapt them to the situations they encounter in practice and the problems they have to cope with at work. Indeed, in social welfare law, the actual implementation of each piece of legislation is dependent on pre-existing decision-making structures, organisational patterns of dealing with different groups of clients (possibly by means of a categorisation inconsistent with the legal provisions involved), sets of values prevailing in society or in the agencies concerned, and so on (Lipsky, 1980: 55-69, 88-104; Tala, 2001: 266-267).

From a strictly legal point of view, however, the officials and bodies implementing the law are deemed to put legal provisions into effect in a neutral way. Moreover, all their decisions are regarded as legal unless they are challenged, and altered or rejected as the result of a judicial review or other corrective procedures. (e.g. Mäenpää, 2000: 47, 391-392). Such challenges are not frequent and, at best, lead to mere fragmentary corrections of the mass of decisions in question. Hence, the assumption of the *prima facie* legal validity of these decisions, together with the often extensive discretionary powers of the officials, gives the decision-makers considerable autonomy, which in a way isolates them from the legal sphere. This isolation is a paradoxical feature of implementation. The assumption of legal validity presupposes reliable decision-making institutions which can be trusted to abide by the law without being constantly supervised. However, the autonomy of the apparatus allows it to develop its own decision-making practices, possibly including extra-legal or even unlawful ingredients.

An official inquiry into the implementation of activation provisions in Sweden revealed that certain municipalities applied activation measures to all claimants of social assistance, regardless of their situation or age. With regard to the activation of clients aged 25 and over, this is clearly against the law as individuals belonging to this group may be activated only if they have "a special need for activation measures increasing their abilities". As for recipients aged 18-24, the Social Services Act requires that activation measures should be adapted to the individual's conditions and that they should aim to develop her/his possibilities to earn a living and to improve her/his employability or, if appropriate, her/his chances to engage in further training. This implies that the application of activation to all young clients does not conform to the law either, because it is not intended e.g. for recipients who only need assistance temporarily. (The inquiry was carried out in 2004 by the National Board of Social Welfare and the county governments, see Socialstyrelsen, 2005: 19-22). Another study showed that, in many municipalities, there were serious deficiencies in the local activation programmes (Salonen and Ulmestig, 2004: 37-38, 74, 83-84, 89, 93). The findings referred to a lack of clearly defined goals, the absence of a timeframe established in advance, inadequate content and documentation, neglect of follow-up, and so on. In these municipalities, activation apparently focused on the placement of clients in a programme as such, regardless of whether the measure could improve their skills with a view to entering the labour market or engaging in further training as required by the law. Moreover, the programmes in question did not take the participants' individual wishes and abilities into account. The survey concluded that in many municipalities local activation programmes are used to reduce expenses and to merely occupy clients in some way or other.

The same study described how an older claimant's special need for activation measures increasing his abilities had been interpreted in practice. Such measures included, for example, courses designed to improve language skills or proficiency in using information technology. This kind of training is, indeed, likely to promote the client's chances of entering the labour market or engaging in further training, as the Social Services Act prescribes. However, the officials sometimes interpreted the expression very loosely and made adherence to a certain timetable (including getting up early in the morning) the main objective of the activation programme (Salonen and Ulmestig, 2004: 40-41, 92). In my view, it is very doubtful whether this kind of compulsory measures – only remotely connected with employability – is acceptable. Such exercises hardly fulfil the requirement of effective implementation. Moreover, according to the same Act, the authorities should base their action on the respect of their clients' right to self-determination and integrity (Swedish Social Services Act – 2001/453, chapter 1, section 1). Compelling somebody to follow a certain timetable is permitted under a contract of employment and can also be accepted in labour market policy measures. However, when compulsion is used in connection with other activities which are only weakly oriented to the labour market, this transgresses the borderline between unlawful social control and respect for the client's integrity. In a democratic society the authorities have no right to interfere with the private life of the citizen without due reason.

From the recipient's perspective, the frontline decision-maker and the agency she/he represents determine the factual pseudo-legal conditions of the decision on the benefits or service applied for and of the realisation of this decision (Cf. Järvinen, 2002: 75-77). If the legality of these conditions is put to the test in court, the lawfulness of the implementation practice is affirmed or denied, which submits the decision-making again to the legal sphere in which implementation took its starting-point. To evaluate the effects of activation policies on the client's position, we need to keep in mind the two components of decision-making. The client's rights and obligations are laid down in a more or less general fashion in legal texts. The texts are transformed into reality by agencies, which shape the implementation process not only according to the assignment given in the legislation, but also by integrating it into their own culture and range of interests.

Different Conceptions of Rights

To a certain extent, activation implies a shift from rights to obligations. From a social policy perspective, the term "rights" (or "social right") focuses on the claimant's right to receive the social benefit concerned, mainly in accordance with the conditions of entitlement and their interpretation. For its part, "obligations" as a social policy concept means a way of acting, or a pattern of behaviour, on which this right depends. From a legal point of view, the concept of "rights" is much broader. All rights are embedded in the legal system which imposes:

– the implementation of basic rights (constitutional rights and human rights). In this context, relevant basic rights are e.g. the right to equal treatment, the right to liberty, respect for private life and freedom of movement;

– the application of procedural safeguards. These safeguards include, among others, the right to be heard, the right to receive information on one's own case, the impartiality of the decision-maker, the independence of the tribunal or other body judging appeal cases and the demand that decisions be properly justified (especially when a claim is rejected or a sanction is imposed);

– the protection of other individual rights, such as the protection of personal data, the secrecy of confidential material, access to public documents, and so on.

These (other than social) rights also restrict the scope of the obligations imposed on the recipient of social benefits, because the legal system limits the powers of the authorities in favour of the citizens (clients). Because of this intertwining of particular rights and obligations with other legal norms, one could characterize the "legal system construction" of clients as follows:

- the client has the same rights as any other citizen
- she/he needs protection against unlawful decisions and maladministration
- the authorities are responsible for the implementation of her/his rights
- social benefits are universal, though each case should be judged on its own merits. According to the principle of equality, similar cases should be treated in the same way, unless there are acceptable reasons to depart from this rule.

Within the legal system as whole, legal safeguards protecting the rights of the citizen in her/his dealings with the authorities have been specified and strengthened in the legislation of all three countries concerned during recent years. This development should counterbalance possible negative effects of activation – at least after a certain time lag. Indeed, the impact of legal provisions limiting the powers of the authorities and protecting the rights of the clients often lags behind because these norms presuppose corrective measures targeting decisions made in the first instance. When a wrongful decision has been made, the client has to take the initiative and invoke the protective legal provisions in question by appealing against it or contacting supervisory bodies. The outcome of the corrective proceedings is basically restricted to the case at hand, though it may sometimes be used as a precedent with a wider sphere of application or lead to an adjustment of administrative practices. Hence this kind of feedback is generally fragmentary, all the more so because only a relatively small part of wrongful decisions are formally objected to by the clients involved.

Another factor diminishing the effectiveness of corrective legal safeguards is that a decision unduly limiting the rights of the client will be revoked or altered by a tribunal or supervisory body only if it is clearly unlawful. This means that in practice the legal system allows, to a certain extent, a weak implementation of the client's rights by permitting restrictive interpretations of the authorities' duties.

Basic Rights at Risk

The process of activation starts with selecting jobseekers for different programmes. This poses a problem of equal treatment. In all three countries, equality before the law and the banning of discrimination are firmly established legal norms. However, it is not forbidden to divide people into groups with different rights and obligations when the criteria used to distinguish between them are legally acceptable. In the case of activation, this means e.g. that some recipients entitled to activation can be chosen to participate in specific programmes on account of their education, skills and work history, while others are excluded. Problems of equal treatment arise when improper criteria are used to select participants, or when certain categories of beneficiaries are systematically prioritised because they have good employment prospects. Such "cream-skimming" practices seem to be a recurrent problem in the three Nordic countries under examination (e.g. Salonen and Ulmestig, 2004: 63). Moreover, in some cases, activation measures have been applied in a discriminatory way. This has been established at least in Sweden, where the local authorities have extensive discretionary powers to activate recipients of social assistance. Certain officials had adopted a practice of singling out for activation clients who had drinking or drug problems or whom they suspected of working illegally. These officials clearly exceeded their authority, as their practice had no foundation in law (unless the activation measures would be connected e.g. with care of alcohol or drug abusers), (Salonen and Ulmestig, 2004: 40; Socialstyrelsen, 2005: 11).

Another question concerning equality is to what extent, and on which grounds, positive discrimination can be allowed – a matter especially important from the point of view of disadvantaged clients. Finally, the divide between programmes organized by the local authorities and those arranged by employment agencies also has equality aspects. The former may be more limited in scope and pursue other goals than integration into the labour market. Moreover, they may provide a smaller income than the latter (Salonen and Ulmestig, 2004: 37-38, 90-93). Officials working at local social services have other priorities than employment officials and are less competent to deal with labour market issues. Efforts have been made to further joint administrative action involving both branches of administration in activation measures. These efforts correspond to what I have called "the labour market construction" of clients. From the perspective of equal treatment, joint action and a uniform choice of activation programmes constitute a positive development. However, it is an open question how new demands for engagement in measures intended to improve employability affect disadvantaged recipients who cannot live up to the standards of the labour market.

Limitations of rights and obligations imposed on people should fulfil the requirements of legality. This implies that they should be based on the law (and not, for example, on mere administrative practice) and that they should be formulated with sufficient precision. Precise formulations enable the individual to evaluate the content and scope of her/his duties and to regulate her/his conduct accordingly. Unfortunately, activation legislation contains some passages whose wording is vague. For example, according to the Swedish Social Services Act, (2001/453, chapter 4, section 4) the local social authorities may oblige a recipient of social assistance to participate in training or "activities improving her/his abilities" which aim at developing the recipient's possibilities of earning a living. The "activities improving her/his abilities" should make it easier for recipients to enter the labour market or to continue their education. Recipients of over 24 can be obliged to participate in these "activities improving their abilities" only if they need them "for special reasons". The Swedish National Board of Social Welfare has criticized these two terms (and some other formulations) as being unclear (Socialstyrelsen, 2003: 91). Another lose expression is to be found in the Finnish Rehabilitative Work Activities Act (189/2001, section 2). The Act stipulates that one of the aims of both the individual activation plan and the work activities is to improve the recipient's "command of her/his own life". As a recommendation this expression is acceptable, but its vagueness is inadmissible when officials impose penalties on a client because she/he does not follow instructions concerning this "command". In such a situation, arbitrary decisions seem difficult to avoid unless they can be based on judicial decisions.

Officials have to implement legislation in an effective way. Their first priority is to concentrate on the tasks based on the specific piece of legislation most obviously relevant to their everyday work. There is a risk that in practice other legal norms are considered remote or irrelevant, even when their purpose is to protect the recipient's rights. This risk should be taken into account, especially when officials can forcefully intervene in the client's life as in the case of activation. Respect for private life and the right to personal liberty and self-determination are principles integrated into the legal system of all three countries. They are limited in many respects by legislation adopted to achieve societal goals, but this legislation or the authorities implementing it should not interfere in the rights of an individual in a way which is not in an acceptable proportion to the lawful goals pursued. This is called the principle of proportionality. In all three countries benefit penalties are used as sanctions, which is a tough measure as the benefits in question are on a low level and the punishment affects people already in a weak position. The main arguments put forward to justify the penalties are the legitimacy of promoting employment and the societal importance of this objective. However, these grounds for intervening in the private sphere of the recipient should be balanced against her/his fundamental civil rights.

In a democracy, the trade-off between civil rights and obligations connected with social rights is a frequently recurring problem. With regard to the principle of proportionality, the curtailing of the individual's civil rights by the authorities on account of other interests should be examined in the light of the following factors (e.g. *Perusoikeudet*, 1999: 175-176; Åhman, 2005: 37):

– whether the limitations are necessary to achieve a legitimate objective,

– the importance of the societal interest in question in proportion to the rights subjected to restrictions,

– the nature of the intervention (e.g. its scope, duration, ordinary or exceptional character) and how much it affects the individual,

– whether the person concerned needs special protection because of her/his weak position in society,

– whether other, or less severe, measures could be taken to accomplish the same result,

– whether there is a compensation for the intervention.

As a result of this analysis, one can conclude that compulsory activation measures and the penalties attached to them are problematic from the point of view of basic rights. The recipients' weak position especially and the considerable impact of penalties on their situation lead to this conclusion. One could argue, however, that effective activation enabling the recipients to secure gainful employment and improve their living conditions counterbalances the temporary loss of rights. Against this argument, one can object that the results of activation and active labour market policies are uncertain in terms of employment when the focus is on the open labour market (e.g. Malmberg-Heimonen, 2005: 20-21) In any case, this argument would preclude the use of penalties when activation measures are not directly and closely connected with the labour market.

Empowerment by Participation?

One of the rights strengthening the client's position introduced in all three countries is the client's right to participate in the decision-making process concerning her/his case. In Denmark, this is called the principle of dialogue. It means that the authorities should give the claimant an opportunity to influence the decision-making process, though she/he is under no obligation to play an active part in it (sections 1 and 4 of the Legal Security Act (LBK nr 858 af 08/08/2006); section 1, subsection 3 of the Active Social Policy Act (LBK nr 1009 af 24/10/2005); Ketscher, 2002: 317-320).The principle emphasises the active role of the claimant as someone with rights, as opposed to the conception of the recipient as the submissive object of administrative action. However, under Danish law, the client can only participate in the processing of her/his case, not in formulating the actual decision.

In the Swedish and Finnish legal provisions, participation is connected with individualisation, (sections 8 and 13 of the Finnish Rehabilitative Work Activities Act – 189/2001 (and section 8 of the Client Act – 2000/812) and chapter 4, section 4, subsection 2 of the Swedish Social Services Act – 2001/45) which is an important feature of activation policies. Individualisation has a dual nature. It permits the client to put forward her/his personal views and wishes, while at the same time requiring of her/him to subject her/his personal affairs, abilities and weaknesses to an even closer scrutiny and assessment than in the case of traditional social work. Moreover, in practice, the meaning of participation and individualisation depends on the organisational conditions in which they are realized. The term participation can be used in different ways (e.g. Borghi and van Berkel, 2005: 7). In its weakest sense it means that clients take part in the decision-making process only by giving information to the officials. The authorities proceed by discarding the data which do not fit into their pre-established decision-making patterns and convert the selected material into a formal decision. The decision may, or may not, take the claimant's personal wishes and abilities into account, depending on the limitations resulting from the number of alternative measures available, the administrative culture of the unit involved, and so on. In any case, the programme is chosen by the officials.

Naturally, this is not genuine participation (and hardly "dialogue" either) and does not satisfy the requirements of the Swedish and Finnish legislation, which oblige the administration to respect the client's right to self-determination. Real participation presupposes that the client gets adequate information on all possible alternatives and on the consequences of her/his choice. She/he should be allowed to influence the planning of the activation measures concerning her/him or to change their contents. Furthermore, the client should have an opportunity to consult an adviser and be given time to make up her/his mind. Ideally, she/he should be permitted to try out different programmes. It is obvious that authentic participation puts heavy demands on the administration, and the same applies to genuine individualisation, which aims to adapt services to individual needs and preferences. Both arrangements call for flexible decision-making supported by considerable resources. In situations where either of these elements – or both – is lacking, there is a risk that the concepts in question are only catchwords resulting in tokenism. This can be illustrated by a study of the implementation of the Danish legal provision in question, which showed that in many cases local social services did not implement the participation rule properly (Socialministeriet, 2004: IV-VI). Decision-making concerning activation measures were not included in the data, but there is reason to presume that these research results also apply to activation.

Conclusions

Activation policies increase the officials' power and, correspondingly, make the client more dependent on the balanced implementation of the legislation involved. When evaluating the impact of activation, not only the results of various programmes should be taken into account, but also the effectiveness of legal provisions protecting the client against unlawful administrative action. In the three Nordic countries, many such protective provisions have been enacted, but their realisation should be improved. One of the difficulties attached to implementation deficits in this area is that in all three countries, especially activation measures applied to the disadvantaged unemployed are the responsibility of the local (municipal) authorities. These units have a considerable degree of self-government, which allows them in certain situations to pursue their own organisational or other interests when implementing the protective legal provisions.

It is difficult to determine at which point sanctions imposed to enforce compulsory activation violate the recipient's basic rights. However, to avoid such violations, voluntary measures should be preferred, as well as programmes facilitating entry into the labour market of people with reduced employability e.g. by creating or subsidising jobs especially suitable for them. Moreover, the individualised treatment of clients should be sensitive to other problems they may have and not concentrate exclusively on work-orientation.

References

Åhman, Karin, "Europadomstolens principer", in Marcusson, Lena (ed.) *Offentligrättsliga principer*, Uppsala, 2005.

Arbejdsdirektoratet, Being Insured against Unemployment in Denmark, 2006.

Borghi and van Berkel, Activation, Participation, Individualisation: Shifting Public-Private Boundaries, Shifting Roles of Citizens, paper prepared for an ESPAnet conference, September 2005.

Hytti, Helka, "Miksi ruotsalaiset ovat sairaita mutta suomalaiset työttömiä?" *Yhteiskuntapolitiikka* 2002, p. 333-345.

Järvinen, Margarheta, "Mötet mellan klient och system – om forskning i socialt arbete", *Dansk Sociologi*, 2002.

Ketscher, Kirsten, *Socialret*, Copenhagen, 2002.

Lipsky, Michael, *Street-Level Bureaucracy*, New York, 1980.

Malmberg-Heimonen, Ira, *Public Welfare Policies and Private Responses*, Helsinki, 2005.

Mäenpää, Olli, *Hallinto-oikeus*, Helsinki, 2000.

Perusoikeudet, Helsinki, 1999.

Salonen, Tapio and Ulmestig, Rickard, *Nedersta trappsteget. En studie om kommunal aktivering*, Växjö, 2004.

Socialministeriet, *Undersögelse af retssikkerhedslovens 4 §*, Copenhagen, 2004.

Socialstyrelsen, *Ekonomiskt bistånd. Stöd för rättstillämpning…*, Stockholm, 2003.

Socialstyrelsen, *Hur tillämpas bestämmelsen i 4 kap. 4 § socialtjänstlagen?*, Stockholm, 2005.

Tala, Jyrki, *Lakien vaikutukset*, Helsinki, 2001.

Vår sociala trygghet, Helsinki, 2005.

Implementing the New Swiss Employment Policies in the Context of Globalisation

Olivier GIRAUD

Centre Marc Bloch Berlin, CNRS

Introduction

This article focuses on the issue of what is known as "executive federalism" in Switzerland. The key issue discussed in this paper is the impact of "policy and administrative styles" at cantonal level on the implementation of a federal programme. The new employment policy at stake in Switzerland combines various policy goals and instruments in way, which is typical for the globalisation ages. Mixing active measures of employment policy and instruments of control, this law is closely related to the policy program in terms of activation (Barbier, Ludwig-Mayerhofer, 2004). This agenda has been spread around the world from the Third Way revolution developed and experienced in Britain from the late 1990s. The LACI of 1995 as well organizes a regionalisation of the implementation of employment policies in Switzerland. This relative centralisation does not prevent the prevailing logic of the system from being a clear decentralised. This pattern matches the logic of empowerment of local/regional actors also very characteristic of the contemporary, globalisation related, agenda of the labour market policies.

Furthermore, the 1995 Federal Law on Unemployment Insurance (LACI) constitutes a particularly suitable object of investigation as regards the issue of implementation analysis. The LACI law follows the usual configuration of multilevel governance in Switzerland: the federal government, owing to its limited administrative resources, needs to rely on the cantonal public employment service for the implementation of its strategies. The LACI provides stringent measures aimed at monitoring cantonal implementation. However, in spite of these, various studies aimed at assessing implementation in this field have highlighted important cantonal disparities between the cantons in the actual modes of implementation (Curti, 1999). Disparities in implementation may in fact be even more pronounced in this domain than in others, since the LACI resulted from a compromise between Swiss social partners and political Left and Right, with a subsequent juxtaposition of instruments which reflect expectations on both sides (Giriens, Staufer, 1999). The LACI law indeed combines, on the one hand, active labour market programmes (ALMPs) aimed at supporting the reintegration of the unemployed with control measures designed to prevent "abuse" of unemployment benefits on the other. The LACI therefore provides for different potentialities in implementation. Firstly, when focusing on degree of implementation, it is quite possible to imagine that some cantons implement the law in a more intensive fashion than others. Secondly, one may envisage that some cantons may primarily use instruments aimed at improving the reintegration of unemployed persons in the labour market, while others may be more intent on preventing unemployment benefit abuse.

Thus, our aim here is firstly to *measure* possible disparities between cantons in LACI implementation. The second main step is to *explain* these potential disparities by applying the analytical framework of *policy and administrative styles* to the Swiss federal arena.

First, we will determine whether the juxtaposition, within the LACI, of instruments aimed at reintegrating job-seekers into employment and instruments designed more for control over job-seekers may lead to different modes of LACI implementation at cantonal level. This first part will enable us to discuss more precisely the contents of these two main implementation strategies, to present the criteria of empirical testing we have chosen, and also to present the results of the first part of our investigation. We shall thus highlight different "groups" of cantons depending on the modes of LACI implementation they have sought to follow.

The rest of this article deals with the second phase of our research, viz., elucidation of these cantonal differences in LACI implementation. This section will focus on a policy styles analysis of the implementation modes of the LACI.[1] Founded in 1982 by Jeremy Richardson (1982), this concept was dedicated to the study of "policy-making and implementation style" and was oriented towards the analysis of "deep-rooted values in society" (*Ibid.*: 2). Frequently applied to national cases – France stands for an *étatist* policy style, the United Kingdom for a

[1] This article derives from a research project (NPR 43 Swiss National Science Foundation "Steering and Implementation of Active Labour Market Policies in Switzerland: Employment Regulations Analysis from Federal Strategies to Localised Needs", co-directed by D. Braun and I. Papadopoulos (IEPI, Lausanne University). A first version of this argument had been co-authored with Monica Battaglini and published in the Swiss Political Science Review.

liberal policy style and Germany and the Netherlands share a rather similar neo-corporatist one (van Waarden, 1997) –, this analytical framework has very rarely been applied to infra-national cases, such as federal cases (Schiller, 1991). Both the high decentralisation degree of the Swiss federal institutions as well as the high level of heterogeneity characterising the cantonal political cultures in Switzerland[2] indicate to our mind the appropriateness of this concept for the case of Swiss federalism. From a theoretical point of view though, we will need to elaborate the application of policy styles analysis to our case as an introduction to the second section of this article.

1. Cantonal Strategies of LACI Implementation

The following are elements, which explain more precisely, what LACI entails and provide more details as to how implementation disparities between cantons may actually be measured according to the aforementioned axes.

1.1 The Two Main Implementation Strategies

As a reminder, unemployment policy should, according to the LACI, focus on *two main sets of measures*:

a. More social oriented reintegration measures:

– To improve placement capability (employability);

– To fill in various gaps in the qualifications of the unemployed through vigorous training programmes, and to help them reintegrate the labour market;

– To diminish the negative consequences of unemployment at social and professional level.

b. Measures aimed towards control over the unemployed:

– To diminish abuse of the unemployment insurance benefit system.

Following these premises, there are basically *two questions*, which highlight the modes of implementation of the LACI:

1. Is the LACI implemented *entirely*, viz., in a way that all goals are reached? In other words, to what degree is the law actually implemented?

2. If not, what path or orientation is the implementation actually following?

2 Both persisting religious (Geser, 1997) and linguistic disparities (Kriesi *et al.*, 1996) are well known for being significant causes of differences in terms of political culture.

Concerning the first question, a basic assumption is that all Swiss cantons are implementing the LACI. However, the various cantonal administrations may be applying it in ways, which may or may not be in full accordance with the LACI prescriptions, and to varying degrees. Implementation in full accordance with the LACI comprises all the items inherent in the two sets of measures mentioned above, viz. *reintegration* and *control.* Implementation, which covers only one of these sets, is not in full accordance with the LACI. Finally, implementation, which covers both, but only partially, is consequently only partially in accordance with the LACI, with a low degree in implementation.

By combining these two factors, intensity and accordance, one may bring out a typology comprising three different categories of cantons in terms of LACI implementation:

1. "Maximalist" cantons, which implement the LACI to a higher-than-average degree and in full accordance with its prescriptions.

2. "Partial" implementation cantons, in which implementation focuses on only one of the two sets of LACI measures.

3. "Minimalist" cantons, where implementation covers both sets of LACI measures, but to a low degree.

These categories can be summarised as follows:

Table 1. Modes of implementation

		Reintegration	
		High	Low
Control	High	"Maximalist" implementation	Control-oriented "partial" implementation
	Low	Reintegration-oriented "partial" implementation	"Minimalist" implementation

1.2 A Statistics-based Typology

1.2.1 Reintegration Indicators

In order to find a suitable means of measuring the tendency towards reintegration in LACI implementation, attention has been drawn to three *structural* indicators: (a) the level of development of the ALMP logistics; (b) experimental programmes or cantonal initiatives; and (c) the cantonal fulfilment rate of ALMPs demanded by the Confederation for the year 1999.

The ALMP logistic is a LACI-specific organisational device set up by the cantons with the aim of analysing systematically on the one hand the needs of employers and the skills or qualifications of job-seekers on the other, and to set up accordingly various ALMPs including training – or retraining – measures. The level of development of ALMP logistics differs considerably from one canton to the other, and therefore measures the degree to which LACI implementation is oriented towards reintegration.

The LACI (Art. 110a) law enables cantons to set up provisional experimental programmes or cantonal ALMP initiatives that may depart from the federal law while still being funded by the Confederation. Such "trials" which are considered effective may be included in the existing ALMPs for a maximum period of four years. Some cantons even finance certain ALMPs not included in the LACI themselves. The presence of such programmes in a given canton is an indication of a certain amount of diligence as regards unemployment policy, meaning a clear orientation towards reintegration of job seekers.

The LACI law obliges cantons to set up more ALMPs than before the law was amended in 1995. This extension of ALMP supply seeks to improve the placement capability of job seekers and to ease their access to employment. Here again, cantons differ in the way they carry out these programmes. Measuring the cantonal fulfilment rate of ALMPs demanded by the Confederation for the year 1999 gives a clear indication as to whether or not a canton has an inclination towards active reintegration of job-seekers.

1.2.2 Control Indicators

Structural indicators do not provide a suitable means of assessing the "control" inclination of a given canton, since there is no specific control structure. However, the provision of service indicators delivers a clear picture of control, through the number of "penalties" per job seeker decided by the cantonal Public Employment Service (PES); this is the control indicator we use in this research. As mentioned above, the LACI law requires that the counsellor/placement officer verify that job seekers find and *accept* as soon as possible what is to be considered "suitable work" (as defined by Article 16 of the LACI law). Indeed, there are instances where job seekers normally entitled to unemployment benefits refuse a job unjustifiably on the grounds that a better job may be found. They may also be found to not have made enough efforts to find a suitable job, or to have abused the system in some other way. In theses cases, they may be subject to "penalties", namely by a reduction of transfer payments.

Detailed questionnaires on the reintegration indicators were sent by mail to all cantonal administrations for work and employment. Only two cantons did not provide us with the necessary information. The research results available are consequently confined to 24 cantons. The control indicator is standardised data provided by the SECO.

1.2.3 Classification of Cantons

According to the indicators mentioned above, close investigation based cantonal data enables us to sketch a preliminary classification of cantons in terms of modes of LACI implementation. In the following table, cantons above average for each of the depicted indicators are market with 1, while cantons below average are marked by 0.

Table 2. Coding and typology of Swiss cantons according to LACI implementation

		Reintegration *High*	***Reintegration*** *Low*
Control	*High*	"Maximalist" implementation **BS 1111** **LU 1111** **SO 1111** GR 1101 SZ 1011 BE 1011 *AG 1001* *GL 0101* *BL 0101* *SG 0101*	"Partial" control-oriented implementation **UR 0001** **OW 0001** **NW 0001**
Control	*Low*	"Partial" reintegration-oriented implementation **JU 1110** **VS 1110** **TI 1110** **FR 1110** **VD 1110** GE 1100 NE 0110 ZG 1100 *ZH 1000*	"Minimalist" implementation **AR 0000** **AI 0000**

1	1	1	1
a	B	c	D

a: 1st reintegration indicator: ALMP logistic;
b: 2nd reintegration indicator: canton initiated experimental ALMP scheme;
c: 3rd reintegration indicator: cantonal fulfilment rate of ALMPs objective set by the Confederation;
d: control indicator: number of penalties decided by the cantonal PES.

In our classification we consider as "maximalist" all cantons that have above average control and reintegration indicators. Cantons with low levels of both types of indicators are considered "minimalist" in implementing LACI. Finally, cantons that have low levels of reintegration and high levels of control and vice versa are respectively "partial reintegration-oriented" implementers and "partial control-oriented" implementers.

As shown in Table 2, we find some "ideal cases" (in bold) and some "hybrid cases" (plain characters).[3] For hybrid cases we consider that they are included in the "maximalist" group if they have at least one indicator of reintegration indicator and one control indicator that is above average. If they have only reintegration indicators that are above average we consider them as "partial reintegration-oriented" implementers.

The typology of the various modes of cantonal implementation demonstrates its capacity to discriminate most cases in a coherent manner: 13 out of 24 cases show configurations of variables fitting exactly one of our four possible modes of implementation and only five cases show rather unclear configurations of variables. These results also corroborate the distinction we make between implementation modes according to both intensity and orientation of the cantonal execution of the LACI. In the latter respect, they confirm the clear distinction between executions oriented towards reintegration and executions oriented towards control.

The first conclusion to be drawn at this stage regards the gathering of all French and Italian speaking cantons in the "partial-reintegration" type of LACI implementation, while most of the German-speaking cantons of Switzerland belong to the "maximalist" type.

2. Explaining Divergences by Cantonal Policy Styles

The high level of disparity in the implementation of the Swiss federal law on unemployment insurance (LACI) revealed in Section one should now be addressed. Different explicative hypothesis are discussed in the literature on implementation in the context of Swiss federalism. In this article we shall focus on the impact of diverging *policy and administrative styles* at cantonal level.

The concept of policy style has been criticised for its vagueness and theoretical weakness (Feick, 1990: 185), but, at the same time, it has been praised for being the missing link between important factors in comparative policy analysis – institutional, cultural and inter-individual factors – and the qualitative output of policy systems, *i.e.* the policies themselves and the way they are implemented by administrations (*Ibid.*: 187).

3 Characters in italics refer to cases that are even more ambiguous, with the special case of Zurich, where apparently the municipality, and not the cantonal administration, is most highly involved in unemployment policy.

In order to develop an operational conception of policy and administrative styles, we should begin with a review of the available literature focusing on elements useful for our purpose. We will then apply this operational concept to the different groups of cantons identified in Section one and thus compare the results of our typology of LACI implementation with a typology of policy and administrative styles in the context of Swiss federalism. We will first have to make use of standardized (quantitative) indicators to be able to work on the complete range of Swiss cantons. The second step of our investigation will based on the case studies investigated thoroughly for the purpose of our research. We will then make use of qualitative data based on cantonal case studies.

2.1 Applying the Theory of Policy Style to the Context of Swiss Executive Federalism

The principal goal of Jeremy Richardson in 1982 in founding the concept of policy styles was to discover whether "*societies develop 'standard operating procedures' for making and implementing policies*" (Richardson, 1982: 2). Influenced by Lowi's typology of policy issues (1964), Richardson's own matrix of national policy styles is developed according to two main aspects: the consensual versus the imposing type of decision making and the anticipatory versus the reactive type of problem solving (*Ibid.*: 13). Richardson evokes the possible influence of "*deep values rooted in societies*" but does not elaborate any explicative framework of possible causal links between culture and policy styles.

Among the more recent works, which have further investigated the possible links between institutions, culture, modes of inter-individual coordination and policy outcomes, we shall limit our discussion to the most useful contributions for our research.

Jürgen Feick (1990) provides a stimulating analytical discussion of the existing literature on policy styles and shows precisely how policy styles are "the processes of decision making and/or implementation, in which actors handle in interaction with each other, according to institutional rules, to their own cognitive and normative orientations, to their personal preferences for different procedures and according to their own interests positions" (*Ibid.*: 209). He defines three basic aspects of policy styles to be found in various policy sectors or nations (*Ibid.*: 210): the preferred modes of conflict resolution, the preferred modes of problem resolution, the patterns of interaction and participation in the relevant policy network. For our purpose, the configuration of variables adding institutional rules, individual cognitive and normative orientations and interests positions with traditions of conflict resolution, or network shape, represents a first important step. In line with the present institutionalist position, Feick establishes a clear link between individual patterns of behaviour and different types of institutional constraints.[4] To us, the important point in Feick's view is that he stresses the distinction between two types of institutional constraints: those which are formalised (laws, rules, etc.) and the historically developed orientations of co-ordination among actors (explicit or implicit mutual understanding, historically developed type of social or political regulation, etc.). As Feick lucidly points out, the difficulty relates to both the measurement of the latter kind of institutional constraints and their possible impact on policy process.

The contribution of Frans van Waarden (1987) goes a step further in the definition of relevant policy styles[5] and in the explanation of the impact of policy styles on policy-making and policy implementation. Adopting a historical institutionalist position, he proposes a causal model explaining both the formation and the influence of national policy styles on policy-making and implementation. Van Waarden states that there is a process of mutual reinforcement between political culture and institutional development. The basic institutions of the political system reinforce the political culture, which then strengthens in a congruent direction the functioning and development of the main traits of the institutional framework (*Ibid.*: 346). Van Waarden explains the impact of a few selected influential institutions according to his model: conceptions of the state in legal systems; presence or absence of judicial review; public administration[6] (degree of professionalisation and social prestige); embeddedness (in the social structures) and persistence (*Ibid.*: 347-361).

Both these analytical models of policy and administrative styles complement rather than contradict each other. Feick's and van Waarden's models concern the persisting coherences linking broad cultural and institutional environments during the entire policy process

---

4 This standpoint is for instance a key element in the theory of actor-centred institutionalism (Scharpf, 1997).

5 Liberal-pluralist vs. corporatist styles; active vs. reactive styles; comprehensive vs. fragmental or incremental styles; adversarial vs. consensual vs. paternalistic styles; legalistic vs. pragmatic styles; formal vs. informal network relations (van Waarden: 335-336).

6 A recent contribution by Terpstra and Havinga (2001) focuses more precisely on administrative culture, or at least on the interpretative schemes and norms dominating in a specific administration and differentiates between four clear types of policy implementation: a traditional policy implementation mostly based on customs, traditional morality and local authority; a bureaucratic policy implementation based on formal rules and bureaucratic impartiality; a professional policy implementation based on professional decisions within the legal framework; a managerial policy implementation based on productivity and cost-efficiency (*Ibid.*: 102).

(decision making and implementation phases). In these models, the most basic factors of policy and administration styles are both the scope and style of state intervention, the mode of actors' co-ordination and interaction and the basic values of the political culture. All the policy style defining patterns according to Feick and van Waarden derive from a combination of these four factors. From the perspective of actor-centred institutionalism, one could state that the style of state intervention and the mode of actors' co-ordination and interaction are to be analysed simultaneously. Renate Mayntz and Fritz Scharpf (1995) show convincingly how the regulation mode in a social sector depends on the regulation capacity of the state, the regulation capacity of organised social actors, but also, the willingness of the state to give some social actors access to the policy network, and conversely on the readiness of the social actors to participate to this network. In Scharpf and Mayntz's view, a regulation mode is not an equilibrium resulting from the different parties' regulation capacities. In our view, style of state intervention and mode of actors' co-ordination are precisely related more to the ability of certain actors to act in a more or less exclusive or co-operative way as regards their power implications, than to the direct expression of their respective regulation capacities.

Three of these four factors are qualitative factors. The style of state intervention (legalistic, authoritarian, consensual, etc.), the mode of actor's co-ordination (based on market, corporative or public instruments), or the basic features of the political culture (preferences, norms, orientations) are strictly qualitative factors. They are not to be translated into quantitative data and thus do not permit a systematic analysis of all Swiss cantons. They were though analysed using qualitative methods in detailed case studies and will be presented in Section 2.3. From a policy style analysis perspective, the only variable easily applicable to the entire range of Swiss cantons is that measuring the level of development of state intervention. Quantitative results are presented in the next section.

In focusing on the scope of state intervention, we of course miss the questions of actors' co-ordination and interaction, of the style of state intervention, and of the patterns of the cantonal political culture. However, the issue of state development and intervention has been central in all Western states at least since the end of World War II. The Swiss cantons, which enjoy a particularly high degree of sovereignty and autonomy, are intent on preserving their political and administrative traditions, and are able to choose their own level of public intervention. Thus they may also be categorised according to this criterion.

2.2 Using Comparative Quantitative Data

For the time being, with the exception of a few other studies which have certain points in common with this type of approach (Urio, 1986; Germann, 1986), analysis in terms of *policy style* has not been applied in the context of Swiss federalism. In Switzerland, however, there are marked disparities in political traditions between cantons. Inequalities in cantonal administrative capacity or in the levels of cantonal welfare spending,[7] for instance, do not only reflect structural or economic disparities, but also proceed from long-term political choices. The impact of long-term partisan leadership is a difficult matter in the case of the Swiss cantons. In the first place, there is a marked contrast in cantonal partisan traditions from one region to another and their influences are consequently difficult to compare (Ladner, 1999: 215-216). In most cases moreover, the cantonal executives are composed of more or less broad coalitions of parties. The influence of each party over the cantonal policy tradition is then difficult to demonstrate. Direct democracy or any other kind of decentralised power institutions blurs even more the links that might be drawn between a party – or a stable coalition – and a recurrent policy outcome (Freitag, Vatter, 2002). In our view, this point strengthens the utility of the policy style perspective to explain the particularities of cantonal policies or policy implementations. In our view, the analysis of the partisan influence has to be apprehended in the Swiss context through qualitative analysis (see 2.3.) and not through standardised quantitative analysis.

In Chart 1, we selected an indicator, which points to the level of cantonal spending in public employment per capita (cantonal population). This ratio provides us with a synthetic indicator as to the level of public (or administrative) interventionism in each canton. It thus reliably measures the scope of state intervention and its stability, over 30 years.[8] We then try to compare the correlation between this indicator and the typology of the cantonal implementation mode with different control variables.

Firstly it can be seen that, the ranking of cantons is stable over the time-period shown in Chart 1. With the exception of outstanding cases, the positioning of which has changed considerably, the relative ranking of nearly all Swiss cantons, over 30 years, is indeed very stable. This

7 Annuaire statistique de la Suisse 2000.

8 We could have used indicators comparing the level of public spending in all cantons. But since public money can be dedicated to privately implemented actions, the level of cantonal spending in public employment per capita is, to us, a more realistic indicator of the scope of public intervention itself.

first observation in itself gives credence to the stability of policy styles and to their applicability in the case of the Swiss cantons.

The second stage of our statistical investigation is dedicated to analysis of the impact of our variable measuring state intervention development on the mode of LACI implementation (Table 3). Since we are dealing with a partial indicator of policy style, we controlled the correlation of the public employment expenses with two variables that might also have an impact on implementation: the cantonal level of urbanisation and cantonal financial capacity. According to Table 3, neither the results of the "urbanisation" variable, nor those of the "financial capacity" variable could possibly explain the distribution of the cantons in the different modes of implementation.

Chart 1: Cantonal and communal spending in public employment *per capita* (cantonal population) from 1968 to 1998

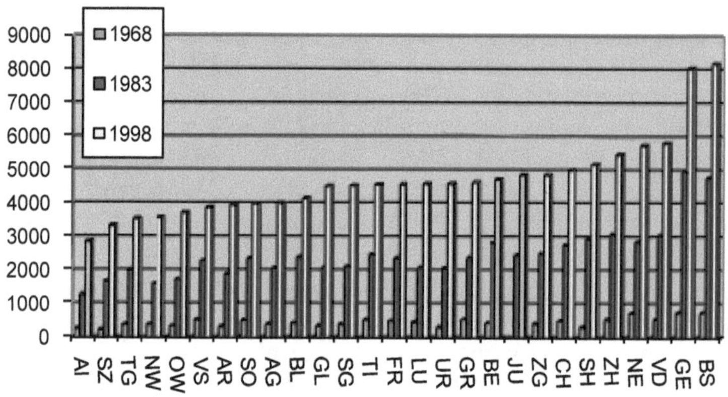

Table 3. Multinomial logit regression coefficients (standard errors in parentheses, * p < 0.1, ** p < 0.05) (comparison category: minimalist implementation)

	control	Reintegration	maximalist
public employment expenses (mean 68-98)	0.006	0.014*	0.013*
	(0.006)	(0.008)	(0.008)
urbanisation	-0.081	-0.019	-0.03
	(0.079)	(0.075)	(0.073)
financial capacity	0.113	0.098	0.104
	(0.093)	(0.083)	(0.082
Constant	-14.856	-33.291*	-31.05*
	(13.795)	(17.612)	(17.554)
LR chi2 (df)		17.70** (9)	
N		24	

The coefficients of public employment expenses (as a mean for the period 1968-1998) are significant at the 0.1 level for the "partial-reintegration" mode of LACI implementation and for the "maximalist" one, but not for the "partial-control implementation" mode of LACI execution.[9]

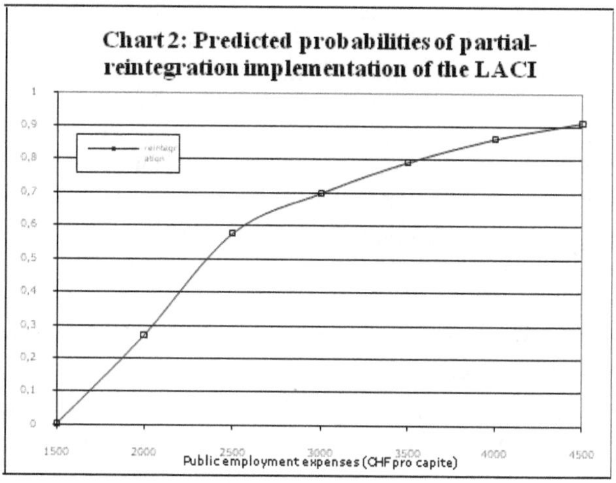

Chart 2: Predicted probabilities of partial-reintegration implementation of the LACI

Chart 2 demonstrates a clear correlation between the level of public employment expenses and the probability that the mode of LACI implementation is the "partial reintegration" one. At high levels of expenses, reintegration becomes clearly the most likely implementation mode.

This quantitative data analysis demonstrates a link between a fairly long term development of the state intervention's scope and an implementation of the LACI that favours the instruments of reinsertion over the instruments of control, or over a minimalist or a maximalist use of both types of instruments. However, this first conclusion cannot explain why cantons presenting quite similar levels of state intervention development – Basle-town and Geneva or Bern and Fribourg for example – adopted different modes of LACI implementation (compare Table 1 and Chart 1). The qualitative criteria measuring modes of actors' coordination and the style of state intervention should now be considered to examine some of the questions reminding unanswered.

9 The significance level is not high, but this can be attributed to the small sample.

2.3 Interpreting Case Studies

The first part of our analysis indicates a relation between the orientation of cantonal state intervention traditions and the LACI implementation modes. The last stage of our study is dedicated to the investigation of the complementary aspects of policy and administrative styles. Qualitative case studies were necessary to investigate the entire range of factors influencing the different cantonal policy and administrative styles, *i.e.* the qualitative factors concerned with the modes of actors' co-ordination and interaction and with the style of state intervention. To this end, six case studies were picked among the Swiss cantons. We selected the case studies according to their importance within our typology of implementation modes (see Table 2).

– Three case studies were dedicated to the largest group – the *reintegration-oriented partial implementation* group: Fribourg, Geneva, Ticino.

– Two case studies were dedicated to the second largest group – the *maximalist implementation* group: Basle-Town and Bern.

– One double case study was dedicated to the third largest group – the *control-oriented* partial implementation group: Nidwald and Obwald.

We did not make a case study in the *minimalist implementation* group because the patterns of this group's cantons turn out to be only slightly different from those of the latter group. Moreover, it appeared irrelevant to us to carry out detailed investigations in more than two cantons presenting extremely low unemployment levels, as is the case in the cantons belonging to both the control-oriented and the minimalist implementation groups.

We shall present here a brief analysis of the relevant features of policy and administrative styles to be found in each group. This analysis is based on a set of qualitative data collected in our 6 cantons. In each case,[10] 15 to 25 interviews were conducted with the most relevant political, administrative, corporative or associative actors. The cantonal legislation and all available administrative sources of information were analysed.

The three main indicators of policy style that were revealed by our qualitative inquiry are the style of state intervention and the mode of actors' co-ordination on the one hand, and the main traits of regional political culture on the other. The analysis of the labour market policy network provides us with essential information on both the style of state intervention and the mode of actor's co-ordination and interaction in the

[10] For further details on the actors interviewed, see research report forthcoming.

different cantons. In the labour market policy domain, it turns out that besides the public actors, the key organisations in the policy network are, with different emphasis in the different cantons, the trade unions, business associations, and the organisations in charge of unemployment insurance funds. The dominant traits of the cantonal political culture's orientation are apprehended through analysis of electoral results over the past 30 years. Given the degree of segmentation of the Swiss party system in the different cantonal arenas, the nature of the different parties' influences will have to be re-contextualised. Several federal referendums results were analysed to measure the sensitivity of the cantonal population to social issues and its degree of openness as regards national/international issues.[11]

2.3.1 The Reintegration-oriented Partial Implementation Group: Fribourg, Geneva, Ticino

All French and Italian cantons of Switzerland are classified within this group. These cantons indeed implement most of the structural items of the LACI, develop to a large extent the active labour market schemes aimed at the reintegration of unemployed but are reluctant to make use of sanctions. Two main points of the policy and administrative style of these three cantons appear to be linked to the *reintegration-oriented partial implementation mode*.

In the first place, trade unions are traditionally strong and still are today – at least in the Swiss context – in the labour market policy domain of these cantons. The case of Geneva is the most striking in this respect. In this town-canton, the unions are strongly organised. They are considered as unavoidable partners of the public authorities and can count on strong partnership relations in the cantonal parliament. Consequently they can transfer their positions or opposition towards the administration into the political arena when negotiation has turned out to be inefficient to fulfil their goals. In Ticino and Fribourg, the unions' influence is less institutionalised and obvious than in Geneva. The continuing pressure the unions of both these cantons can exercise on both administration and government helps to hinder an interpretation of the LACI towards control.

---

11 These two cleavages are often considered in the literature as the most crucial in the context of Swiss federalism (Kriesi *et al.*, 1996; Hug and Sciarini, 2002). Fifteen federal referendums or initiatives from 1978 to 2001 are considered. Most of them concern strictly social issues ("paid leave extension" – 1985; "working-time reduction" – 1988; "federal maternity-insurance fund" – 1999; "pension reform" – 2000, etc.). The national/international cleavage is relevant for our research mostly as far as it concerns the issue of protection of the Swiss labor market ("nationality law reform" – 1994; "immigration reglementation" – 2000; "bilateral agreement with the EU" – 2000).

In the three cantons standing for the *reintegration-oriented partial implementation mode*, the influence of unions is backed by a traditional orientation of the regional political culture towards rather strong social policy. This orientation was measured by the cantonal results of different federal referendums concerning social policy issues. The rate of approval of these issues is systematically higher in these cantons than the average throughout the country.[12] This trend in public opinion is coherent with the strong representation of the socialist party and / or of the Christian democracy in the cantonal parliament and executives. These parties traditionally tend to promote social policies or a social orientation in the implementation of federal programs, especially in the Latin cantons of Switzerland.

The influence of unions over cantonal politics and policies combined with a general social orientation of political culture shared by both the political élite and the population are determining factors explaining a cantonal LACI implementation strategy favouring the objective of reintegration of the unemployed over that of control of the unemployed. Despite strong differences in the social, economic or labour market structures of the cantons of Fribourg, Geneva and Ticino, the cantonal configurations of these three cantons in terms of policy and administrative style are very similar to each other. These policy styles configuration are moreover consistent with the implementation mode of the Federal Law on unemployment policy oriented towards reintegration.

2.3.2 The Maximalist Implementation Group: Basle-Town and Bern.

Compared to the former, the *maximalist implementation* group enforces the LACI in a more orthodox way. In the cantons belonging to this group, governments and administration demonstrate an equivalent involvement in both major aspects of the law. They actively promote the reinsertion of job seekers but do not do so at the cost of a reinforced control of the unemployed population. With the exception of Bern[13] and to some extent Graubunden, all cantons belonging to this group are located in the north-western part of the country and are all exclusively German speaking.

As was the case with the previous group, the policy and administrative styles of both our case studies belonging to this second group demonstrate a certain level of homogeneity.

---

[12] The stronger orientation of the French and Italian speaking Swiss towards social goals was demonstrated quite recently (Kriesi *et al.*, 1996).

[13] Bern is considered as a bilingual canton; the French speaking population is a small minority. This canton is also usually considered as being part of Western Switzerland.

In the first place, the influence of unions is, in this second group, notably weaker than in the first one. Unions are organised but cannot count on direct support emerging from the political arena and do not enjoy immediate access either to the administrative or to the political networks. In both cantons, the unemployment policy network is state-centred. In the case of Bern, the business associations are pushing for reinforcement of the control aspect of the LACI implementation, which is not the case in Basle-Town.

This type of unemployment policy network is congruent with the population's political culture that appears to be rather moderate and strongly oriented towards consensus. In Bern, the moderate Christian-Democratic party dominates the cantonal executive. The socialists are also strong but are very consensus oriented too. In Basle-Town, very centrist socialists[14] dominate the executive and the second leading party is a moderate right-wing party. The social orientation of both cantonal governments seems to comply with the expectancy of the cantonal populations. Measured by cantonal results of national referendums on social issues, these cantons' public opinions appear to be more moderate than in the first group. In neither Bern nor Basle-Town is there a clear demand emerging from the population for more social protection.

The qualitative interviews conducted in the administrations of both cantons reveal an administrative style strongly marked by legalism and conformity with the federal law. In Bern, the geographical closeness to the federal authorities is said by local actors to reinforce the pressure on the cantonal administration for more compliance with the original intentions of the confederation. In Basle-Town, the executive has granted a high degree of autonomy to the administration as concerns unemployment policies. In this case, the continuous process of federal control over implementation activities in the cantons could suffice to impose a high degree of conformity with federal goals. Moreover in both cantons, the interviews carried out at all levels of the cantonal unemployment department show strong approval of the core values of the law. Both control and reinsertion are understood as complementary and necessary instruments of state intervention in unemployment issues.

2.3.3 The Control-oriented Partial Implementation Group: Nidwald and Obwald.

For the first time in their history, the half-cantons of Nid and Obwald are acting together to implement the LACI. The two cantons have reached a sufficient level of co-ordination and agreement in unemploy-

14 The socialist party is so centrist oriented that a small minority of its members left their organisation in order to found a more radical party, regularly represented in the cantonal parliament.

ment policy to create a single regional placement office. Thus they both implement the LACI in a way favouring a high degree of control of job seekers – these cantons reached one of the highest penalty rates per unemployed – and neglecting active reinsertion of the unemployed. This specific mode of implementation is also to be found in another small canton of central Switzerland: Uri.

These cantons share most features of their respective policy styles. They are small entities; their urban and industrial structures are weak. They are strongly influenced by conservative political parties. However, the Christian Democracy that dominates in this region of Switzerland differs from the equivalent parties in western and Italian-speaking Switzerland. In central Switzerland, this party is not oriented towards social goals and does not favour any kind of state intervention. Moreover, the lack of industrial tradition partly explains the extreme weakness of labour unions in both cantons. These characteristics of the regional policy styles are furthermore highly consistent with the orientation of the population's political culture. The results of federal referendums on social policy issues are regularly radically more conservative in these two half-cantons than they are on average throughout the country.

The qualitative research conducted in our six case studies was able to take account of variables assessing the modes of actors' co-ordination and interaction emerging from the societies of the different cantons – frame of policy network, preferred modes of conflict resolution, self-organisation ability of actors – as well as some basic features of the regional political culture. The second stage of the analysis explains in a more detailed manner the nature of the link between policy styles and mode of implementation, which has first been indicated by statistics mostly measuring the degree of interventionism of all Swiss cantons. It is for instance possible to understand why Basle-Town and Geneva, which developed the two largest cantonal states in the country, measured in terms of public employment, do not implement the federal law on unemployment policy in the same way. In Geneva, the context of policy network is much more open to the influence of the organisations of industrial relations and the demand emerging from the people for more state intervention is much higher than it is in Basle. The same kind of analysis could be made for Ticino and Bern, which demonstrate levels of public employment which are very similar but enforce the LACI along different lines.

Only the combination of both types of indicators, assessing the strength of the scope of state intervention, as well as the mode of inter-individual co-ordination, the style of state intervention and some basic traits of political culture, can lead to full understanding of the interplay between institutional, cultural and inter-individual variables.

Conclusions

The major aim of this article is to reach a better understanding of executive federalism, a process by which federal legislation is implemented by the cantons, and is thus re-appropriated and re-translated by actors at cantonal level.

Having classified the cantons according to their type of implementation, the next step was to explain these differences. In other words, to understand how and why federal legislation with explicit legal and administrative norms aimed at homogenising the Swiss labour market policies may be re-appropriated by cantonal actors in such disparate manners. The main hypothesis presented here is that modes of implementation may be strongly influenced by policy styles, consistent with traditions related to culture, institutions and preferred modes of inter-individual co-ordination and interaction at cantonal level.

Indeed, by focusing on a clear-cut indicator, it is possible firstly to determine whether a given cantonal administration is oriented towards interventionism, or on the contrary towards liberalism. One of our contentions is that policy styles influenced by interventionist traditions and more leftist political forces are more prone to use job-seeker reintegration instruments. On the contrary, policy styles influenced by more liberal traditions and conservative political forces give preference to control instruments or the simultaneous use of both types of instruments.

By making use of qualitative case studies, the second stage of the research demonstrates that the mechanisms of the influence of different policy and administrative styles on implementation have to be explained by more complex configurations of variables. Only the interplay between the strength of the state apparatus, the modes of actors' co-ordination and interaction, the style of state intervention and the main patterns of political culture can explain the diversity of our cases. As we have seen, interventionist cantons – Basle and Geneva for instance – in fact apply the LACI in contrasting ways because public intervention is embedded in these different cantons in quite differently organised societies and in diverging political cultures. These conclusions confirm at infra-national level, these conclusions confirm two of the basic assumptions of the literature on policy styles.

Firstly, it is possible to identify in the Swiss cantons "standard operating procedures" detected by Richardson in the context of cross-national comparisons. There is indeed a link between culture, institutions and actors' modes of co-ordination and interaction that frames encompasses configuration of factors. Separate analysis of the influence of political parties, institutions or the level of state development appears to be insufficient, particularly in the Swiss case. Secondly, Frans van

Waarden revealed a few years ago a mechanism of mutual reinforcement of culture and institutions. Here we could complement this conclusion by stating that all the main components of policy and administrative styles – degree of state authority and development, shape of policy networks, preferred modes of conflict and problem resolution and self-organisation ability of social groups – tend to evolve in an interdependent manner. In our research, we need to include analysis of all these variables in order to be able to explain all types of variations between our cases.

The Swiss law on unemployment (1995) is the result of a political compromise between the left and the right. During the decision making phase, the political left promoted instruments of reintegration of the unemployed into the workforce. The political right focused on instruments of control over job-seekers aimed primarily at preventing abuse of the unemployment benefit system. Both sets of instruments have been integrated into LACI, reaching a political compromise. It consequently offers a certain amount of leeway in interpretation, since actors entrusted with implementation may give more weight to one or other of these sets of instruments. In the Swiss context, the heterogeneity of regional power relations opens a considerable space for diverging implementation regimes. The empowerment of decentralised actors, distinctive features of the globalisation era, opens in the Swiss case room for the development of considerable inter-regional inequalities.

References

Barbier J.-C. and Ludwig-Mayerhofer W., "The many worlds of activation", European Societies, Vol. 6, No. 4, 2004, p. 423-436.

Braun D., "Interests or Ideas? An Overview of Ideational Concepts in Public Policy research", in D. Braun and A. Busch (eds.), *Public Policy and Political Ideas*, Cheltenham, Edward Elgar, 1999, pp. 11-29.

Curti M. and Meins E., "Politiques suisses du marché du travail – Différences résultant de sa mise en application au niveau du service de l'emploi", *La Vie Économique*, 2/99, 1999, pp. 64-70.

Feick J., "L'analyse comparative des politiques publiques: un chemin vers l'intégration des résultats?", *L'année sociologique*, Vol. 40, No. 1, 1990, pp. 179-225.

Freitag M. and Vatter A., "Die Janusköpfigkeit von Verhandlungsdemokratien. Zur Wirkung von Konkordanz, direkter Demokratie und dezentralen Entscheidungsstrukturen auf den öffentlichen Sektor der Schweizer Kantone", *Revue suisse de science politique*, 2002, 8, (2), pp. 53-80.

Germann R.-E., "Die Beziehungen zwischen Bund und Kantonen im Verwaltungsbereich", in R.-E. Germann and E. Weibel (eds.), *Manuel du système politique de la Suisse/Fédéralisme*, Berne, Haupt, 1986, Vol. 3, pp. 343-369.

Geser H. "The Persistence of Confessional Political Cultures in Switzerland: Some Puzzling Empirical Evidence from Local Parties", *Revue suisse de science politique*, 1997, Vol. 3, No. 2, pp. 1-29.

Giriens P.-Y. and Staufer J., "Deuxième révision de la loi sur l'assurance-chômage: genèse d'un compromis", in A. Mach (eds.), *Globalisation, néo-libéralisme et politiques publiques dans la Suisse des années 90*, Zürich, Seismo, 1997, pp. 105-143.

Hug S. and Sciarini P. (eds.), *Changements de valeurs et nouveaux clivages politiques en Suisse*, Paris, L'Harmattan, 2002.

Kissling-Näf I. and Wälti S., "Der Vollzug öffentlicher Politiken", in U. Klöti, P. Knoepfel, H. Kriesi, W. Linder and Yannis Papadopoulos (eds.), *Handbuch der Schweizer Politik*, Zürich, NZZ Verlag, 1999, pp. 652-689.

Kriesi H., Wernli B., Sciarini P. and Gianni M., *Le clivage linguistique – Problèmes de compréhension entre les communautés linguistiques en Suisse*, Berne, Office Fédéral de la Statistique, 1996.

Ladner A., "Das Schweizer Parteiensystem und seine Parteien", in U. Klöti, P. Knoepfel, H. Kriesi, W. Linder and Y. Papadopoulos (dir.), *Handbuch der Schweizer Politik*, Zürich, Verlag Neue Zürcher Zeitung, 1999, pp. 211-257.

Linder W., Schweizerische Demorkatie: Institutionen – Prozessse – Perspektiven, Bern, Haupt, 1999.

Lowi T.-J., "American business, public policy, case-studies, and political theory", *World Politics*, No. 4, July 1964, pp. 677-715.

Mayntz R. and Scharpf F.-W., "Steuerung und Selbstorganisation in staatsnahen Sektoren", in R. Mayntz, and F.-W. Scharpf (eds.), *Gesellschaftiliche Selbstregelung und politische Steuerung*, Francfort s.l.M.: Campus, 1995, pp. 9-38.

Richardson J., Gustafsson G. and Jordan G., "The Concept of Policy Style", in J. Richardson, *Policy Styles in Western Europe*, Londres, George Allen and Unwin, 1982, pp. 1-16.

Scharpf F.-W., *Games Real Actors Play – Actor-Centered Institutionalism in Policy Research*, Boulder, Westview Press, 1997.

Schiller T.,"Politikstil als vergleichendes Untersuchungskonzept", in U. Kempf, H.-J. Michelmann and T. Schiller (eds.), Politik und Politikstile im kanadischen Bundesstaat – Gesundheits- und energiepolitische Entscheidungsprozesse im Provinzenvergleich. Opladen: Leske und Budrich, 1991, pp. 33-52.

Terpstra J. and Tetty H., "Implementation Between Tradition and Management: Structuration and Styles of Implementation", *Law & Politics*. 2001, Vol. 23, No. 1, pp. 95-116.

Urio P., "Les administrations cantonales", in R.-E. Germann and E. Weibel (eds.), *Manuel du système politique de la Suisse/Fédéralisme*, Berne, Haupt, 1986, Vol. 3, pp. 107-134.

Van Waarden F., "Persistance of National Policy Styles. A study of their Institutional Foundations", in B. Unger and F. van Waarden, *Convergence or Diversity? Internationalisation and Economic Policy Response*, Aldershot, Averbury, 1997, pp. 333-372.

Diversity? Internationalisation and Economic Policy Response, Aldershot, Averbury, 1997, pp. 333-372.

Part II

Decentralisation and Specialisation of Labour and Employer Associations: Emerging Negotiation Paradigms

Entrepreneur Associations and Trade Unions

Towards a Merging of the Labour Policy Agenda?

Paola CAPPELLIN

Sociologist – Universidade Federal do Rio de JaneiroIntroduction

Since the 1960s, large corporations and firms throughout the world have taken up the challenge of attempting to combine corporate success and social responsibility. Indeed, over time, it has become clearer how solidarity principles can be conjoined with business success (Carroll, 1999: 268-295). From this integration, there emerges a more complex image of companies, a sum of the different components of their actions. The form and nature of relationships developed between various social actors also play a role. In other words, the imperatives of financial profit, of defining the 'right price' and of offering a quality product are no longer the sole guarantees of success. In evaluating a company's performance, its social conduct also comes into play.

Companies have long operated essentially according to the logic of productivity and profitability, while their social responsibility remained hidden or subordinated to this logic: should profits be threatened, social progress would be too. In fact, in the eyes of businesses, social issues were solely limited to how much they paid their workers, how much money they made, and how much they produced. However, international experience indicates that this perspective is changing: because of the profound transformations within today's working world and the crisis scenario that has accompanied ever-stiffer competition, many companies are now turning to the public for support in overcoming their competitors.

With this in mind, the purpose of this paper is to detect how local, foreign and multinational companies operating in the state of Rio de Janeiro (Brazil) have become involved in different spheres of the social agenda. The idea is to explore new corporate concerns and the changes in firms' behaviour that promote citizenship inside and outside the workplace. The sections below provide a more detailed analysis of the issue. The first section deals with the development of the concept of

Social Responsibility based on American background reference; in fact, most of the theoretical debate and practicing managers quote this original source. The second section examines how Brazilian business associations and organisations internalize social responsibility concerns, focusing in particular on the widespread and divergent opinions about it. The third section investigates companies' social practices. Finally, the fourth section reviews the local trade unions' opinions about the current social responsibility in companies located in the state of Rio de Janeiro.

Firms and American Society: "Nevertheless, it Does Move"[1]

We use this exclamation of Galileo's as a metaphor, so as to study how firms in the United States have been pressured into relinquishing their isolation and finally becoming part of their social context in order to reorganize a guideline for their economic strategy (Morgan, 1980). This change has also produced a concept: that of Corporate Social Responsibility (CSR). CSR serves three purposes: to enforce legal obligations; to perform voluntary social programmes; and, to introduce ethical belief while sharing the quest for economic benefits. The concept was first introduced when corporate economic power threatened to increase its autonomy. Indeed, in 1920-1930, two hundred of the largest firms in the USA controlled roughly 50 percent of the nation's corporate wealth (Berle and Mean, 1968: 33).

According to Kaufman, Zacharias and Karson (1995), the debate on the modern corporation introduces the issue of managers' legitimacy and of corporate autonomy government. Already, some concerns had been raised: corporate size would result in substantial power or monopoly; corporate deep pockets would corrupt democratic electoral and legislative processes; and, corporate managerial autonomy could lead to managerial opportunism and produce a possible erosion of traditional private propriety. Thus, the debate has been open since 1920-1930.

The post-war period should be seen as a long period during which legislative efforts to involve corporations in regulatory measures were reoriented following pressures to introduce social issues from the movements inside and outside corporations. Four references can be mentioned as examples. First, the civil rights movement shows us how political pressure has economic consequences and can transform firms' behaviour through the consumer's influence (Vogel, 1978). The Kodak case and the boycotts of Pepsi-Cola, Gulf and Sun Oil were responsible

---

1 In 1633, Galileo Galilei was tried by the Inquisition and made to abjure all his beliefs and writings. As he arose from his knees, he exclaimed "sotto voce": "E pur si muove (nevertheless, it does move)"; cf. *New Illustrated Colombia Encyclopedia*, 1979, Vol. 9, p. 2, 596.

for introducing better conditions for black employees. Second, the Vietnam antiwar movement challenged, among others, AT&T and Dow's business to publicly refuse to supply the Defence Department with military material while the USA was at war. Third, a number of religious groups and American partisan movements pressured American companies, such as IBM and Polaroid, regarding their activities in other countries. Thus, for example, the corporate activism initiated by the action of church movements in favour of suspending bank loans and withdrawing investments in South Africa. Lastly, the campaign against old GM social performance and the introduction of the code of investor conduct by Yale University ("University. The ethical investor: Universities and corporate responsibility", 1972) are two of the results in this field contributing to a change in management mentality. All of these actions are in favour of introducing social and ethical accountability into economic strategy (Vogel ,1978: 99).

Hence, Corporate Social Responsibility has become a concept that expresses the philosophical point of view in corporate accountability in the United States since the 1960s. It tries to admit the importance of social issues in corporate governance and conduct. Because of that, its focus also introduces a politicisation of the shareholders' investor role. Finally, Galileo's exclamation "e pur si muove" (nevertheless, it does move) suggests that, like the earth moving alongside the other planets in the solar system, the firm is seen as an institution that abandons its isolation and becomes part of the social context.

Business Associations and the Debate on Social Responsibility in Brazil

In Brazil, business associations and institutions have demonstrated an ability to reach their members regarding product and management innovations (Diniz *et al.*, 2000). This vitality in terms of seeking out innovative sources and resources so as to promote member participation suggests that these institutions constitute a great arena for perceiving if the social responsibility debate is receiving the entrepreneurs' attention.[2]

The study of the attitudes of employers' associative entities towards social responsibility was carried out taking into account the different segments of the Brazilian business class.[3] The development of the social

---

[2] See Levaggi, V., *Organizaciones de empleadores en America Latina. Reflexiones* desde *el cono Sul*. Equipo Técnico Multidisciplinario, No. 93, Oficina Internacional del Trabajo/International Labour Organisation, ILO, Chile, 1999. See also Martinelli, A., *L'Azione collettiva degli imprenditori*, Ed. Di Comunità, Milano, 1994.

[3] I use the results of the research carried out among Brazilian firm associations during 1999. The team conducted interviews with over 50 business associations and trade unions. I thank Gian Mario Giuliani, Regina Morel and Elina Pessanha, and the re-

agenda requires the opening up of new channels of dialogue between businesses and society, channels going beyond the classic functions of employers' organisations and which are related to the challenges of modernisation, technological innovation and administrative management.

The associations, whose vocation is to promote collective employer action, have performed certain functions and roles. The changes that have occurred during the last two decades – economic liberalisation, structural reforms, market reorganizing due to globalisation – have stimulated employers to rethink their models of production, their management styles and the forms of institutional regulation.

We consider the associations and organisations of employers as vehicles or privileged intermediates in the relations between employers, society and the State.[4] As "open systems", employers' entities participate in the control of economic, social and political relations through their capacity to regulate.[5]

The analysis of objectives, and of the modalities and effects of actions of representation, show how today companies' associations aim to influence (by debating, interpreting and evaluating) the public policies affecting their members: monetary, fiscal, labour, industrial, foreign trade, communications, the environment, scientific research, etc. The associative entities are involved in collective decision-making, interfering in and/or influencing government proposals, including the defining of proposals concerning the sphere of industrial relations and the processes of negotiation between trade unions and employers. Further, as it is in the interest of these organisations to influence investment so as to develop the capacity to innovate and to strengthen the autonomy of the companies they represent, their actions have a direct repercussion on workers, shareholders and consumers, thereby conditioning the welfare of the collective.[6] The complexity of these actions demonstrates their dual character: they are politically regulated actions and, at the same

---

searchers Cristina Nobrega and Keyla Oliveira who have integrated the team during this period. This study, *Social Responsibility in Brazilian Firms Associations*, UFRJ/PPGSA, was supported in part by IBASE and the Ford Foundation.

4 I am drawing on a specific strand of the literature of Political Science and Sociology, which has replaced the traditional study of employers' organisations with a new focus on the channels of transmission of interests and demands. See the contributions of the Joint Committee on Western Europe, affiliated to the Science Research Council and to the American Council of Learned Societies (Martinelli, 1994).

5 See the contributions of Galbraith, 1976; Pfeffer, 1981; Burns and Stalker, 1961; quoted in Martinelli, 1994.

6 In this sense, Lindblom states: "In every system based on private enterprise… employers become a type of public employee and perform, in a broad view of their roles, public functions", Lindblom, 1977, p. 181. See Martinelli, *op. cit.*, p. 87.

time, actions that can exert a political influence on the societies in which they operate. This dual character gives these associations an extremely important role.

All of the interviewed associations' leaders answered the main question: "How do you suggest managing the link between economic success and improving firms' social performance and development?".

In the concept of social responsibility, one encounters the reciprocal links between: the distribution of rights and obligations, the acknowledgement of public and private attitudes, the limits of the collective and individual spheres, and the general diffusion of welfare and the concentration of wealth and privilege (Preston and Post, 1981). I feel it is important to map the corporate initiatives by collecting information on programme trajectories and by reconstructing the decision-making process, enforcement mechanisms and company evaluation of results.

The employers' dominant social position is based on the individualistic and competitive nature of their economic actions and their power of investment. Therefore, it is important to understand how associations consider themselves as agents available for re-establishing the reciprocity between rights and obligations, thus redefining themselves in the pursuit of social solidarity. Different moments of national life have shown that the range of attitudes leading to the aggregation of interests can be quite broad and that, on the associations' part, the proposals for collective action can be heterogeneous.

Attitudes and Institutional Practices: Business Organisations' Actions

The range of possible attitudes related to social responsibility can vary from ignorance, through disinterest, to understanding and even to intellectual interest and/or action. For this reason, in order to facilitate the analysis, I have characterized the various responses of our interviews in relation to certain basic elements. The first is certain employer organisations' acknowledgement that dealing with social questions is pertinent to their prerogatives. The second criterion is the business organisations' willingness to allocate resources (material and financial, or in terms of knowledge and organisational experience) to social interventions. Finally, the third element corresponds to these entities' inclination to enlarge the range of social actors available to participate in these proposals and initiatives.

Using these elements, I drew up a typology of attitudes. This should be seen neither as a classification with a valuing connotation, nor as a comparison between "who does" and "who does not". The principal concern is to characterize the diverse discursive and argumentative matrices in order to show how there can be different forms of thinking about social responsibility. During the period the interviews were carried out,[7] the national agenda was occupied by the debate on the implementation of social policies, in particular those aimed at reducing the levels of extreme poverty and social inequality in Brazil.[8] The principal public institutions (federal government, national congress, political parties) fomented the debate that reverberated in public opinion. In our opinion, this raised the level of awareness of our interviewees to at least a level of reflection.

The organisations studied present significant differences in terms of their grasp and the institutional grounding of the social responsibility issue. All of the associations' chairmen proposed some type of solution for social problems, but not all of them shared the same perception of the relevance of the question to the objectives and aims of their associates, nor showed the same willingness to allocate resources so as to promote concrete actions, in pursuit of a social responsibility permitting the interaction of different social actors. The programmes made by firms' associations provide the means to organize a typology that systemizes the diversity of purposes and goals of these programmes.

a) Cooperative Actions

The perception that urgent social problems exist and that these are relevant to firms' activities has caused some associations to take the initiative behind co-operative actions, which engage its member-firms in a dialogue with public agencies. The associations are willing to act and allocate resources and energy together with public agencies (whether local, state, or national) and other institutions so as to implement programmes directed at specific segments of society. A few firms participate with a special monthly amount, sponsoring part of the social programmes defined by the associations. A few such examples include:

- The Union of Employers of Building and Construction of Rio de Janeiro, which set up a course for the unemployed "*To teach (people) to read is to construct*", in cooperation with SESI, the Department of Education and the Roberto Marinho Foundation. It also created the Building and Construction Firms Social Work Department (SECONCI), which for over a decade has provided health and educational assistance, and has also developed an alternative food programme for workers.

---

7 Between 1999 and 2001, 60 directors and chairmen of associations were interviewed in five Brazilian states (Rio de Janeiro, Ceará, Rio Grande do Sul, Minas Gerais and São Paulo).

8 In this respect, the proposal made in August 1999 by Senator Antônio Carlos Magalhães to create an Anti-Poverty Fund should be taken into account. See also *Map of Brazilian Poverty*, source PNAD, 1997, developed by IPEA, in *O Globo*, August 1999.

♦ Since 1993, the American Chamber of Commerce in Rio de Janeiro and São Paulo runs the "Quality in Education Programme", in cooperation with the respective municipal secretaries of education. In 1984, the American Chamber of São Paulo started the "ECO Prize", which rewards, on a national level, the businesses accomplishing the most with respect to social activities.

♦ FIDES, in São Paulo, runs a social programme in *favelas* together with the J. Bosco Foundation, and also organizes meetings between bishops and employers with the support of the Adenauer Foundation from Germany.

♦ Inspired by the Constitution and the Statute for Children and Adolescents, as well as by United Nations recommendations, the Brazilian Toy Industry Association (ABRINQ) in São Paulo has developed nine projects for children. These include: the "*Vaccination Campaign*" and the "*Fight against Dehydration*" in partnership with the National Department of Health; the "*Guardianship Project*", aimed at fostering children in substitute families; and the programme "*Mayor-Children*" which offers subsidies to mayors who adopt child care as one of their administration's priorities.

♦ The Industrial Federation of São Paulo State (FIESP) carried out the *National Campaign for the Prevention of Work-Related Accidents* in conjunction with the National Department of Labour.

♦ The Commercial Association of Minas Gerais has organized activities in the area of *environmental preservation* with the Department of the Environment and IBAMA.

♦ In 1989, the Association of Young Employers of Ceará started, together with other groups, a series of weekly meetings of the "*Co-operation Pact*" promoting debates with various groups in the city of Fortaleza on different social issues in their State. It also organized the "*Re-socialisation of Prisoners Forum*" and the "*School Performance Prize*", specifically aimed at public schools.

b) Combining Ethics and Economics

The admission that firms also have a social function has led a few associations to propose actions aimed at inducing businesses to re-examine the basis of fundamental moral and ethical principles linked to good economic performance and respect for institutional rules. Several basic concepts, such as "Social Management", "Social Responsibility" or "Employer Citizenship", have been elaborated as intellectual references by firm associations. In addition, debates on "Social Exclusion" have been organized, with the explicit purpose of reaffirming the firm's centrality as an actor capable of taking up the challenge of strategically combining economic performance and social commitment. The objective is to stimulate debate among the membership. Various educational activities have been undertaken to encourage new stances among managers that internalize fundamental moral principles, such as actually applying obligatory legal regulations and policies, understanding that tax evasion to be wrong and respecting labour and environment legislation.

♦ The Association of Christian Business Directors of Rio de Janeiro, has promoted seminars, issued documents, and produced studies centred on its proposal for "*Social Management*". It also participates in forums, organizes debates and engages the media (press and television).

♦ The Industrial Federation of Minas Gerais created the "*Employer Citizenship Group*" to promote new initiatives that might become the standard bearers of a new business ethic.

♦ The Employers' National Think-Tank (PNBE) in São Paulo promotes press reports, seminars and employer forums regarding the relationship between structural adjustment and the struggle against social exclusion.

♦ The Brazilian Association of the Fine Chemical Industry and the Brazilian Association of the Chemical Industry, both of which are employers' associations in this sector, have adopted the guidelines of the "*Programa de atuação responsável*", the Brazilian version of the "*Responsible Care Program*", aimed at environmental management. Its goal is to propagate the adoption of codes of conduct, managerial practices, guidelines and indicators related to the environment and occupational health.

c) The Priority is Economic

In contrast with the proposals described above, there are business associations that are convinced that enterprises have primarily economic aims, which are currently being challenged by problems of international and regional adjustment. Their actions seek to prioritize, in a time of crisis, the reestablishment of sectorial competition, before undertaking any involvement, action or investment external to their economic mission.

The concern of promoting enterprise efficacy and efficiency is placed above any and all actions in the social sphere. For a few business associations, initiatives in the social area involve additional costs to enterprises; consequently, they are to be avoided, or postponed, until the sector, in crisis, has once again achieved equilibrium. In all five States covered by the survey, one observes in these organisations, preoccupied almost exclusively with the defence of employers' interests, an absence of plans and programmes oriented to a social agenda. This is especially common among firm associations in the economic sectors most affected by international competition. The urgent need to reorganize the technological apparatus and reconstitute the market results in imposing a priority that relegates the management of human resources, the preservation of the environment and the interaction between the social and institutional spheres to a minor concern. Among the entities which predominantly adopted this attitude we find the Union of Fruit Producers of Ceará; the Association of Brazilian Software and Computer Service Companies; the Association of the Textile Industry of Ceará; the Footwear Industry Union of São Paulo; the Union of the Clothing Industry of Rio Grande do Sul; the Union of the Rice Industry of Rio Grande do Sul; the Brazil-Argentina Chamber of Commerce; the Agricultural Federation of Rio Grande do Sul; and, the Agricultural Federation of Ceará.

d) A Personal Option among Managers

Another group of associations does not intend to adopt direct institutional involvement as an employers' group. However, the directors stress the initiatives and individual programmes of their members, which have a certain tradition in taking initiatives inside and outside their company. These practices are often referred to as being "personal options of business managers". The latter are managers/owners who are individually engaged in philanthropic activities, operating as partners with NGOs or responding to the demands of local communities (for instance, the neighbourhood or the parish). Some association directors consider that the adoption of initiatives aimed at coordinating and/or proposing institutional action by the organisation itself could have the effect of inhibiting, or impeding, the individual actions already underway. In other words, they believe that instead of stimulating such actions, "guidance from above" could have the opposite effect. Through their directors, these associations demonstrate an attitude of restrictive representation, relying on their ability to rapidly mobilize all of their members, but wanting to remain the 'spokesperson' of mainly economic interests. This attitude, which sometimes contradicts the initiatives of important firms, is characteristic of several associations in different States. One finds it in the Association of Supermarkets of Rio de Janeiro and Minas Gerais, in the Industrial Federation of Rio Grande do Sul, in the Association of Christian Directors of Minas Gerais, in the Brazil-Argentina Chamber of Commerce, and in the Association of Banks of Ceará.

According to the Federation of Banking Institutions of São Paulo (FEBABRAN), many banks already have their own projects underway, often through foundations. For example, Bradesco Bank has set up its own foundation, which provides schools for the families of employees and involves more than 98,000 children; Itaú Bank operates a programme for the renovation of public schools, distributing educational material for the training of teachers, etc. Similarly, according to the Commercial Association of São Paulo, several of its members support the 'CAMPI' project, aimed at training 'boy scouts', and which is concerned with training and accompanying the insertion of young people in the labour market and supervising their performance.

e) When there Are Positive Externalities

Several associations' directors stated that their institutions have established a clear separation between public and private social responsibility. For them, the promotion of education and health is the responsibility of the State, not the firm, as employers are agents of economic promotion. Even when they agree with the idea that higher education levels are strategic factors for companies' development, they expect the State to fulfil its obligation of providing basic public education. Therefore, a few associations become promoters of debates and initiatives only when such actions result in positive externalities or in comparative advantages for firms. The only other factor mentioned as an important public commitment relevant to employer objectives, is the preservation of the environment, which, consequently, should be a part of the associations' discussion. It is interesting to note that this group comprises associations that were formed with the objective of organizing and defending a broad range of interests and includes the newer generations of employers.

For example, the directors of the Association of Young Employers of the State of Rio de Janeiro said that this entity is preoccupied with monitoring the technological choices necessary to preserve the quality of the environment. The commitment is permanent, since a member of the board always represents this organisation in forums related to this issue, such as the Employers' Council for Sustainable Development and the American Council of Commerce. The other members of this group include the Association of Young Employers of Minas Gerais and of Rio Grande do Sul; the Liberal Institute and the Institute of Employer Studies of Rio Grande do Sul; and, the Association of Young Employers, and the Institute of Liberal Studies, both from Rio de Janeiro.

f) Public Security

Several entities have a clear perception of the relevance of the question of violence, and consequently are willing to act in relation to public security, allocating resources and abilities to deal with the gravity of the situation. The security issue is considered as important, given that it poses a threat for the actual life of employers, puts companies' installations at risk, and, at times, inhibits the firms' proper functioning even to the point of putting their actual survival at risk. Many different ways of intervening have been proposed. Leaving aside the initiatives involving private self-defence, it is worth mentioning those involving a broader strategy dealing with some of the social causes and/or proposing policies of a more collective or institutional scope, namely:

♦ Among its 19 employer-councils, the Commercial Association of Rio de Janeiro has one specifically concerned with public security. Between 1993 and 1997, this institution ran the programme "*My Neighbourhood, My Police Station*", which re-equipped 34 local police stations. It also sent the public authorities (the President of the Republic, National Congress, and the Judiciary) a written proposal for the reformulation of the Police Academy School's curriculum, and also suggested establishing a permanent campaign on the evils of *drug use*.

♦ The Federation of Employers' Association of Rio Grande do Sul (FEDERASUL) has promoted the programme "*Pescar*" (Fishing) concerning the professional training of young people in situations of risk, which is based on the idea that professionalisation contributes to reducing the risks of social marginalisation.

♦ The Federation of Industries of the State of Rio de Janeiro (FIRJAN) has contributed to various initiatives of the Viva Rio movement against violence.

g) Medium- and Long-Term Aims

Various firms' associations, as employers, saw other types of problems as being relevant to the business world, because of the seriousness of their social impact and the urgent need for solutions. Among them were the issues of unemployment and professional training, racial discrimination in the workplace, and the still common practice of child labour. These are considered as challenges that not only require action on their part, but which also call for new stances and attitudes towards economic action. They are understood as issues affecting several of the important values of employer culture. Their solutions, however, cannot be found in partial or short-term solutions, but only through medium- and long-term initiatives.

Several associations have made these themes their flagship activities and, because of their participation in national and international organisations, have reinforced their mediation capacities with employers and public authorities. In some cases, proposals for joint action between employers' organisations and those of workers have seen the light, in the wake of various international experiences, such as those presented at the ILO's Second Enterprise Forum in 1999. Some examples include:

♦ Through its Foundation, the Brazilian Toy Industry Association (ABRINQ) has implemented specific actions, such as the programme

"*The Company: The Children's Friend*", initiated in response to the ILO's 138th convention and UNICEF recommendations. It has also developed and signed different *Sectorial Pacts*: in 1996, for instance, with producers of the alcohol sector, citrus growers, car manufacturers and producers in the footwear sector. In these cases, the National Departments of Labour, Justice and Industry were also involved.

♦ The Italy-Brazil Chamber of Commerce is drafting a bilateral cooperation agreement with planning and professional training institutions in areas of recent deindustrialisation (the areas of the Greater São Paulo ABC cities and Greater Milan), investing in the search for solutions and for adult workers' professional retraining.

♦ The Association of Businesswomen and Professionals of Porto Alegre (BPW/POA) has set up the *Popular Entrepreneurial Prize* as an incentive for low-income women entrepreneurs to improve their enterprises. Also in this state can be cited the Employers Union, and the Brother José Otão Foundation.

Within this group of preoccupations, one should mention certain interventions aimed at long-term solutions, namely a series of declarations signed by associations up to 1999, i.e. against sexual and racial discrimination, against child labour, in favour of the incorporation of physically disabled workers. For example:

♦ The Industrial Federation of São Paulo (FIESP) recently signed a declaration with the Inter-American Union Institute for Racial Equality (INSPIR) against racial discrimination in the workplace.

♦ Through its Social and Labour Policy representative, the Union of Building Firms (SINDUSCON) is a member of the network promoted by the Brazilian Council of the Building Industry (CBIC), called "*Building is the Solution*". This is a national movement of employers and workers which, according to its founding declaration, proposes to unite forces around a national agenda of action aimed at *employment generation policies*, by implementing housing and infra-structural programmes. The initiative was justified due to "*the serious situation of the growing unemployment rate and the population's deteriorating quality of life*" (SINDUSCON, 1999: 121).

Firms and Social Responsibility

International literature suggests that companies are motivated to engage themselves in social issues in new ways, which take into account the progress made in broader spheres of collective life and, above all, the progress resulting from the enlargement of democratic relations and the dissemination of information, which make consumers more watchful. According to the European Commission's paper "Démocratie et

Créativité",[9] many companies have learnt to recognize the power of the media, as well as the new attitude expressed by the public at large and by consumers in particular. Therefore, firms devise policies aimed at shaping their image so that it reflects their contribution to updating internal codes, promoting social and cultural progress, and protecting the environment. This also reveals that companies are redefining their human resource policies and accepting trade unions as valid discussion partners. Some examples of innovative policies highlight the different forms that companies adopt so as to introduce citizenship in the workplace: the introduction of human resource-management mechanisms to overcome racial and sexual segregation; the adoption of non-discriminatory treatment; the institution of training programmes to promote equal opportunities for career advancement; and promoting a reconciliation of work with family responsibilities so as to improve employees' living conditions for both men and women.

Our object is to bring to light the ways in which companies in the State of Rio de Janeiro combine financial goals (profit and performance) with the adoption of 'good conduct' practices toward their employees and their community. Since 1997, and in response to an IBASE-sponsored campaign, certain companies now draft and publish a Social Report. This initiative is one of the signs of a new corporate culture that addresses social responsibility.

Our study covers twelve firms, located in the State of Rio de Janeiro and operating in different sectors: building and construction; the chemical and pharmaceutical industries; metallurgy; publishing; the textile sector; the food industry; oil industries, and supermarket services. These firms are national and international companies.

All the companies' directors we interviewed answered the basic question: "What does your firm do towards social development inside and outside the company?". The question was motivated by the assumption that economic success has an effect on social relations. It is known that the reason of a company's existence resides in a combination of different objectives: to offer products and services, and to produce profits and distribute dividends. Such objectives refer more appropriately to a market society's productive aims. But the reasons for a company's performance can go beyond mere economic objectives. Socially legitimate reasons can include a firm as source of employment and as a space where workers can find dignity.[10] I suggest that companies have a

[9] See Atelier No. 3, *Solidarité des Entreprises*, Commission Européenne, DG XII, 1996.

[10] I refer to the definition of "decent work" proposed by the International Labour Organisation (ILO), concerned about diffusing dignity in labour relations, in collabo-

different conception of social responsibility. This diversity is related to the economic sector, the companies' product and the consumer market's proximity, more than to the relations with civil society. The economic sector is one of the most important references for perceiving the context in which firms identify their concern and worry about social responsibility. In fact, during the interviews, it was clear that chemical, pharmaceutical and oil industries introduced the debate about environmental issues because of international agreements about responsible care (Giuliani, 2001). Metallurgical firms, building and construction, publishing and textile industries have focused the debate on the importance of work processes and labour-force training, due to technological modernisation. Supermarket services appear particularly concerned about the consumer market, whose influence orients their external policies. These prior concerns show that every sector identifies its own link with society, and then defines the sphere of their relationship with it.

The companies' product also has a number of implications for the management's perception of, and practices regarding, social responsibility. Managers select the forms of interaction with customers, employees, suppliers and domestic competitors, with whom they have direct contact. However, they are not constantly related with governments, consumer advocates, environmentalists, media, local communities and other groups. Some companies have selected their social programmes in relation with their product's image. These firms think about social needs by reacting to public opinion. For example, as a pharmaceutical firm's products are linked to health-related issues, the company might organize a social programme improving or introducing health services for the external community. However, these services are not always available for the company's workers. On the other side, since factories are exposed to public view, in the building and construction industry companies are worried about accidents and injuries, which are immediately visible and could damage their brand name. Similarly, in the case of supermarkets, the proximity of consumers stimulates firms to implement social programmes that can be used as an efficient vehicle of propaganda among its clients; one supermarket, for instance, is partner of the recycling waste programme, advertising this programme on its bags as well as with leaflets distributed in its stores.

Other firms (especially in the metallurgical, oil, textile, building and construction sectors) combine social policies with other special activities related to their productivity strategy. Indeed, new policies centre on cutting costs and expanding efficiency. Therefore, the purpose of social

---

ration with segments of employers, unions and government institutions. See ILO, *Decent Work*, 87th Meeting, Geneva, 1999.

responsibility becomes a support for managing industrial reorganisation. A few companies (in the sectors of publishing, textiles, and building and construction) have introduces professional training programmes related to technological modernisation. Only in the case of one building and construction firm, is the social activity part of agreements resulting from negotiations with the local trade union.

Companies belonging to the oil, chemical and food sectors adopted programmes oriented towards human resource policies and internal climate. For example, these firms are interested in improving women's participation in managerial staff and, over the last year, introduced a special policy in gender diversity (even if limited to white-collar occupations) as a part of their international policy. In other sectors (metallurgical, pharmaceutical and supermarkets), some firms have introduced temporary AIDS programmes in response to employees' needs. Finally, a few companies (essentially in the oil and metallurgic sector) have introduced unpaid jobs in the community for white-collar employees in their administrative centres.

Some firms (publishing, metallurgical, textile, building and construction) also take into consideration the community's demands. Generally, the community is represented by local organisations (associations, NGOs, churches or individuals) in search of specific support (e.g. equipment) or social work (such as literacy courses, part-time after-school activities for children, or sponsoring municipal schools and hospitals).

All these activities suggest that companies practice social responsibility through voluntary programmes that are strictly related to their strategic interests. In fact, the elements that generally define companies' social commitment are: their product, consumers market and concern with their internal climate. Only in few cases (supermarkets, textile and food industries) is the company's social performance defined in response to community needs as a philanthropic action.

Brazilian Trade Unions and Corporate Social Responsibility

From the perspective of Corporate Social Responsibility, trade union participation stands out on two counts: the degree of openness of the institutional dialogue between firms and society, and the breadth of sectoral and local variations in employers' care of workers (who should normally be the direct beneficiaries of companies' social policies).

As agents of representation, Brazilian trade unions have historically played the role of enforcing the exercise of rights on the shop floor, based on confrontation tactics rather than a dialogical approach with employers. Complex processes introduced by industrial reorganisation and modernisation have since changed companies. According to employers, new policies are centred on cutting costs, increasing productivity and expanding efficiency. Hence, in the midst of these profound transformations, corporate social responsibility (CSR) became one of the strategies in Brazil for managing these changes. However, as trade unions report, this has had repercussions for the workers: flexibility, an expansion of strategies such as "just in time" (JIT) and "total quality control" (TQT) and, finally, the lessening of labour rights regulation. Our concern is to enlarge the significance of this remodelling process and to report the opinion prevailing among trade unions about CSR. I suggest that, even if they recognize this approach's positive aspect, trade unions consider that, so far, its use has not reversed local companies' purposes and practices.[11]

According to trade unions, the CSR approach demands that firms modify their role beyond the classic expectations related to paternalism in the past. Indeed, throughout the history of Brazilian society, employers used to play a paternalistic role so as to protect their interests. For example, the industrialisation process at the beginning of the 20th century was sustained by employer actions aimed at the "domestication" of the emerging working class through the Company Town and Cottage System models, or the so-called "working class city". Later, employers were compelled to interact between employees and public authorities introducing regulatory roles. As a result, during the Vargas period and its ensuing social pact, labour legislation was implemented introducing the first regulation of employers' responsibilities towards the workforce. Finally, in the last Constitution (drawn up in 1988), firms were obliged to modify their actions regarding internal and external partnerships, developing and increasing innovations in their social role and offering human dignity and new rights to employees. However, this period exposed the intensity of the disputes and rifts between employers' and workers' demands. According the trade unions, this last national agreement highlights how difficult it was to force employers to modify their range of paternalistic attitudes.

Nowadays, the demands formulated by civilian associations, NGOs and, recently, also by national and local agencies of the State, suggest that firms and employers should embody a new social role. The introduction of social responsibility and stakeholder relations, such as busi-

[11] This affirmation is based on the results of the research carried out in the State of Rio de Janeiro among local trade unions. In particular, I shall refer to two cases in this paper: the Building and Construction Industry Trade Union and the Metallurgy Trade Union. Here, I would like to thank Cristina Nobrega and Keyla Oliveira who integrated the team on this part of the research. This study was supported in part by FAPERJ and CNPq, the National Centre of Investigation, during 2000-2002.

ness contributions, suggests it is necessary to enlarge the partnership so as to include suppliers, clients, consumers, workers and the community. Indeed, according to trade unions' leaders, the CSR approach implies the introduction of new values, both inside the firm (in respect to workers and white-collar employees' rights) and outside it (with suppliers, clients and community demands). For them, social responsibility should redefine and thus renovate business goals. One of these goals is that the tension caused by conflicting interests should be resolved through negotiations and be regulated by collective agreements.[12] During the 1990s, there were only a few cases that showed this business attitude. For example, the initiatives of the Sectorial Councils (between 1992 and 1993 and between 1995 and 1996) provided moments of institutional opening for three-party negotiating in respect to defining targets and performance in the automobile and the chemical sectors. Therefore, trade unions know that collective agreements with employers do not need to have a precedent in terms of a national legacy.

The following trade unions' opinions illustrate two different conceptions of corporate social responsibility. According to the findings of our survey among local trade unions, the leaders in the Building and Construction Industry consider that corporate responsibility has shrunk on a number of issues.[13] It should be noted that the first agreement concerning social issues – the Social Programme in the Building Industry (SECONCI/RJ) – was signed in 1988 as part of the local bargain. This programme focused on providing different types of care for workers on the shop floor and was organized and administrated by employers. It included medical and dental care, an audiometric service and a few social programmes (a literacy course, professional training and a nutrition programme) targeted exclusively at workers. Although positively evaluated, these services are considered limited in purpose and restricted in terms of results. In fact, the trade union argues that this kind of service has a reduced the impact among workers and does not address the issue of assistance to their families.[14] In addition, considering the shop

12 The ILO's Second Enterprise Forum, held in 1999, arose from preoccupations such as these. An example of an initiative of this type is that of the agreement between the Danone firm and the European Union of Food Workers and Connected Trades (SET UITA) See the *Convention Groupe DANONE and UITA* signed by the president of the company and the Secretary General of the European Union of Food Workers and Connected Trades in September 1999.

13 According to the secretariat of the Building and Construction Trade Union, in 2002 approximately 36,000 of the 100,000 workers in the city of Rio de Janeiro were trade union members, an appreciable increase considering that trade union associations only represented 27.76% of the workers in 1991.

14 The leader explains that the workers' actual profile changed a few decades ago. Nowadays, individual immigrant workers are not representative of the workforce. In

floor's reorganisation, the high turnover of labour and the large periods of unemployment faced by workers, this programme is very selective. Indeed, the trade union's criticism stresses that the programme concerns only a small proportion of workers, namely white-collar employees – but not the bricklayers, who are the most important part of the workforce in this sector. To overcome the limits of this employer programme, the trade union has started a similar one of its own, which can be utilized by workers and their relatives even after the cessation of job relations. Moreover, the disregard shown by firms regarding the application of labour rights has motivated the trade union to monitor cases of injuries, a service it ensures since 1996, and which includes a daily supervision by technical experts. Finally, the local agreement between the trade union, the State and employers led to the creation, in 2000, of the Prior Conciliation Committee (*Comissão de Conciliação Prévia*) with the explicit power to find solutions regarding workers' rights, thus reducing the delay of Justice.[15]

The metallurgic trade union's assessment of how corporate social responsibility is interpreted among companies suggests new references, namely that employers' actions in this regard can be dispersed and heterogeneous. As an example of this, activists in the metallurgy sector compare two corporate cultures that present a stark contrast in employers' practices: on the one hand, an old American company that has been located in the region for many years and, on the other, a German firm that recently opened a plant in the same region. These two cases highlight how company social responsibility acts and manages work demands in opposite ways. Using the motto of social responsibility, the first firm has, since 1993, organized different social programmes: in the community (municipal school and hospital, and social and sport activities for children) as well as for white-collar employees at its administrative centre (unpaid jobs and AIDS programme). In contrast, this firm neither has a partnership on the shop floor, nor with the local trade union. Also, for many years, it used to demand that the business association's lawyer negotiate the annual agreement, without the managers' presence. Hence, the activists explain their special interest in the debate with the firm: "the company does not open the door to the trade union". In opposition, the second company, without using this motto, since early 1990 when it opened its factory, has solicited a partnership with the

---

fact, workers in this special sector have their permanent residence in Rio de Janeiro and live in nuclear families.

15 According to available data, during the first nine months of its existence, this Committee solved 68% of among more than 3,000 cases. Without this mediation, these cases should follow the traditional route of going before labour justice. See Gazeta Mercantil, 05/03/2002.

trade union. Moreover, it has accepted the constitution of a trade union committee on the shop floor, while the annual negotiations take into account the technical advice of trade union activists.

In conclusion, trade unions tend to emphasize the gap between business rhetoric and practices. Considering the long tradition of maltreating workers in these important sectors, leaders recognize that few achievements have been reached in terms of labour protection. However, they consider the business motto of corporate social responsibility as still being uncertain. According to them, even if it could signal a change of approach in companies' labour policies, to date it has proved to be an inadequate slogan for differentiating companies' practices.

Conclusions

The analysis has given an accurate picture of the place of social responsibility in the national and regional business environment in Brazil. The conception of social responsibility in American literature and the interviews with Brazilian firms' associations constitutes a useful reference in perceiving how companies in Rio de Janeiro approach the issue. Moreover, the opinion of the trade unions located in Rio de Janeiro helps understand how strongly this issue rebounds on balancing power relations and on the equitable distribution of benefits.

The confrontation of these different opinions suggests that, in the national environment, there are ongoing changes. The business associations offer to their members different options on managing the advantages of introducing social responsibility in their firms. The strong impact of the production's restructuring in terms of systems and markets has given a great emphasis to programmes, actions, projects, petitions and meetings in the business field. Business associations express their concern about social responsibility by collecting data, evaluating programmes, debating and broadcasting initiatives coherent with this perspective. They thus improve the quality and quantity of available information and invest in communication through seminars and exchanges, which offer important clues regarding the social agenda. They also manage institutional social programmes, generally directed at equipping schools, training workers and organizing basic education for the population. Most of these programmes are carried out through a partnership with local and regional State agencies. Furthermore, many of these programmes have been an integral part of associations' activities since the 1990s.

Therefore, the proposal of pushing employers' strategies in a direction that combines the economic success of firms with their commitment to social development, is neither an unknown formula to business, nor an attitude created by fashion. The typology that I presented, and that systemizes the diversity of associations' purposes and goals, shows that some associations are more directly engaged in the social responsibility perspective. For example, the associations classified in the categories of "Cooperative Actions", "Combining Ethics and Economics", and "Medium- and Long-Term Aims" invest in social actions. The research also shows that this attitude is present in a few companies in Rio de Janeiro. In fact, some companies (metallurgical, oil, textile, building and construction) found their practices in Cooperative Actions, acting in partnership with local State agencies and concentrating their actions in the educational and health areas. Concerning the firms from Rio de Janeiro, I found that the concept of "social responsibility" as understood by the associations (i.e. "Combining Ethics and Economics") is put into practice only in a few cases, in particular by oil, metallurgical and chemical companies.

Associations adopt the concept of social responsibility from different perspectives. Several actors contribute to this diversity: the press, international organisations, NGOs and their campaigns, researchers, local and State executive powers.

On the other hand, firms have different backgrounds. In multinational firms, suggestions about social responsibility programmes originate in the extension of the mother-company's international policy to its local factories. The survey suggests that when firms wish to finance some programme, they prefer training programmes and indirect assistance to people outside the labour market, rather than initiatives destined at workers inside their factories. For example, among the twelve firms of our survey, not one of them mentioned an explicit intention to perform according to the International Labour Organisation's conventions, which include the promotion of human rights, labour standards and the analysis of environmental impact. None of them, either, made any reference to "good practices", or to affirmative action on gender or racial concerns, even though business associations had referred to this kind of convention.

The research also identifies an ambiguous relation between belief and behaviour. A few firm associations, even though they recognized the seriousness of social problems (such as unemployment or environmental degradation), find it very difficult to adopt the social responsibility belief and practices. Because of that, there is a huge distance between "what should be done" and "what can be done". This resigned attitude is present among the associations classified in the categories: "The Priority is Economic", and "When There are Positive Externalities".

Among the firms consulted during our survey, no two presented similar arguments. It is possible that three of them (a supermarket, a tyre producer and a clothing industry, which – it should be noted – interrupted their collaboration in our research after the very first meeting) are among the firms that cannot include social responsibility in their business strategy.

The analysis of employer organisations revealed a varied range of conceptions of social responsibility. However, it was clearly obvious that this engagement goes on in a selective manner, and business organisations orient their member firms in different ways. The different conceptions, methods and strategies for action generated by associations, turn social responsibility into a concept that is "disputed" by ideological and political concerns. It is as yet impossible to establish a general consensus on what social responsibility actually means. What is significant, however, is the growing on-going movement in Brazil, which is placing the interests, proposals and values of economic agents face to face with the demands, needs, expectations and aspirations of different social sectors, which expect some form of benefits from these economic agents' actions.

On the contrary, the research among companies revealed a predominant pragmatism in the attitude of companies that undertake voluntary initiatives in social areas. Firms' concerns and motivations are strictly related to four elements: the economic sector, the company's product, the proximity of a consumer's market, and its relations with civilian society. The characteristics of the sector in which firms operate impose technological challenges, which in turn serve to indicate the social areas in which they could invest, generally prioritizing the challenges related with their current constraints. On the one hand, firms are worried about technological reorganisation, organisational performance, and quality of the social climate, above all in their administrative centre. These are the keys that trigger investments in social programmes aimed at increasing workforce productivity and white-collar employees' motivations. On the other hand, consumer expectations and the value of brands are also keys that can motivate firms to back social programmes directed at people outside the workplace. Sometimes the ideas come from community demands with firms generally assuming the role of sponsors or integrating institutional partnerships.

The absence of interactions with trade unions show that firms are rigorously selective in whom they consider as social actors. This therefore suggests that "social responsibility" is more of a business point of view than the result of a dialogue between social partners. It is a business interpretation of social demands that especially neglects the trade union agenda.

References

Caloia, A., *L'imprenditore-social*, Asti, Edizione Piemme, 1995.

Cappellin, P. *et al.*, *As organizações empresariais face à responsabilidade social das empresas no Brasil*, Rio de Janeiro, UFRJ/PPGSA, 2000.

Carroll, A., "Corporate social responsibility, evolution of a definitional construct", in *Business and Society*, Vol. 28, No. 3, pp. 268-295, 1999.

Chiesi, A. and Martinelli, A., *La rappresentanza associativa imprenditoriale di fronte al cambiamento degli anni noventa*, Milano, Istituto Superiore di Sociologia, 1987.

Coleman, W.D., "Meeting on The Regional Organisation of Business Interests and Public Policy", *Quebec Nationalism and the Organisation of Business Interests*, McMaster University, Hamilton, 22-24 May, 1985.

Diniz, E., Boschi, R. and Santo, F., *Elites politicas e econômicas no Brasil contemporâneo*, São Paulo, Fundaçao K. Adenauer, 2000.

Durand, F. and Silva, E., *Organized Business, Economic Change, Democracy in Latin America*, University of Miami Press, 1999.

Galbraith J., *Designing Complex Organisations*, Reading, Addison Wesley, 1973.

Giuliani, G. M., *XXIII International Congress of LASA, Environmental responsibility of Brazilian companies: practices and rhetoric*, Washington, 2001.

Gonçalves, E. L., *Balanço social da empresa na América Latina*, São Paulo, Livraria Pioneira Editora, 1980.

ILO, *Decent Work*, Geneva, 1999.

Kaufman, A., Zacharias, L. and Karson, M., *Managers vs Owners. The struggle for corporate control in American Democracy*, New York, Oxford University Press, 1995.

Kriesi, H.P. and Farago P., "The Regional Organisation of Business Interests and Public Policy Meeting", *The Regional Differentiation of Business Interests Associations in Switzerland: Economic, Political and Social Determinants*, McMaster University, Hamilton, 22-24 May, 1985.

Martinelli, A., *International Markets and Global Firms. A Comparative Study of Organized Business in the Chemical Industry*, London, Sage, 1991.

Martinelli, A. M. *et al*, "Organisation of Business Interests Meeting", *The Organisation of Business Interests in Italy: A Preliminary Report*, Istituto Universitario Europeo, Firenze, 19-21 May, 1985.

Martinelli, A., Schmitter P. and Streeck W., "L'organizzazione degli interessi imprenditoriali", in *Stato e Mercato*, No. 3, 1981, pp. 423-445.

Morgan, G., "Paradigm, metaphors, and puzzle solving in organisation theory", in *Administrative Science Quarterly*, 1980.

Offe, C. and Wiesenthal, H., "Duas lógicas da ação coletiva: notas teóricas sobre a classe social e a forma de organização", in C. Offe, *Problemas Estruturais do Estado Capitalista*, Rio de Janeiro, Tempo Brasileiro, 1980.

Pessanha E. and Morel R., "Mudanças recentes no modelo de relações de trabalho no Brasil e novo sindicalismo", in I. Rodrigues, *Novo Sindicalismo, Vinte Anos Depois*, Rio de Janeiro, Ed. Vozes, 1999.

Pfeffer, J., *Power in Organisations*, Boston, Pitman, 1981.

Preston Lee, E. and Post, J.E., "Private management and public policy", in *California Management Review*, No. 3, pp. 56-62, 1981.

SINDUSCON, *Programa a minha casa e a minha vida*, Brasilia, 1999.

Solé, C., "The Regional Organisation of Business Interests and Public Policy Meeting", *The System of Organized Business Interests in the Spanish Textile Industry*, McMaster University, Hamilton, 22-24 May, 1985.

Torre da Silva, C.V., "Entre o bem estar e o lucro. Histórico da responsabilidade social das empresas através de algumas experiências selecionadas de balanço social", Master's dissertation in Political Sciences, UFF, Niterói (mimeo), 2000.

Vogel, D., *Lobbing the corporation. Citizen challenges to business authority*, New York, Basic Book Inc., 1978.

Territorialised Industrial Policies and New Spatial Division of Labour

What is at Stake for Socio-economic Actors?

Jacques PERRAT

Scientific Director of Adees-Rhône-Alpes (Lyon)

Introduction[1]

A constant reshaping of firms (mergers, corporate restructuring, outsourcing, etc.) is presently taking place, against a background of increasing internationalisation characterised, in developed countries, by the threat of relocation abroad and the call for a "compulsory" reduction of labour costs and constraints. Therefore, both national economic policies and national normative frameworks for labour relations are strongly challenged. In this context, the territorial level seems to be called upon to bring new opportunities in terms of both industrial dynamics and economic and social governance. For the past few years in France, public authorities' tendency to rehabilitate the notion of industrial policy, at both the national and the regional level, has explicitly targeted the territorial dimension, especially through the *pôles de compétitivité* programme. This policy reveals many of the current changes in the relationship between productive requirements, labour division and territorial organisation.

The aim of this paper is to highlight what really is at stake in this upgrading of the territorial level. Examining the new French industrial policy will bring us some lessons on the positioning of the different territories concerned. We shall then try to specify what this means in terms of productive, organisational and institutional dynamics, in order to shed light on some of the challenges these developments represent for socio-economic actors, and especially trade unions.

1 We particularly thank Mireille Breton and Marianne Georgopoulos for their valuable assistance in mastering the English language.

From a Functional to a Territorial Division of Labour?

Analysing French industrial policy in the light of the theoretical notions it mobilises may help define the way in which new productive organisations are reshaping their relation to space.

French Industrial Policy: from Territorial Productive Systems to Market-pulled Clusters

For the last few years, territorial – and especially regional – authorities in France have applied themselves to nurturing a financial and organisational improvement of territorial resources. The logic behind this is: we cannot resist globalisation and the power of the market, but we can help our region adapt itself in order to ensure a good positioning in global competition, for instance by introducing clusters of activities and/or firm networks. At the national level (where, in the 1970s, the creation of *technopôles* had been promoted in a few areas), the Datar[2] decided, in 1998, to develop Local Productive Systems (LPSs) and Industrial Districts (IDs), over a hundred of them being identified. Lastly, during the September 2004 Ciadt[3] meeting, the French government, referring to the European Lisbon Process relative to the "knowledge economy", decided to promote a selective choice of *pôles de compétitivité* (competitiveness poles), whose selection was made public in July 2005.

All these notions mobilised by public actors are well known to Regional Science researchers. Thus, it is interesting to examine more thoroughly what it means to shift from one to another as regards the reality of the industrial policies these can relate to. We do not intend to review the works analysing these notions, preferring instead to briefly present the elements allowing one to grasp the change of logic in which the most recent decisions have taken place, compared with what prevailed previously, namely:

. creating *technopôles* aimed at boosting synergies (at least theoretically) between research, training and production in the long run and opening up the fields of innovation likely to nurture the industrial fabric;

. supporting Local Productive Systems and Industrial Districts aimed at accelerating the specialisation of the greatest number of territories according to their industrial capabilities, inducing both endogenous and exogenous development;

. promoting competitiveness poles refers, in a fuzzy way, to several notions. First, it relates to the *technopole* idea of research-training-

---

2 A state office for Territorial Planning and Regional Action.

3 Inter-ministerial Comity for Territorial Development and Planning.

production synergies but in a reduced way (temporary set up, focalised targets of innovation, etc.). Second, the highly selective choice of a few territories where public financial and organisational investments are to be concentrated tends to draw a competitiveness pole towards the reality and logic of either a joint laboratory (temporarily created between a large company and a public research centre), or an industrial pilot (temporarily created to manage the shift from an innovative project to an industrial process). Third, it refers to the notion of Local Productive System, but both the selectivity related to the actors and the indistinctness related to the geographical scale refer more, in fact, to the notion of cluster.[4]

This helps us understand why the more pliant notion of cluster is used nowadays so frequently, as its definition can range from almost referring to an Industrial District (Porter, 1998[5]) to indicating a lose network of firms with no precise geographical scale. If it is true that all these approaches stress the leading role of firms in the governance of these different spatial configurations, the (implicit) aim of an Industrial District was endogenous development in the long run, whereas the (explicit) aim of a "firm network" is to match the market changes "on the fly". The contradiction being, when speaking of competitiveness poles, that large corporations are to be the key-actors, whereas filling the scientific and technologic gaps requires high, risky and long-term funding and non-market coordination that only public intervention can ensure (Boyer, Dehove, Plihon, 2004; Beffa, 2005).

Thus, such a change marks a shift from an industrial policy aimed at fostering long-lived productive systems to a policy targeted at upholding short-lived firm networks, by selectively backing choices that are pulled by both the market and the strategy of multinational corporations.

Territorial Rating and Changes in the Division of Labour

These developments lead to a stronger differentiation of the industrial landscape, with a *de facto* rating of territories according to the interest they represent for leading companies:

. first-rate "territories of excellence" with an international/national label, that will be supported by the new public policy: in fact, they are most often territories that have been able, and for a long time, to nurture a dynamics of productive innovation, such as the technopolitan arias of

---

4 It is symptomatic that the English version of the French government's website translates *pôles* by "clusters"!

5 "A geographic concentration of interconnected companies, specialised suppliers, service providers, firms in related industries and associated institutions (universities…), in fields that compete but also cooperate" (pp. 197-198).

Grenoble and Toulouse. We shall see whether such a policy can consolidate their dynamics or if it tends to favour a limited part of their potentialities;

. second-rate "territories of excellence" with a national and/or regional label, that will emerge or consolidate their position through public support, whether they originate – or not – in existing forms of territorial organisation (Local Productive Systems / Industrial Districts), with the same question as above;

. third-rate "non-labelled" but dynamic territories, such as urban or regional diversified productive areas or, at a more local scale, big sites of extended corporations (with sub-contractors, utilities, etc.);

. fourth-rate traditional Local Productive Systems, Industrial Districts and, more generally, regional or local industrial areas, which are unable to meet the new productive and financial requirements; they depend strongly on public support and on the various mechanisms created to this purpose by the French government ("territory contract", "site contract", tax exemptions, etc.).

Of course, reality is much more complex and, quite frequently, several of these situations get regionally or locally entangled. However, we believe that the criteria linked to the "labelled cases" can teach us something about the characteristics of the whole process, even if things differ according to the story and dynamics of each of these territories.

Several official reports that helped the French government define the competitiveness poles policy shed light on this evolution. In his report, Blanc (2004) stresses the role of the innovation factor in international competition and states that the scientific and economic systems can no longer be organised on a national basis: "today, information networks are global, but knowledge networks must be conceived in the perimeter of people's daily return trips, on foot or by car". This reference to proximity and to the interactive relations between productive firms, research centres and clients runs throughout the report. At the same time, Blanc explains that what made the force of the Industrial District ("a post-artisan model which, today, is partially threatened"), i.e. "the proximity and short distance between conceptive and productive agents", is "no longer sufficient" and that the "winning areas" are those where "global player corporations" emerge.

Another report, by Fontagné and Lorenzi (2004), calls for a greater selectivity and focus in public funding ("too scattered, till now") and promotes the cluster logic in these terms: more than the capability of an area to offer synergies between R&D, production and adaptation to the local market, "it's the tendency [of such a complex] towards a limited field of knowledge application that guarantees success". But this report is also interesting in what it tells us about the specialisation of territories in terms of their relation to both innovation and time, by distinguishing two main types: the great complexes of large European firms and research potential that need to be promoted in a short-term logic ("behind each research project there must be a concrete industrial application") and in a restricted range of sectors ("high technologies, energy, environment, transport, etc."); and, "at the other extremity of the spectrum, the medium industrial and social term", referring to "regional scale, SMEs, clusters, *bassins d'emploi*".[6]

According to Morvan (2004), we are going to pass "from a somewhat casual distribution of firms on the territory, related to the needs of a functional division of tasks between them, to a more polarised distribution around blocks of knowledge and capabilities, necessarily extremely localised, and around functions that are well integrated thanks to interface structures that improve the circulation of information among actors". These polarised areas are combining with "a new interregional and international labour organisation, through networks that are structuring an open space economy". Further, one should not, according to this author, oppose endogenous and exogenous types of development, nor excellence and equity as "percolation effects" can exist between "territories of excellence" and the other ones.

Thus, we can retain the idea that there is a shift from a functional labour division, with a vertical differentiation of productive segments that led to a certain rating of territories, to a territorial one, with a horizontal differentiation of localised blocks of capabilities that leads to a different territorial rating. However, it is necessary to specify what this means in terms of productive, organisational and institutional dynamics.

A Contradictory Requirement of Territorialised Capabilities

The ongoing changes in the relations between industrial dynamics and territorial forms are to be apprehended through two contradictory tendencies regarding the mobilisation of resources: we can identify a call for the systemic construction of complete sets ("blocks") of productive capabilities, but, at the same time, this trend is permanently challenged by the dominating presence of competition and cost criteria. Thus, it both opens up and closes off opportunities for the resources concerned, for territorial authorities, SMEs and workers.

---

6 A French concept for local employment policies (lit. "employment basins").

Towards the Mobilisation of Complete Sets of Productive Capabilities?

Today, leading corporations do not simply need to mobilise material resources and a workforce, but also a complete set of capabilities. And these sets are composed of several levels of elements that interact in a systemic way:

. technical know-how regarding products and processes;

. organisational know-how regarding the division and coordination of tasks throughout the process of conception, production and distribution, this process being increasingly divided up among several actors;

. institutional know-how regarding the normative context in which the two other levels are embedded, which can be referred to as the governance notion (i.e. the system of powers and rules that presides over such a setting).

Most of all, these capabilities have to be permanently adapted to match the changing requirements of large extended firms, and our past research enables us to observe that there is a connection between the adaptation trends related respectively to workers, SMEs and territories, whose evolutions are supposed to be going on at the same pace.

Concerning workers, we showed that a new employment model is emerging (Perrat, 2004). Drawn by the constitution of a high-skilled category of professionals acting in a para-salarial way, it spreads the idea among all employees that it is compulsory to involve oneself in both the productive ends and their risks, and to privately and permanently ensure one's capability and "employability".

In the same way, territories are called to permanently ensure their competitiveness, their attractiveness and their adaptability to circumstantial and structural changes. Hence, what is valid for a worker is also applicable for a territory. Furthermore, the latter appears to be the best place to ensure the permanent upgrading of workers' skills and employability in all their dimensions: since the recent decentralisation laws, regional authorities have clearly been in charge of the strategic decisions regarding vocational training, and increasingly intervene in the institutional aspects of employment (new forms of contracts combining mobility, flexibility and elements of security; promotion of territorial social dialogue, etc.); as for the local level (*bassin d'emploi*), it is tending to become the appropriate place to ensure the provisional management of both employment and capabilities, and to help SMEs join this dynamic, including its institutional aspects (local instances of social dialogue and/or labour negotiations).

Finally, by analysing the new employment model, we have indicated the type of labour market segmentation it may bear according to the manner in which workers integrate:

. the "new professional" model (Gazier, 2003), with the aforementioned para-salarial characteristics,

. the traditional model of qualified and relatively protected employees with long-term contracts,

. or what could be called a "non-labelled" model, with short-term contracts, little protection and few benefits.

Furthermore, what we previously said about the new industrial policy could mean that there is a link between the tendency to specialise and rate territories and the tendency to specialise and rate employment forms.

But if the territorial level's role in these processes is to be further analysed, it is relatively clear that it needs to be approached essentially with respect to time, as territorial proximity (i.e. the whole systemic set of geographical, technical, organisational and institutional proximities) is strongly required for a change to occur, either punctually (productive and/or innovative "leaps forward") or more permanently (incremental adaptation of technical and human capabilities, provisional management of employment, organisational evolution of firm networks, institutional upgrading of governance rules, etc.). And that reality opens the way to several contradictions.

A Contradictory Mix of Market and Non-market Criteria

A territory cannot be reduced to the way it carries out operative functions "for others", i.e. the way in which it helps large firms mobilise complete and permanently adapted sets of capabilities; it has to work – at least partly – for itself (*per se*) and in a – relatively – lasting manner. This is especially true when the very firms' logic contains a lot of contradictory tendencies.

First, it is uncertain that the officially highly praised relationship between innovation and geographical proximity is entirely true, as several studies demonstrate that such a relationship is far more complex (Lung, 1997).

Second, it can be observed that territories are asked both to specialise in precise fields of activities (several official reports stress that French productive and territorial systems are not specialised enough) and to be versatile enough to continuously adapt themselves to strategic economic changes (Viet, 2003).

Above all, what we have observed through recent studies,[7] especially in the aerospace sector in the Aquitaine region, is that when trustworthy, non-market, relationships are called in to ensure the full mobilisation of the workforce, SMEs and territories in common projects implemented with manufacturing integrators, such relationships are said to hamper the upgrading of the productivity and competitiveness of these very potentials. Thus, a report of the Regional Chamber of Industry and Commerce of Aquitaine[8] states that:

. there is a development of alliances between suppliers in order to present a more complete and high-level offer to leading integrative firms wishing to establish partnership and co-productive relations, and these networks can often be made to work better by territorial authorities;

. there is a trend towards "marketisation", through a coding of the criteria of relations, this coding being systematic and centred around commercial services;

. a basic requirement is that of shifting from relations (inside the firm, but also between parts suppliers and integrators) that were built over time and upon non-market criteria ("trust relationships in which know-how was the main bargaining element") to relationships in which "prices and productive conditions become the main factors of contracting";

. this is also true in territorial terms: territories are called to play the Local Productive System card, "the geographical proximity of the partners ensuring flexibility and reactivity"; but at the same time, the report observes that "the advantage of LPSs does not particularly reside in price-competitiveness", upon which large integrators' new requirements now focus; therefore, it weakens "the industrial culture that had been historically built in certain productive areas", where the contracting between partners was "essentially of a non-market type, the main factor being a cutting-edge and locally-developed know-how".

These contradictions may explain both the praise and distrust of the Industrial District that permeates many official reports: indeed, the notion proves useful when promoting certain particular aspects of actors' interrelations, such as cooperation and common rules among employers, or the "porosity" between the statute of employee and that of employer (Perrat, 2001); however, at the same time, IDs are also consid-

---

7 These studies were carried out in the form of a "action-research" with trade unionists, through a research contract with the Cgt union and the Ires (Institute for Economic and Social Research).

8 *Diagnostic industriel 2003 – Les entreprises de sous-traitance du secteur aéronautique-spatial-défense en Aquitaine*, Chambre Régionale de Commerce et d'Industrie d'Aquitaine, 2004.

ered outdated as regards their productive and territorial purposes of endogenous and perennial development (see Blanc, 2004).[9] Actually, we could say that large corporations would like territories to combine both the advantages of the two polar notions of Industrial District and cluster.

What Manoeuvring Margins for Territorial Development?

The most contradictory aspect of this development is that the complete sets of capabilities are asked to work as territorialised systems, because of the coherence that has to be organised between the different levels of proximity (technical, organisational, institutional), when the keys of their development and durability lie elsewhere, i.e. in the large corporations that control the integration of the various productive sets that are supplanting (or completing) the traditional value chains.

For the territories where such productive sets exist (and for their actors), the main question is: what margins do they have to manage these capabilities as a system of their own? One of the possible answers could reside in the manner in which the "externality relationship" is mobilised. This notion expresses the need for a dominant actor to establish a relationship with other actors, which is no longer a hierarchical relation but one that offers these actors a margin of autonomy so that they might implement their productive and innovative capabilities (Perrat, 1997). More precisely, we could say it expresses a transfer of both sides of the entrepreneur's statute: involvement in production, innovation and profit improvement and involvement in the resulting risks. This also happens within the new employment relationship (on the shop floor, in the factory and within the whole corporate system), within the partnerships established between integrators and suppliers, within the territorial system of actors and within the inter-territorial system of relations (between European, national, regional and local authorities, especially through the "subsidiarity" logic and "project-oriented" policies), so that we can speak of a fractal-type diffusion of this externality relationship.

When that relationship is at work, and even if it remains a non-symmetrical one, it opens up possibilities for the actors concerned to manage their development for themselves, at least partially. But the contradiction is that when that relationship is strongly required in a productive logic way, it is also constantly challenged by the financial logic, which aims at short-term results and which balances the advantages and constraints of territorial potentials, in real time and on the most global scale, according to those criteria.

---

9 Similarly, according to *L'Usine Nouvelle* (2005/04/28), Italy's feeble growth in recent years calls into question its industrial model based on Industrial Districts.

In this context, territorial actors have to try to "square the circle" by nurturing sets of capabilities which can both be pertinent for companies' profit aims and able to ensure a durable territorial development. This means, for instance, not to simply ensure the launching of new products or processes, but also to have an important share in the subsequent productive processes. It is just such a complex environment that socio-economic actors, and especially trade unions, have to deal with.

New Opportunities and Constraints for Socio-economic Actors

In order to shed light on these transformations and on what is at stake for socio-economic actors, we believe it is necessary to stress the link between the changes in both productive and territorial organisations and the changes in the employment relationship, as opposed to viewing employment conditions as a mere social fallout from economic strategies.

A More Individual, Local and Autonomous Employment Relationship

For the last few years, the whole French legislative and normative labour system has been challenged by the strategy of employers aimed at individualising, localising and autonomising the employment relationship. On the workplace level, the individualisation trend is on the increase in terms of wage policy and career prospects, as proved by the management's periodic control of the employee and the definition of individual projects and objectives. At the institutional level, employers exert strong pressures on authorities to dismantle the existing legal framework that guarantees a hierarchical link between the different levels of collective rules (the Labour Code at the national and inter-professional levels being improved by Collective Agreements at the level of professional branches, which can then be eventually improved by Company Agreements at the firm level). The explicit aim of employers' organisations is to invert this hierarchy and to obtain both the primacy of the Company Agreement and the autonomy of its negotiating.[10]

In a previous study (Perrat, 2004), we insisted on the vocational training policy as a key-vector for the transformation of the whole set of employment norms. The Law for Lifelong Vocational Training and Social Dialogue,[11] that refers to the European recommendations on these issues, makes the building and validating of capabilities the basis of the employee's professional security: it offers the employee new rights in

[10] See the numerous declarations and reports by the Medef (the main employers' organisation) representatives that express this strategic target.

[11] Passed in May 2004.

terms of vocational training, and even a certain transferability of these rights (in the case of dismissal, for instance). At the same time, it points out that she/he must use these rights – more than the traditional collective ones – to ensure her/his own labour protection, by continuously increasing, adapting and promoting her/his "employability", with an implicit reference to the human capital theory (Becker, 1964). Further, this same Law introduces a link with the negotiation issues by enabling the Company Agreement (under certain conditions, but for the very first time in France) to go against the established professional and general agreements.

This process is currently being implemented at the level of large firms. For instance, Messier-Dowty (a Snecma subsidiary), a constructor of landing gears for planes and helicopters, signed several agreements with its unions (in January and April 2005) strongly connecting the development of individual capabilities, vocational training planning (including the new legal measures which, in theory at least, promote individual prospects) and career progression with the development of non-wage incomes, linked with the firm's results.[12] This verifies the fact that the "new professional" model is actually reshaping the employment relationship, at least as regards its strategic perspective.

Similarly, one can observe that in many activities (automotive, chemicals, aerospace, etc.), the leading integrators try to impose the same process among their suppliers, at least their direct ones. The territorial level thus appears as the right one for these SMEs to adapt to this complex change as, individually, they would be unable to attain this objective on their own.

Lastly, the complex context of both high unemployment and a lack of qualified labour incite regional and local authorities to involve themselves in the nurturing of new employment and training mechanisms. Favouring an individual treatment of these issues, their aim is not only a quantitative and qualitative adjustment of labour markets (for instance, relating to a sector of activity on a given territory, thanks to procedures – such as *Contrats d'Étude Prospective* or *Contrats d'Objectifs* – that attempt to coordinate the development of different vocational training modes), but also a better diffusion of the new employment model by linking vocational training, employability and professional security (several regional authorities are experimenting with different forms of labour contracts that can match this target).

Thus, what is at stake on the territorial field is a whole range of adaptations that include firms' productive and innovative capabilities as regards employment management, vocational training and labour norms

12 *Liaisons Sociales*, 2005/05/12.

as well, which leads us to the issues of collective bargaining and/or social dialogue.

Territory as a New Social Bargaining Place?

Collective bargaining is "a rule-making process" marked by "voluntary negotiations between employers or employers' organisations and workers' organisations, with a view to the regulation of terms and conditions by collective agreements".[13] The places of such a process used to be the national level, the sector level and the company level. What we said about the individualisation of the employment relationship implies that collective bargaining tends to wane in the face of a varied set of inter-individual agreements (formal or tacit). The reduction of firms' size contributes to the same evolution, as in most cases trade unions are absent within SMEs. Nevertheless, companies claim to be the key-place for collective agreements, in order to react speedily to global competition and manage their individualised wage and employment policies. Thus, the number of firms' agreements is on the increase and the sectorial level tends to lose ground before the onset of industrial relations' decentralisation, even though several new laws have strengthened its abilities, especially in the key-issue of vocational training. Consequently, territories ought to become key-places for collective bargaining, which at present is not yet the case.

In fact, there is a double process at work regarding labour agreements (Jobert, 2004). On the one hand, traditional collective bargaining is weakly taking place at the regional or local levels, either in activities long used to it (metal-mechanics, building-trade, etc.) or through new mechanisms, punctually (site agreements) or more durably (regional or local/inter-professional or professional joint arenas[14]). On the other hand though, a large set of non-classical forms of agreement is rapidly developing at these levels, in particular as regards regional planning for vocational training, local mechanisms of ongoing economic changes, the organisation of "social time", etc.

The main tendency of this new trend is to marginalise collective bargaining in its classic form and to favour either consultation ("an advisory process in which one party seeks the advice of the other, but retains the power of unilateral decision-making"[15]) or social dialogue (i.e. "the process in which actors inform each other of their intentions and capaci-

---

13 *Industrial Relations in Europe*, European Commission, Employment & Social Affairs, p. 29.

14 The Law for Lifelong Vocational Training and Social Dialogue (May 2004) promotes the creation of such arenas for social partners and gives employees new rights to participate in them.

15 *Industrial Relations in Europe, op. cit.*, p. 29.

ties, elaborate and exchange information provided to them and clarify and explain their assumptions and expectations [thus preparing the ground] for joint problem-solving, collective bargaining or unilateral decision-making"[16]). Indeed, one of the facts that favours such a shift is that these agreements mobilise a great number of different actors: public authorities, public and private training centres' managers, public and private job agencies' managers, members of numerous associations for labour insertion, etc., " none of the levers being in the hands of a single actor" (Edouard, 2005).

In a configuration such as this, the place for social partners is profoundly called to question: they become actors among others and tend to lose their specificity through the common search of "good practices" capable of solving the problems encountered. Besides, regional authorities most often ask either social partners as a whole, or trade unions as a whole, to elaborate common answers and proposals regarding economic and social development issues, so that the specificities of each social partner and of each trade union organisation become blurred.

Another problem for both employers' and employees' organisations is that of being able to ensure a presence in all these new arenas, whether these are circumstantial or more permanent, as they have difficulty situating themselves in such a prolific and ever-shifting setting. Furthermore, they are obliged to face the challenge of organising the best connection between what is at stake in these places and their other fields of activity, i.e. not simply delegating these missions to individual "specialists" to carry out.

An Agenda for Unionists... and for Researchers

We thus observe that, though the individualisation trend tends to exclude trade unions from employment management, they are recalled on the scene by the territorialisation trend, for the main reason that these problems' complexity cannot be addressed without a more collective governance. Consequently, it opens up new scopes for their activity. Indeed, whereas in the traditional Industrial Districts they were rejected from industrial relations, they can now actually prove to be key actors in the new territorial organisations.[17]

However, at the same time, they are forced to face great challenges, for this shift to the territorial level carries a decisive change in the employment relationship: on the one hand, it fuels the diffusion of the

[16] *Id.*

[17] Indeed, in many a difficult situation, employers have had to more or less resign themselves to the fact that unions could reopen the individual and collective prospects, boost local governance and bring back public and private investments.

new employment model while, on the other, it fuels a surpassing of the labour relationship itself (Perrat, 2004) through the fusion it tends to bring about between market and non-market activities, between work-time and other social times, between productive decisions and societal ones (sustainable development, consumption choices, firms' social responsibility, etc.).

Another complex issue for unions is the fact that the territorial level is the easiest place for osmosis to take place between public and private actors and mechanisms. This is the case, for instance, in the current restructuring of employment and unemployment management (see the new French mechanism of "Houses for Employment"), or in the geographical redistribution of healthcare potentials. For unionists, there is a contradictory challenge: they must intervene so as to preserve the interests of all employees, both public and private ones; they must sustain criteria enforcing the role of public orientations in the strategic evolution of the mechanisms concerned; and, they must worry about the best services offered to users and, if need be, reach an agreement with their representatives.

In any case, the individualisation and localisation trends of the employment relationship are pushing trade unions to reformulate their targets and reorganise themselves towards both more generality and more territoriality: they try to foster rights and guarantees that secure individual trajectories and prospects for workers (see the Cgt's demand regarding an "employee statute" and a "professional social security"), merge their professional branches[18] and extend their territorial presence. There is even a debate at present to know whether it might be pertinent to favour the territorial scope instead of the professional one and whether, for workers, territorial identity is possibly supplanting professional identity (Pruvost, 2005).[19] In order to shed light on this complex context, we would like to point out certain leads that might take this analysis further and which call to question both unionists and researchers.

Who Decides?

Faced with either the employability target put to workers or the attractiveness target put to territories, one must ask the question: who actually decides on what employability or attractiveness should be? According to which and whose criteria and interests? From within the

---

18 See the creation of Ver.Di, in Germany, covering all activities related to the sector of services.

19 Referring to the tendency of current employment policies to "fix" the workforce on a territory (with the exception of the higher echelons), instead of promoting mobility as happened during the previous period.

labour relationship, from the territorial system or from an external point of view? This brings us back to the complex issue of evaluating the manoeuvring margins for the actors concerned but, with relation to trade unions, it also calls up the need to assess the characteristics of governance rules and the way their production and evolution are organised: individual and/or local agreements (explicit or tacit), collective bargaining, consultation, social dialogue, etc. Eventually, unions would be forced to demand the creation of real bargaining arenas whenever a governance process takes.

The Crucial Link between Economic and Social Issues

Another aspect of the previous question is to call into question the usual dichotomy existing between economic and social issues, and especially between industrial decisions and the way workers, activities and territories are expected to adapt themselves. This is true for the rights and guarantees that need to be ensured in order to secure workers' individual trajectories, which cannot be uncoupled from the rights related to employers' strategies (productive investments, closing down or relocation of an activity, etc.). It is also true for the nurturing and promotion of territorial complexes of activities and capabilities, for instance French competitiveness poles. A characteristic of these mechanisms is that trade unions are rarely approached to participate in their elaboration and implementation, but are requested to facilitate the handling of their social aspects, especially as regards the provisional management of employment and capabilities. But it is crucial for them to claim they are associated to both, and this is legitimate, considering the systemic setting of productive, organisational and normative capabilities this mechanism mobilises. To this one must add a further difficulty, linked to the aforementioned fact that the governance of these mechanisms is almost exclusively a private one: the content of their projects is marked with the seal of confidentiality.

From Generality to Materiality

In a previous work (Perrat, 2002), we stressed labour's two main characteristics: i.e. its "materiality", meaning the way it becomes embodied in concrete productive operations and processes, and its "institutionality", or the way it is embodied in normative and social relationships. We believe that one way of shedding light on the complexity of the industrial relations that seem to push unions to more and more generality would be to explore the different expressions of this "materiality":

What about professional identity? Isn't there a new distribution of capabilities, classifications and jobs? For instance, the aforementioned Messier-Dowty agreements target the establishment of a reference panel of capabilities structured around ten "families of jobs"; is there a general trend pushing job to take over a greater part of the role played to date by branches? In his report, Edouard (2005) advances that the outsourcing trend challenges "the continuous search for professional identities that professional sectors and branches can define and give life to, such as labour communities and places for carrying out collective projects". And if he insists on the role that branches need to continue playing in defining professional identity, he calls for more partnership between branches and other territorial actors in order to master these complex evolutions.

. Regarding workforce mobility: does it exist essentially within the firms? Within the firms' networks? The sectors? The territories? According to a governmental institute (Insee), "most of the employment reallocations going on each year take place within each sector rather than between sectors".[20]

. About sectors: how can we evaluate the dominance of the new employment model? What about the segmentation between high-skilled professionals (with non-pay incentives), "rank-and-file" employees, temporary and agency workers, etc.? What proportion of workers (category by category) does it concern? With which segmentation of firms (main integrators, first rank suppliers, second rank suppliers, subcontractors, etc.)? What difference between sectors' productive models? between large companies' productive models? The Gerpisa[21] work-programme (Freyssenet, Lung, 2003) teaches us that we cannot simply oppose productive and financial logic to appreciate the scope of the externality relationship (and therefore the manoeuvring margins of the actors concerned): it is important to identify where a specific firm is located amidst a large panel of models that combine a profit strategy in different ways (whose choice depends on the international, national and sectorial conditions of consumption, incomes, labour markets, rivals' strategies, etc.) and a governance compromise, the latter combining a product policy, a productive organisation and a labour relation, also in different ways.

. On territory: what about the real synergies mobilised by a "territory of excellence" mechanism? Which resources are to be integrated in this process? Which are not? Which type of specialisation of the productive, organisational and normative set of capabilities is at work? With which type of spatial division of labour? For instance, we might think that the new relationships between main integrators and suppliers (i.e. the shift from traditional subcontracting to outsourcing and "modularisation" –

---

20 *Les Échos*, 2005/05/16.

21 Groupe d'Études et de Recherches Permanent sur l'Industrie et les Salariés de l'Automobile.

Frigant, 2005), combined with the reduction of the number of parts in each finished good, tend to enforce the horizontal and territorial distribution of capabilities, instead of the vertical segmentation induced by traditional subcontracting relations. But what about the real suppliers or subcontractors' pattern on the territory, i.e. which spatial concretisation of the productive models mentioned above? And which spaces for trade unions' interventions? For collective bargaining and/or social dialogue pertaining to these different models?

Conclusion

The new French industrial policy is to be taken as a revealing factor for a wider movement of significant bearing. In a context of individualisation, localisation and autonomisation of the employment relationship, it highlights the new specific part played by the couple regional level (for strategic positioning) / local level (for field achievement) in issues connecting industrial reshaping, employment management reshaping and territorial forms reshaping. Of course, we must take care not to over-evaluate the French case. Reality may differ from one country to another, especially relating to the role played by the local level.

An issue that needs to be studied more thoroughly concerns the international aspects of labour division: does what stands for territorial differentiation in developed countries also stand at the global scale? Though the division into productive segments according to labour costs continues to be predominant, the rise of countries like China or India begins to strongly question not only this distribution, but even the one based on the high-range / low-range distinction. If we are moving towards a relative equivalence of delivered goods, would not the differentiation criteria pass to the manner in which the different productive "packages" (sets of capabilities) are composed throughout the world, i.e. to the manner in which they combine their technical, organisational and institutional components, favouring either a low-wage and less regulated workforce (in terms of time, protection, autonomy, etc.) or the high productivity of para-salarial professionals and adapted rules of employment governance, so as to in any case offer investors the profitability they are looking for?

Further, in France itself this local level is still in a largely experimental stage: the relevant scale has not been entirely defined and it seems that social actors both acknowledge the necessity of regional and local bargaining places and are afraid of their unpredictable consequences: the Medef does not want to give a bargaining mandate to its local representatives, but is trying to master all those new arenas; trade-unions call for the creation of such arenas, but distrust the internal problems it could introduce into their organisation as well as the possible bargaining differentiation between territories and workers that could result from such an evolution.

Nevertheless, we think that the new productive models cannot function without certain territorial requirements. The development of skills cannot be entirely individualised and demands a part of organisational and institutional governance. The same remark can be made concerning employment management: from the employers' point of view in a context where there is a shortage of high-skilled workers, and from the employees' point of view in a context of high unemployment and an unstable labour market. Is it not compulsory to mobilise local resources and actors in order to address the challenges of resolving the issues at stake? And if what we said is true about vocational training being a key-vector of the employment relationship's transformation, does not the territorialisation trend of training policies (and not only in France) imply that it is that very relationship as a whole that is concerned by such a process?

So, if what we observed actually foments a real trend towards territorially-built solutions and mechanisms, it seems that social partners are acquiring new spaces for their interventions and relationships, at the same time that their traditional spaces of negotiation (inside the firms and branches) are shrinking. The main issue is that of the pertinent collective bargaining places, knowing that one of the stumbling blocks regarding their implementation is the link that needs to be established between industrial strategies and their structural social components and not only with their social repercussions.

References

Becker, G., *Human Capital. A Theoretical and Empirical Analysis, with Special Reference to Education*, New York, National Bureau of Economic Research, 1964.

Beffa, J.-L., "Pour une nouvelle politique industrielle", *Rapport au Premier Ministre*, Paris, Assemblée Nationale, 2005, 58 p.

Blanc, C. (ed.), "Pour un écosystème de la croissance", *Rapport au Premier Ministre*, Paris, Assemblée Nationale, 2004, 78 p.

Boyer, R., Dehove, M. and Plihon, D. (2004), "Les crises financières", *Rapport du Conseil d'Analyse Économique* No. 50, Paris, La Documentation Française.

Edouard, F. (ed.), "Conséquences sur l'emploi et le travail des stratégies d'externalisation d'activités", *Rapport du Conseil Économique et Social*, Paris, Ed. des Journaux Officiels, 2005.

Fontagne, L. and Lorenzi, J.H., "Désindustrialisation – Délocalisations", *Rapport au Premier Ministre*, Paris, Conseil d'Analyse Économique, 2004, 127 p.

Freyssenet, M. and Lung, Y. (eds.), "Les acteurs de l'entreprise à la recherche de nouveaux compromis?", *Actes de la Onzième Rencontre Internationale du GERPISA*, 11-13 juin, Ministère de la Recherche, Paris, CD-Rom, 2003.

Frigant, V., "Les proximités dans la production modulaire: une analyse de l'internationalisation des équipementiers automobiles", *Cahier du GRES*, No. 11, Bordeaux, 2005.

Gazier, B., *Tous sublimes – Pour un nouveau plein emploi*, Paris, Flammarion, 2003.

Jobert, A. (2004), "Le dialogue social territorial: entre logique de projection et logique de projet", *Notes Thomas*, No. 7, Avril, Paris, CGP.

Lung, Y., Organisation spatiale et coordination des activités d'innovation des entreprises, Convention d'Étude du Commissariat Général du Plan, 1997.

Morvan, Y., "Aménagement du territoire et pôle de compétitivité: l'indispensable réconciliation", *Inter-Régions*, No. 256, Sept.-Oct. 2004, pp. 10-14.

Perrat, J., "Une clé de lecture du rapport firmes/territoires: la notion d'externalité", *Espaces et Sociétés*, No. 88-89, Paris, L'Harmattan, 1997, pp. 207-236.

Perrat, J., "Districts industriels et territorialisation du rapport salarial: un éclairage à partir des réalités vénitiennes", *Revue d'Économie Régionale et Urbaine*, No. 4, Bordeaux, 2001, pp. 641-663.

Perrat, J., "Dynamiques territoriales et dynamiques salariales: de nouvelles règles pour une nouvelle donne?", *Géographie, Économie*, Vol. 4, No. 4, Paris, Elsevier, 2002, pp. 405-426.

Perrat J., "Formation, emploi, travail: régulation sectorielle et/ou régulation territoriale?", *Communication aux Quatrièmes journées de la Proximité*, Idep, Lest, Greqam, Groupe Proximité, Marseille, June 17-18, 2004.

Porter, M., *On competition*, Boston, Harvard Business School Press, 1998.

Pruvost, F., "La politique de l'emploi comme accompagnement social des restructurations", in H. Jacot and J.-C. Le Duigou (eds.), *Délocalisations, restructurations, exaspérations, ripostes, Rapport sur la situation économique et sociale 2004-2005*, RRS-CGT, 2005, pp. 65-84.

Viet, C. (ed.), "L'accompagnement des mutations économiques", *Rapport au Premier Ministre*, Paris, Ministère des Affaires Sociales, du Travail et de la Solidarité, 2003, 35 p.

PART III

INDIVIDUAL AUTONOMY *VS.* COLLECTIVE RESPONSIBILITY IN A WORLD OF FLEXIBLE LABOUR

Part III.A

Autonomy at Work

Autonomy, General Working Capacity and Collective Action

Patrick DIEUAIDE

Center of Economy of Sorbonne
University of Paris – Panthéon Sorbonne

Introduction

Widely discussed today, the concept of autonomy is part of a radical change of model in terms of labour organisation. As P. Bernoux points out, the latter "*is no longer centred on the workstation and individual performance but, rather, on the coherence and integration of subgroups, on communication between departments and beyond with the subcontractors (partnership relations)*" (Bernoux, 1998: 398).

In a model such as the one rapidly presented here, work is enriched with new determinations that transform both its nature and its forms:

Firstly, work is defined in regard to a series of actors and to a wide range of different yet highly integrated socio-technical systems and methods, with the whole outlining spheres of activity that, frequently, extend beyond the confines of the company. The result is that labour is no longer as firmly entrenched as in the past within the opposing relation of employer/employee but, rather, falls within a larger, "triadic" (Borzeix, 2003) space formed by employee, employer and customer (or supplier).

Secondly, work becomes increasingly complex and changes nature under the effect of new determinations (cognitive, linguistic, relational, even emotional), so that in real-life situations workers are increasingly called upon to show initiative and intelligence. Thus, more and more often, work resembles a subjective activity (judgment, discussion, assessment), which mobilizes information and uses discursive and linguistic means. This activity sits ill with a logic of command as, being largely subjective and having its own temporality, it cannot be easily integrated into the "Process Planning Department's" planned time.

These transformations in the form and content of work within a firm make us consider autonomy as the expression of a certain relationship between individuals and their immediate environment and the existence of specific problems that appear within it. More precisely, autonomy at work appears as having a double dimension: as being the expression of a particular space and a particular temporality, which are open to forms of free and subjective commitments (I); as being the expression of a form of authority vis-à-vis oneself and others during the creation of general working capacities and representations (II). These distinctive features will allow us to clarify the question of the relationship between autonomy, rationalisation and control (III).

I. Autonomy as a Form of Free and Subjective Commitment to Work: Elements of Context

Since the early 1980s, statistics and field surveys regarding labour conditions in France reveal a notable increase in autonomy at work, for all socio-professional categories (Bué, Rougerie, 1999; Cousin, 2004). However, the phenomenon is paradoxical, or at least difficult to define. Two conceptions of autonomy can be discerned.

A first conception, stemming from the works of J.D. Reynaud (1989), apprehends autonomy as operators' capacity to acquire the margin for manoeuvre to correct, or indeed to compensate, the shortcomings of prescribed work (Terssac, 1992; Terssac, Maggi, 1996). For this school of thought, autonomy is synonymous to independence. It refers to more or less arbitrary and clandestine behaviours, which are nonetheless in keeping with tacit expectations regarding the handling of a wide range of unknown factors.

A second conception lays more stress on the mobilisation of cognitive capacities and subjective commitment during work so as to underline "the return of work to the worker" (Zarifian, 2000b: 27; Chatzis *et al.*, 1999). Here, emphasis is put on the positive dimension of autonomy as the capacity to define and organize one's own working conditions (method, sequence, relocation, working tempo), legitimate and acknowledged as such by firms' management.

These two conceptions are not *per se* mutually exclusive. Both aim at consistency and a result in terms of efficiency. On the other hand, they are at odds as regards the organisational context within which the work is executed. This opposition largely results from a range of tensions which, since the mid-1980s, reveal the limits of the decision-making and management processes based on instructions and hierarchy:

Firstly, companies' production goals can no longer be decided and expressed under the same conditions as those of the past. Faced with a versatile demand (massively turned towards the consumption of high-tech goods and personalized services), faced, also, with the development of globalized competition (increasingly dominated by innovation), firms are now under an "obligation to invent". As a result, companies are constantly developing "design-oriented" or "customer-oriented" strategies. The outcome is a profound renewal of handling and management methods, breaking with the concept of sequential work in favour of alternative models based on the concepts of "core competencies", of continuous processes or apprenticeships, or of shared knowledge (Hatchuel, 2004).

Secondly, the radical incertitude weighing on production goals is inevitably accompanied by an identical incertitude regarding firms' capacity to define and schedule their own medium-long term requirements in terms of capital goods, intermediate consumption and skilled labour. This "blindness" of companies regarding the type of human or material capital that should be mobilized or produced introduces a second requirement: that of considering the production and management of these specific resources as a specific set of goals corresponding to an equal number of crucial preliminary conditions necessary for companies to give themselves the means of a long-term competitive advantage.

Lastly, hired personnel needs to constantly adjust to the variety of working situations in which the goals pursued and the means necessary to attain them are never totally fixed nor wholly controlled. Consequently, the work demanded of this personnel becomes extremely vague. This is explained, at least partially, by managements' difficulties to conceive and organize the correct pairing between jobs (more and more difficult to define), technologies (less and less stable) and individuals' working capacities (less and less legible on the market).

Therefore, in a context such as this, autonomy would refer to a spectrum of non-programmable situations, in the sense that the integration of a working process' various constitutive components for each individual (activity, work objects and means) would not be given *a priori* but, rather, would appear as a slow and progressive structuring process of these various components. In other words, the work of each person would in no way be immediate. Its process would, in part, belong to a specific space and a specific temporality imposed by the social problems and organisational techniques encountered by the employees while executing their activities. In general, it would be up to the interested parties to take up these problems and become involved with the production of new representations about and for the general working capacity.

Seen from this angle, autonomy at work cannot be disassociated from a general working capacity mobilized according to a logic of experimentation. This is the case, we say, every time that the work no longer directly depends on the ultimate goals set by the management and (as P. Naville had stressed in his time) on the socio-technical requisites imposed on everyone by the machines system (Naville, 1963).

Under these conditions, autonomy is an integral part of a certain form of liberty at work, which surpasses a practical intelligence used for unauthorized on-the-spot solutions. When related to complex and unpredictable environments, autonomy covers a singular productive moment of the work process: that corresponding to the very time of its composition. This means that, in order to work, the workers must already begin by producing themselves, that is to say begin by integrating one with another the capacities they have and the working means that surround them. And yet, this integration cannot be reduced to a "Crozier-Friedberg"-style game dynamics. If this integration corresponds to what is at stake in terms of strategies or of power relations among actors, these components only count inasmuch as they participate in a "counter-effectuation" process (to use the expression of G. Deleuze, quoted by P. Zarifian), that is to say in a moment of investigating and producing sense when confronting the problems that appear (Zarifian, 2000a: 114). Thus, in order to become integrated with their work or give it a meaning, the workers must first go through a series of intermediate activities and objectives, from the simple act of reading technical documentation to that of negotiating or swapping experiences (Valeyre, 1999), all sorts of activities which, in one way or another, contribute to forming an opinion on the different ways of thinking and handling one's conduct at work.

Under this angle, far from being a residual moment outside managerial control, autonomy is more of a moment bearing a "capacity of transformation of self, of others and of activities" (Bercot, 1999: 89). This moment is singular as it has made of the liberty and subjectivity mobilized by the worker the condition and the result of work itself. In this respect, autonomy constitutes a powerful moment of a "professional socialisation", constructed according to a logic of producing and swapping experiences and practical knowledge/know-how.

II. Reflectivity as a Principle of Undertaking and Producing Capacities at Work

What emerges from the above is that autonomy continues to be an integral part of a certain form of power redistribution during production. As C. Everaere points out, in the autonomy model "*power blends in to the very act of working thanks to the local mobilisation of knowledge: the person who executes (a task) is, simultaneously, the one who thinks, who discovers on his own the best way of proceeding, either individually or collectively, and who assumes the responsibility of his work*" (Everaere, 2001: 19). Thus, with the aid of knowledge, work manifests itself as a contingent moment, structured on the basis of non-hierarchical relations and behaviours.

This perspective radically affects the issue of autonomy, inasmuch as the conditions of carrying out a job can in no way be conceived as either mechanical or spontaneous processes. In other words, and for a given environment, labour would consist of specific forms of individuals' mobilisation and undertaking that simultaneously encompass the type or nature of problems to be resolved, the possible solutions towards this and the conditions of putting them into action. In short, and to quote E. Charlon, "*it is no longer a case of doing without understanding but, rather, of understanding what one does*" (Charlon, 1996: 147).

Hence, it is no wonder that, in the firms, mobilized knowledge (for the greater part, tacit knowledge) always surpasses that required by the job description. This knowledge in fact corresponds to "models of action" (Schön) created in a real-life situation on the basis of structures of perception that are specific to their originators. This knowledge or these "models of action" are therefore *cognitive constructions with a specific historicity*. They are the product of a reflective act of work, which is all the more intense and permanent for individuals being continuously confronted with work situations that are not entirely codified and foreseeable.

A/ Work Situations and Modes of Action: a Typology

From the above, it is possible to clarify the conditions of carrying out an autonomous act of work. Indeed, reflectivity is not a fact per se, independent of the context in which individuals in the firm put this faculty of the mind to work. On the contrary, it appears as a mode of action or a specific method of applying oneself to work.

In order to understand this specificity, a reference to K. Marx is not without interest. Indeed, in his famous parable of the bee and the architect, Marx distinguished between a "*primordial state*" of work, which had yet to divest itself of its purely "*instinctive*" mode, and a state that "*belongs exclusively to man*" and whose distinctive feature is that "*its product ideally pre-exists in the worker's imagination*" (Marx, 1968: 728).

Thus, during a first reading, the distinction between an "instinctive" mode and a "reflective (or thought-out)" mode brings to the fore the singularity of man's forms of undertaking and experience while at work compared to that of the animal world. But it is possible to consider this distinction under a different light, namely by stressing the fact that, for man himself, *work is simultaneously an action and a representation*. In this respect, one can say of (human) labour that it is the condensed expression of a specific set of relations between different "production factors" (Marx), both objective and subjective, this set defining work as a process (or procedure).

Consequently, according to the degree of complexity encountered in the work situation, three modes of action, specific to human labour, may arise (we adapt, here, the typology proposed by Dibiaggio, 1999: 120).

If the work situation is *simple*, the job poses no problem inasmuch as the "representation" of its product is immediate. The job can therefore be assimilated to that of a bee, as its completion is almost "*instinctive*" (Marx). This situation is typical of the Taylorism era and mass production where the required know-how and cognitive capacities while carrying out the job prove to be minimal.

If the work situation is *problematical*, the act of carrying out the job is hindered by the fact the worker has no immediate representation of its product. If the causes of this vagueness can be clearly identified, the latter can be overcome through selecting and applying heuristic methods to resolve the problems. Under these conditions, work begins with an act of thought (a reflective act), that is to say that its approach is one of analysis or seeking how to apply a sum of available knowledge to a particular problem. This situation is linked to the development, since the 1980s, of competition processes based on products' differentiation and quality.

If the work situation is *complex*, the job *a priori* defies the imagination. Its execution does not belong to any of the knowledge system's categories. The representation of its product is therefore a matter of conjectures, of thought processes using analogies or metaphors (Reix, 1995). The job is elaborated on a *reflective* mode, that is to say through a series of "to and fro" between the existing knowledge and the new knowledge it is necessary to construct in order to identify and resolve the problem that arises. At this level, the problem and its solution are inextricably linked. This situation corresponds quite well with the forms of competition dominated in the 1990s by the development of product and process innovations.

Of these three modes of action, the reflective mode appears to be of a higher quality compared to the two others, inasmuch as reflectivity allows one to become a "*stakeholder*" as opposed to solely the executor of the improvements or innovations desired by companies' management. It should also be noted that reflectivity is not exclusive of the two other modes of action for a determined activity. This is why it is important that one should not underestimate its importance even in the most simple of work situations (Cavestro, 1988). It should also be pointed out that reflectivity refers to a particular form of individuals implication in their work, which relies on a recursive process between the available knowledge mobilized during the job and the new knowledge derived from the result of its application. In this respect, reflectivity carries in itself an irreducible dynamic and productive dimension.

B/ Reflectivity, Evolution of Knowledge and Know-how, and Dynamics of the Transformation of Working Capacities

In order to simplify the analysis, let us consider the (pure) case of complex work situations. From these situations, it becomes obvious that reflectivity as a mode of action supposed the interaction of two types of rationality:

A cognitive rationality, through which the creative, discursive and linguistic capacities of individuals are mobilized in order to identify and resolve problems,

An instrumental rationality, through which the knowledge produced in real-life situations is (partially) applied to the work itself.

As these rationalities or these logics of action are situated and hence irreducible one to the other, one can suppose that the job is nothing more than equivalent to recording their reciprocal interaction or their coexistence. In other words, the work would appear more like a subjectively constructed local experience, i.e. a "choice of intelligibility" specific to a given situation to quote F. Dubet (1994: 152), and less like the direct expression of an "external rationality" that obliges workers to act or to behave "blindly" according to a unique model and a temporality, both of which are predetermined.

This conception of work is consubstantial with the concept of autonomy presented in the previous paragraph. On the one hand, it leads to considering the labour as a moment of validation of a whole set of activities conceived and carried out *on the worker's initiative* so as to create or organize the specific pieces of knowledge. On the other, the labour invested in the production of knowledge dedicated to the resolution of specific problems is, at the same time, equivalent to producing experiences *for the worker himself.*

Thus, work is based on a dual process of producing knowledge and the practical experiences that support it. If, in the work process itself, the two coincide that is far from meaning that these moments are other than radically different:

The production of knowledge resulting from the workers' initiative commands – to a large degree – the manufacturing process of the final products. More precisely, the intermediate activities underlying this production generate a series of transfers, combinations or creations of knowledge which, directly or indirectly (via the activity of a third party), participate in the internal structuring of the job's organisation. These activities ensure firms' viability in an evolving environment and define its specificity in terms of know-how related to the production of particular goods, services or technologies.

The production of practical experience results from the transformation of the activities decided and acted upon by the workers with a general working capacity in order to elaborate or improve new "models of action". This transformation can be defined as a cognitive activity of synthesis and representation of oneself in a real-life situation, as a thinking and acting individual at work. These general working capacities or capacities for action are similar to inferences constructed by abstraction (Barbier, Galatanu, 2004: 55). In fact, their enunciation, whether it covers a pragmatic or epistemic finality, for oneself or for another, becomes the context of their development for the execution of other activities (*op. cit.*).

The interaction between these two moments is a source of efficiency for the firms, under the condition that the general working capacities generated by individuals' reflective recall of their own practical experiences are an integral part of the continuity of firms' activity in relation to markets' dynamics. Under this condition, the production of knowledge and the production of practical experience mutually reinforce each other in the source of specific trajectories (*path dependent*). Work is simultaneously a process of producing knowledge and a source of capacities' permanent adjustment to incessantly changing contexts of action.

A number of evolutionary works have underlined this point, in particular by stressing the importance of apprenticeships/training and routines in the formation of firms' scope of activities. Relatively few, however, have pointed out its counterpart in terms of the collective action's coordination and management. In this respect, adopting the concept of "organisational routine" put forth by this school of thought proves relatively unsatisfactory. Indeed, as we have seen, reflectivity appears as a particular moment of the work process when the worker, left to his own devices, creates for himself a representation of his specific capacities, which *a priori* has no reason to correspond to the efficiency criterion nor yet to the required or expected capacities defined by the firm's management, in order to ensure the execution of his subsequent activities.

From this viewpoint, reflectivity can prove to be a source of heterogeneity and, in this respect, constitutes a factor of dispersion of knowledge within the firm. Collective action, constantly threatened in its unity or efficiency, becomes problematic. Its management supposes rules regarding the adjustment of individuals' behaviour which, during work itself, conciliates the liberty to undertake, the actions' efficiency and the capacities' control (assessment).

III. The Supervision of Autonomy and the Construction of a Collective Action

To summarize all that precedes, we can say that the definition of autonomy as a general working capacity opens on a representation of individuals at work that is based on the central part played by cognitive processes, whether these concern resolving the problems that punctuate the working process or producing new capacities, which result from the representations generated by an effect of experience.

In this respect, autonomy introduces a radical incertitude regarding the conditions of collective action. Whereas in the past, during the Fordism era, collective action was predefined by the planning of individuals functions, work positions and performances within the organisations, at present (especially where an increasingly knowledge-intensive productive logic prevails) collective action is increasingly subject to individuals' (or subjectivities') prior integration among themselves, *directly* through the activities for which the initiative is theirs.

Thus, the unity and efficiency of collective action are not a given fact, nor can they be established in advance. Constructed within the work process itself, collective action closely depends on the speed and quality of the convergence process regarding the representations of the workers who are part of the work process. Under these circumstances, collective action is an integral part of a dynamic, interactive game of confrontation taking place in real time among individuals, so as to create common or shared practices or representations. This confrontation results in a set of discursive and linguistic practices, which do not act as a substitute for the activities resulting from the workers' initiative but – on the contrary – forms a body with them.

Hence, from the firm's viewpoint, the economic risk is that this confrontation could lead to a dead end or, at least, prove to be unproductive if the workers' autonomy of action becomes an obstacle through the development of activities or capacities that are far removed from its strategy and/or efficiency criteria dictated by the markets. Because of this, the supervision of autonomy appears to be an essential condition for the development of firms' performance. Specific rules, language and procedures are necessary if a minimal orderliness in the resources and cognitive capacities available within each firm is to prevail.

In order to clarify this point, the last section of this paper offers a few reflections on the management policies adopted by companies' directors and managers in order to take workers' autonomy in hand. Our attention will focus on two of these policies' dimensions: the management of conception times and the assessment and piloting of work groups by means of the "skills approach".

A/ Cognitive Rationalisation and Management Methods of Conception Times

In complex work situations, where mobilized knowledge is for a greater part contingent, it is possible to break down the process of knowledge production into three moments, or three phases of action: a moment of analysis of undertaking, a moment of implementation or contextualisation, a moment of reflectivity or formalisation.

From the firm's viewpoint, these different phases are part of a temporality and dynamics concerning the development of each individual worker's specific capacities that escape direct control, especially through official channels. Under these circumstances, there arises a practical (and policy-related) problem of how to direct the actions conceived and implemented both in the short term regarding the work goals imposed by the company's management and in the medium-long term regarding the firms' strategic positioning, especially in terms of portfolio choice (technologies, products, activities). Firms' difficulty lies, precisely, in bringing under control the material and immaterial resources at their disposal and, over and above this, the flow of information through which the workers think out, elaborate and decide on how to act.

Since the early 1980s, the answer provided by firms' directors in terms of process management progressively imposed itself as an original solution to the problem of controlling individuals' autonomy while in the process of working. Basically, process management relies on mechanisms that normalize behaviours expressed during the entire chain of the workers' cognitive activities. These mechanisms are not aimed at imposing opinions or ways of seeing or doing things, but to suggest or help understand the problems that arise while simultaneously giving actors the liberty of action regarding the necessary adjustments. Three examples of these management mechanisms, chosen among the most significant ones, will be used to illustrate the above: quality mechanisms; the role of facilitator passed on to first-level supervisors; and, vocational training.

The increase in the number of *quality mechanisms* (ISO norm, productive maintenance, total quality) introduced by firms addresses the concern regarding the implementation of tools to formalize the knowledge acquired through experience (indicators, procedures), whether this concerns bolstering the continuity of processes' efficiency assessment, or revealing dysfunctions, improvements that have been introduced or successes that have been achieved (Campinos Dubernet, 2003: 187). In this way, these mechanisms ensure the continuity of data required for the observation and understanding of the phenomena encountered (*op. cit.*). In this respect, they permit a better coordination of activities within the firms by offering everyone the means of a greater (historical and contextual) visibility of the problems and the possible or available solutions. They also allow, to quote H. Simon, to save on "attention resources" (Simon) by avoiding repeated investments of the same kind in the construction of already tested learning processes. In sum, the quality mechanisms can generate gains in terms of efficiency by liberating individuals from routine tasks (Veltz, 1999: 21) and thus, at the same time, free time and means for researching or creating activities or problems of a higher level of complexity.

We should note, however, that the virtuous effects of quality tools are not systematic. Though these tools are predominant in activities that are knowledge intensive (such as in activities of industrial design or service relations, where the cognitive dimension of the underlying work is important), they are in no way inescapable. Through the formalisation of different categories of knowledge, in particular of written procedures, there is a risk that supervisors and management directors turn these tools against their users. As J.P. Durand notes, the item "*I write what I do*" then becomes "*I do that which is written thanks to the magic of social relations within the firm*" (Durand, 2004: 68). From being a prop for the real-life situation's cognitive activity, the tool becomes the instrument of a forced cooperation where a direct technico-economic pressure is exercised on potential individual reluctances (*op. cit.*). Everything hinges on the management's desire to promote change in the prevailing coordination methods. As attested by certain case studies, it is not infrequent that, under the effect of implementing quality mechanisms, individuals gain in terms of work autonomy in the context of a collective job what they lose in autonomy-margin for manoeuvre inherited from (neo-) taylorist situations (Campinos Dubernet, 2003; Bercot, 1999).

In order to guarantee the unity and coherence of collective action over time, the mediation role played on the jobsite by supervisors constitutes a second means of "channelling" individuals' subjectivity into their professional practices. Indeed, it is important that firms' management have the means of following, step by step, from the inside, the process of knowledge production, namely by supervising the conditions under which it take place, by taking advantage too of the new knowledge that might emerge and, lastly, by favouring the sharing, combining, dissemination and integration of individual pieces of knowledge. These requirements sit ill with a conception of supervision in the likes of a "methods engineer", whose organisation activity consists of separating the work from the worker, of defining and stipulating the tasks' content, of developing and managing a whole apparatus for controlling and executing the operations characterizing these tasks. *A contrario* they legitimise a profound renewal of the modes and aims of *first level supervision* within organisations, those of managing, consolidating, even deepening, the learning processes or the organisational routines within the work groups (Delteil and Dieuaide, 2001; Dieuaide, 2005). In particular, from the viewpoint of collective action, it is essential to obtain the full and wholehearted participation of the organisation's members towards achieving the production goals. It is up to the "managers" to build, on the field, such a relationship of trust within the work groups. This relation of trust is vital in order to ensure the convergence of representations and allow a free circulation between tacit and codified or explicit knowledge. For the firms' management, these modes of transferring knowledge, which can take various forms (Nonaka, 1994), correspond to as many issues at stake and questions that need to be resolved. Through their duties as "facilitators", the supervisory staff thus needs to reconcile two requirements: perpetuate the learning processes so as to extract the tacit knowledge and incorporate it into the products and technologies; and, improve the existing operating diagrams, encourage the exploration of new ideas and new combinations liable of generating incremental changes at all levels of activity (logic of *Kaizen*).

Lastly, when it circulates (at least partially) within the jobsite, *vocational training* constitutes a third possibility for supervising individuals' autonomy by favouring the apparition of learning processes and specific know-how according to a horizontal, non-hierarchical and intersectional mode (Charlon, 1996). In order to clarify this point, we should note with M. Feutrie and E. Verdier that "real-life situation" vocational training is at odds with a certain managerial and insurance-related vision of training, which is dispensed in turn so as to update or develop specific know-how (Feutrie and Verdier, 1993: 482). With real-life situation vocational training, the link is no longer solely educational; it is also functional (*op. cit.*). As B. Courtois *et al.* remark, "*the aims of training during work activity merges with the production aim during the training processes*" (Courtois *et al.*, 1996: 180). All things being equal moreover, there results a controlled development of the employees' "professionality" via a direct involvement of knowledge resulting from experiences that are mobilized or produced in work situations characterized by instability or by change. When directed towards the production of useful and efficient knowledge, vocational training becomes a central link in developing a participative approach in the employees as regards the improvement of organisational flexibility and, beyond, of firms' economic performance. But this tool is not really effective unless the employees are actively involved, which supposed that a number of obstacles be removed. On the one hand, and as remarked by E. Charlon, "*the capacity to formalize what one knows is not a form of knowledge mastered by every employee*" (Charlon, 1996: 151). On the other, the involvement expected of employees in the context of vocational training strongly risks being experienced as an imposition, particularly when there exists no previous form of collective work (cooperation, collaboration) on whose basis the employees can create for themselves a clear idea of the content and the limits of their professional experiences (see, for example, S. Caroly and Y. Clot, 2004 on the comparison of how two post offices functioned). Finally, in the context of asserting a "knowledge-based economy", where knowledge is increasingly diversified and is linked to an ever-growing number of internal and external partners of the firm, there exists a non-negligible risk that, in the hands of the management, vocational training can become the instrument of a policy of personnel segmentation, a source of a lack of job security for the least qualified among them.

In all, and subject to the limits mentioned above, these different forms of supervision can be considered as being as many means of controlling individuals' liberty of action, whether they concern quality-tools at the level of the construction of representations, direct supervision of subjectivities and mutual trust at the core of work groups' action, or of vocational training at the level of the formalisation of knowledge stemming from experience and its transformation into general working capacities. From the management's viewpoint, there results all in one go a *permanent endogenous assimilation* of skills and know-how in the form of routines, norms, procedures and a *cognitive rationalisation* that can manifest itself in two ways: either through a standardisation of work processes as long as these are sufficiently explicit and/or stabilized, or through an acknowledgement of practices and action modes of the workers themselves (skills method, see below). In any case, it would seem that these different forms of supervision converge so as to try to ensure, in accordance with the goals pursued, that the time needed to produce and mobilize knowledge during the act of working decreases.

B/ Assessment and Piloting of Work Groups: the Stakes of the "Skills Approach"

If collective action poses a problem as regards its management, this is not only because of the autonomy of action of its members; it is also due to collective action itself, as its dynamics can be neither spontaneously nor totally assimilated to firms' key activities or their development strategy.

This gap is structural. It stems both from the pressure of "external" factors (technological, scientific, commercial, financial) that, regularly, force firms' management to revise their strategic choices, but also from the difficulties encountered by the work groups to incorporate these choices at the daily level of the objectives and means of action that are mobilized.

It is, partially, the Human Resources Department's responsibility to seek ways of reducing this gap, namely by introducing management systems that acknowledge that work groups have a coherence and dynamics which are specific to them. In this respect, the "skills method" constitutes an original approach.

Indeed, the "skills method" is not univocal. According to M. Campinos Dubernet (2005), it consists in defining the "occupation (profession) referentials" either starting from the individuals in real-life situations and the posts they occupy, or from the global strategy and the collective skills required to implement it.

In the first case, the "skills method" is of a more functional nature. Using the case of a large company of the high-tech sector, C. Paraponaris shows that this method is based on a battery of management tools, such as pre-recruitment training courses (internships), the qualitative assessment of project managers, the quarterly appraisal interviews carried out by superiors, the annual appraisal interview carried out jointly (Human Resources Department, direct collaborators, project manager) and by means of a self-assessment on behalf of the interested parties (made on the basis of a comparison between the goals the latter undertook to achieve and the results they obtained). Among these tools, the annual assessment is the most important one. It gives rise to an overall grading and leads to a differentiated payment in the form of a bonus. This interview is completed by a promotion policy based on each worker's report on his/her professional activities as well as his/her vision of his/her own personal positioning within the firm's knowledge network (Paraponaris, 1005, summarized by us).

In the second case, the "skills method" initiated by the firm's management falls under the province of a medium-term projection of the skills the company seeks to possess for the professions exercised within it, while taking into account the developments in its environment (regulatory, technological, scientific). But a number of these skills cannot be hired "ready for use" at the exit of schools or colleges. These need to be produced locally, something that in a first stage requires a meticulous diagnosis of the skills that exist collectively at the level of the chains of the strategic activities. The assessment of the strengths and weaknesses in this field lead to a certain number of measures, from a change in the organisation of work in these different chains (and hence a simple readjustment of individual skills), to projects of in-house training or the implementation of knowledge capitalisation methods, to the construction of specific itineraries within firms in order to favour learning processes of the learning by doing type. In any case, the approach that is adopted is a collective one. It is only during a second phase that the "skills method" is applied at an individual level (Campinos-Dubernet, *op. cit.*).

The two approaches do not necessarily coexist, not because they obey to incompatible logics but, rather, due to the fact their implementation calls for a profound change in the regulation of social work relations within the firms. On the one hand, as A. Dietrich (2003: 228-229) notes, to recognize and remunerate individuals' skills supposes that the fields of action and responsibility are well delimited. On the other, the emergence and structuring of skills at the collective level supposes that conditions for learning and acknowledging new forms of professionalism have been put into place.

There exists, therefore, a subtle balance that needs to be found between an individualisation of the wage relation and its collective counterpart in terms of mobility and professional integration. This balance is not a given fact *a priori*. It supposes the establishment of new work and remuneration rules that explicitly recognize the existence of an enlarged space of activities, both on the level of the involvement and the forms of undertaking work and on that of capitalizing their practical experience within the work groups in the form of expertise or know-how.

Conclusion

The development of autonomy as a general working capacity gives expression to a profound transformation in the forms of the organisation and management of companies' economic performance. The interesting factor of this concept resides in the fact it highlights a non-Taylorism path towards the rationalisation of tasks and, incidentally, the construction of a collective action. Established on reflectivity, this path underlines the importance of cognitive logic in clarifying and ordering the actions of conception. Initiated by the individuals themselves under the "remote" control of firms' management and supervisors, these forms of logic are part of open, a priori non-prescribed intersubjective relations. Through their intermediary, collective action is no longer an ex post concretisation of a set of a priori defined and organized representations and tasks. On the contrary, collective action emerges progressively and directly from the individuals' capacity, means and commitment to organizing themselves, producing and sharing their specific resources. It should be noted that the construction of a collective action, on the interface of working relations between the organisation's various members, is a specific social feature that one can suppose is not exclusive to knowledge-intensive activities. It should be possible to encounter this dimension in all activities, especially in the field of services where person/person relations are dominant compared to person/machine relations in defining and conducting their actions.

References

Barbier J.M. and Galatanu O., "Savoirs, capacités, compétences, organisation des champs conceptuels", in J.M. Barbier and O. Galatanu (eds.), *Les savoirs d'action: une mise en mot des compétences*, Paris, L'Harmattan, 2004, pp. 31-78.

Bercot R., "L'autonomie comme capacité d'action: une expérience de cellules autonomes dans l'aéronautique", in K. Chatzis, C. Mounier, P. Veltz and P. Zarifian (eds.), *L'autonomie dans les organisations. Quoi de neuf?*, Paris, L'Harmattan, 1999, pp. 87-112.

Bernoux P., *Sociologie du changement*, Paris, Seuil, 2004.

Borzeix A., "Autonomie et contrôle à l'épreuve d'une rationalité externe", in G. de Terssac (ed.), *La théorie de la régulation sociale de J.D. Reynaud*, Paris, La Découverte, Coll. Recherches, 2003, pp. 197-206.

Bué J. and Rougerie C., "L'organisation du travail: entre contrainte et initiative. Résultats de l'enquête conditions de travail de 1998", *Première Synthèse*, No. 32-1, DARES, 1999.

Cavestro W., (1988), "Automatisation, organisation et contenu du travail", in F. Stankiewicz (ed.), *Les stratégies d'entreprises face aux ressources humaines. L'après-taylorisme*, Paris, Economica, 1998, pp. 57-64.

Campinos-Dubernet M., "Systèmes qualité et amélioration des processus: savoirs, organisations, marchés", *Études DARES*, Convention No. 2001R08, 2003, 207 p.

Campinos-Dubernet M., (2005), "Stratégie des entreprises: le rôle clé des compétences collectives", *La lettre du GIPMIS*, No. 24, Mars.

Chatzis K., Mounier C., Veltz P. and Zarifian P., (eds.), *L'autonomie dans les organisations. Quoi de neuf?* Paris, L'Harmattan, 1999.

Charlon E., "Transformation de la formation et transformation des savoirs", in J.M. Barbier, F. Berton and J.J. Born (eds.), *Situation de travail et formation*, Paris, L'Harmattan, 1996, pp. 147-164.

Caroly S. and Clot Y., "Du travail collectif au collectif de travail: développer des stratégies d'expérience", *Formation Emploi*, No. 88, 2004, pp. 43-54.

Courtois B., Mathey-Pierre C., Portelli P. and Wittorski R., "Transformations de la formation et recompositions identitaires en entreprise", in J.M. Barbier, F. Berton and J.J. Born (eds.), *Situation de travail et formation*, Paris, L'Harmattan, 1996, pp. 165-189.

Cousin O., "Travail et autonomie", in A. Karvar, L. Rouban (eds.), *Les cadres au travail*, Paris, La Découverte, 2004, pp. 23-38.

Delteil V. and Dieuaide P., "Mutations de l'activité et du marché du travail des cadres: l'emprise croissante des connaissances", *Revue de l'IRES*, No. 37, 3e trimestre, 2001b, pp. 57-88.

Dibiaggio L., "Apprentissage, coordination et organisation de l'industrie. Une perspective cognitive", *Revue d'Économie Industrielle*, No. 88, 2e trimestre, 1999, pp. 111-136.

Dietrich A., (2003), "La gestion des compétences: essai de modélisation", in A. Klarsfeld and E. Oiry (eds.), *Gérer les compétences*, Paris, AGRH-Vuibert, chap. 10.

Dieuaide P., "Mutations in the Function of Team Management, Knowledge and Conflict Management", *European Journal of Economic and Social System*, No. 18, 2005, pp. 99-110.

Dubet F., *Logique de l'expérience*, Paris, Seuil, 1994.

Durand J.P., *La chaîne invisible*, Paris, Seuil, 2004.

Everaere C., "L'autonomie dans le travail: portée et limites", *Revue Française de Gestion*, June-July-August, 2001, pp. 15-26.

Feutrie M. and Verdier E., "Entreprises et formations qualifiantes. Une construction sociale inachevée", *Sociologie du travail*, No. 4, 1993, pp. 469-492.

Hatchuel A., "Repenser la gestion. Un point de vue historique sur les firmes comme innovations institutionnelles", *La Lettre de la Régulation*, No. 47, 2004, January.

Marx K., *Œuvres*, Vol. 1, Paris, La Pléiade, 1968.

Naville P., *Vers l'automatisme social?* Paris, Nrf, 1963.

Nonaka I., "A Dynamic Theory of Organisational Knowledge Creation", *Organisation Science*, Vol. 5, No. 1, 1994, pp. 14-37.

Paraponaris C., "L'instrumentation de la gestion des compétences: une instrumentation à finalités multiples?", in A. Klarsfeld and E. Oiry (eds.), *Gérer les compétences*, Paris, AGRH-Vuibert, 2003, chapter 9.

Reix R., "Savoir tacite et savoir formalisé dans l'entreprise", *Revue Française de Gestion*, sept-oct, 1995, pp. 17-28.

Terssac G.de, *Autonomie dans le travail*, Paris, Puf, 1992.

Terssac G.de and Maggi B., "Autonomie et conception", in G. de Terssac, E. Friedberg (eds.), *Coopération et conception*, Toulouse, Octarès, 1996, pp. 243-266.

Valeyre A., "Activités cognitives et autonomie dans le travail", in K. Chatzis, C. Mounier, P. Veltz and P. Zarifian (eds.), *L'autonomie dans les organisations. Quoi de neuf?*, Paris, L'Harmattan, 1999, pp. 141-160.

Veltz P., "L'autonomie dans les organisations: de quoi parle-t-on?", in K. Chatzis, C. Mounier, P. Veltz and P. Zarifian (eds.), *L'autonomie dans les organisations. Quoi de neuf?*, Paris, L'Harmattan, 1999, pp. 13-24.

Zarifian P., "La confrontation aux évènements; entre sens et communication", *Sciences de la Société*, No. 50/51, May/October, 2000a, pp. 107-127.

Zarifian P., "Sur la question de la compétence", *Gérer et comprendre*, Annales des Mines, No. 62, 2000b, pp. 25-28.

Informational Worker Autonomy

Freedom or Control?

Cinara L. ROSENFIELD

Teacher at the Department of Sociology and in the Post-Graduate Programme in Sociology of the Federal University of Rio Grande do Sul

I. Introduction

A context characterized by job precariousness and flexibilisation associated with changes in the organisation of labour in capitalist societies implies new standards for workers. Work, in its usual form (which does not mean the inexistence of precarious, strenuous or backbreaking Taylorist work), has become more varied and more complex, while its content and nature have become richer, due to a greater demand for subjective investment and the mobilisation of intelligence. Work has become thrilling and, in many cases, immaterial. It is possible, therefore, to assume that this picture presents advantages for the workers, since work has become more interesting and flexible. The objective of this paper is to discuss the meaning of autonomy for this immaterial work (which presumes reflection, the articulation of knowledge and observation, and an exchange of information) connected with information and communication technologies (ICTs), especially telework. The reflections presented here stem from empirical research with wage-earning and/or autonomous teleworkers (including call-centre operators, wage-earning and self-employed workers of the computer science area, and home-based teleworkers) in Lisbon (Portugal) and Porto Alegre (Brazil), totalling 22 interviews carried out in 2004 and 2005.[1] This article discusses the concept and implications of the much-discussed work auton-

---

1 This research, titled "Autonomy and Telework", is included as a work in progress in our postdoctoral study, concluded in February 2005 at the Technical University of Lisbon. The present research was carried out with the support of CAPES, during a postdoctoral study in Portugal within the CAPES-GRICES agreement for international cooperation.

omy, based simultaneously on existing literature and our empirical observation.

In previous studies with production industry operators, we detected changes stressing the need for workers' subjective mobilisation in order to fulfil their responsibilities properly, which constitutes a case of conceded autonomy – autonomy is granted as a "concession" to the workers but, at the same time, it is an order to be obeyed. The old Taylorist or Fordist organisation of work was faced with a need for renewal so as to provide answers to another kind of need: in order to guarantee quality and uncommonly high competition, the work of the industrial labourer must incorporate an understanding of the task at hand, so that teamwork and the exchange of information and know-how are possible not only at the moment of conception, but also during the moment of execution. This would be the new face of capital domination: the worker must identify himself, must mobilize himself subjectively and use all of his psychological and relational capacities to do his job well. To these conclusions, we add the ones concerning work autonomy in jobs involving ICTs. Facing a new technological paradigm typical of the information age (also called, according to different theoretical approaches, new economy, cognitive capitalism, net society, informational society), we are going to analyze the new ways of working and the margins of work autonomy that accompany them. If autonomy in industrial work is a conceded autonomy, when we consider its instrumental meaning (i.e. as a tool for the coordination of labour relations aimed at an economic objective in production management by trying to insert elements that are not prescribed into the work process, such as teamwork and subjective mobilisation), we must measure it against ICTs' work autonomy. *A priori*, these technologies would demand better qualification and ability in tasks of an "intelligent" and immaterial nature, which would indicate a less pronounced division of labour between those who conceive and those who execute the job, as well as a greater margin of work autonomy.

II. Informational Work

The worldwide changes of the economy and of work in the field of ICTs over the last the two decades of the 20th century require different approaches. These approaches are found within more general debates on globalisation and productive reorganisation and differ regarding the way they conceive the nature of these changes, their impact and probable consequences.

A first approach, based on the concept of "net society", revolves around the thesis of Manuel Castells (1999), according to which an analytical differentiation is necessary between the information society –

a new societal type – and globalisation – a new capitalist revolution that creates new polarities, inequalities and forms of exclusion on a global level. A new paradigm of information technology forms the material basis of the information society, which remains a capitalist society in spite of these societies' cultural and institutional diversity.

There exists an infinite number of technical innovations surrounding the information technologies which advances with the creation of an interface between the various fields of technology through a digital language, in which information is produced, accumulated, processed and transmitted. The concept of a technological paradigm formulated by Castells helps understand the essence of the current technological transformation as it interacts with society and the economy. The central aspects of this paradigm, as a whole, form the information society's material basis: 1) information is the new paradigm's raw material; 2) as information is a basic part of human activity, the new technological means directly mould the spheres of individual and collective existence; 3) the networks' logic involves any and all types of relations using the new information technologies; 4) the technological paradigm of information is based on flexibility; 5) specific technologies tend to converge towards a highly integrated system.

The current technological revolution originated and flourished – not by chance – during a historical period of a global reorganisation of capitalism, for which it was a basic tool. Therefore, the new emergent society is both capitalist and informational, even if it presents a considerable historical variation in different countries, according to their history, culture, institutions and specific relations with global capitalism and informational technology. For Castells, even considering the reorganisation of capitalism and the diffusion of informational global processes, it would be somehow improper to talk about a single Informational Society, for each country, each region was and still is attached to this process in a different way. However, one could speak of an Informational Society as one once did of Industrial Societies, to invoke the common characteristics of socio-technical systems. This said, it is necessary to take into consideration two exceptions: "[…] on the one hand, informational societies, as they currently exist, are capitalist (different from industrial societies, some of which were State-controlled); on the other hand, we must emphasize the cultural and institutional diversity of informational societies" (p. 38). Thus, one does not risk homogenizing the peculiarities of each nation, but neither does one lose sight of the greater process they are all submitted to – the fact that in the future, more and more, all countries will be informational societies.

The second approach is one of authors grouped around the thesis of cognitive capitalism (Azaïs *et al.*, 2001). For them, the changes that have occurred transformed the nature of capitalism, which in the past was based on industrial production and which today lies in the production of knowledge and information.

The authors grouped around the thesis of cognitive capitalism affirm that, mainly as a result of the growth and integration of new information and communication technologies, a new stage in the history of the capitalist economy has been inaugurated: cognitive capitalism as opposed to industrial capitalism. In this "new capitalism", the origin of value would no longer reside in the production of homogeneous and reproducible goods, characteristic of the Fordist model of production; rather, in the post-Fordist model it is innovation (the production of the "new") that becomes the main factor of valuation. It is not a question of technological determinism, but rather one of noticing that the new is to be found less in technical objects themselves than in the motives, the logics of accumulation and social valuation, in the sense that the whole of society is moving in the direction of innovation and the accumulation of knowledge.

The changes in course do not provoke the incorporation of new technologies in industrial activities, but rather a transformation in the forms of production, accumulation and social organisation opened up by the ICTs. Thus, what appears is a new pattern of capitalist accumulation based on immaterial work, knowledge and innovation processes. In this sense, the authors of cognitive capitalism stress, among others, the changes in the nature of labour, the transformations in the relations between production and consumption, and the implications of the fact that knowledge has become a resource and a product of itself. When the issue is the production of knowledge by knowledge, as in the case of cognitive capitalism, cooperation can no longer occur in Fordist-Taylorist terms, i.e. through passive, static cooperation, guaranteed by the sequential chaining and the addition of functions and elementary tasks. Cooperation for the production of knowledge is tantamount to the creative activity marked by horizontal, non-programmed communication, and by collective, cooperative and reticular work that goes beyond hierarchical control.

In this sense, the shift to cognitive capitalism represents not the centrality of knowledge as a productive force, but knowledge as a resource and an immaterial product simultaneously, which translates the shift from a regimen of reproduction to a regimen of innovation. What makes knowledge a merchandise different from others? First of all, knowledge as a type of merchandise is not subject to the law of decreasing income, that is, knowledge is not a scarce commodity. Second, using knowledge does not imply exhausting it; therefore its "consumption" is not destructive. Third, to exchange knowledge does not imply losing it; the exchange is a metaphor. The fourth specificity of the merchandise "knowledge" is that it does not possess a utility-value; this is defined within the knowledge production and diffusion process. Fifth, knowledge acquires value when exchanged and socialized at the same time. Lastly, the cost of knowledge is submitted to the uncertainty of the innovation process and its social validation. Therefore, these specificities give the valuation of knowledge different laws from those of Marxist and Neoclassic theories of value; consequently, cognitive capitalism functions differently from simple capitalism. This is the basic thesis of cognitive capitalism, as opposed to Castells' thesis according to which informational society is a capitalist society *tout court*. As we will see later, our approach is supported by Castells'.

III. Telework and Autonomy in Informational Labour

If autonomy and the collective nature of work become intrinsic to the new organisation of post-Fordist industrial labour, the new command is "be subjects" and work in cooperation. The autonomy demanded of the worker implies performing activities, from executing the task to understanding what is being done. The autonomy concept seems equally useful for the analysis of the post-industrial or informational society. The work connected to ICTs is considered autonomous and intelligent in nature. In order to reflect on this question, we shall first discuss the autonomy concept and subsequently present the notion and implications of telework, our chosen empirical object emblematic of informational work; finally, we shall analyze autonomy in informational work.

A. Autonomy

Individual autonomy, in its philosophical sense, can be understood as self-governance, self-determination, the ability to construct one's own objectives and values, the freedom to make choices and plans and to act according to these values and objectives. This leads to self-realisation, the condition to construct a complete and meaningful life. Individual autonomy is a condition for conceiving the human being in a situation of equity, of equality. Without individual autonomy man cannot function as an equal in moral life.

Autonomy is associated with the notion of freedom as self-determination, as possibility of choice or absence of interference. But freedom sends forth an "idea of responsibility towards oneself and the community: to be free means in this case to be available (I clarify: to do something by oneself, to self-determine oneself), but to be available to fulfil certain duties. Since the beginning, therefore, the notion of freedom seems to indicate two directions: one, that of an empowerment to do; the other, that of a limitation" (Ferrater Mora, 2001: 1734).

Therefore, it would be necessary to distinguish at least two kinds of freedom: social and personal freedom. Social freedom is easily confused with autonomy and independence. In a given human community, autonomy means to be master of one's own destiny without the interference of other communities. On the other hand, inside a community, this autonomy consists, above all, not in avoiding the law, but in living in accordance with the collective laws. Personal freedom, in turn, is also conceived as autonomy and independence in relation to constraints imposed by the community, society or the State. In this case, if one admits that there is in the individual a reality that is not only social but also personal, the citizen can in some way and for some time "leave", withdraw in relation to the constraints, to dedicate himself to leisure and self-development for example (Ferrater Mora, 2001).

However, autonomy does not mean absolute freedom, for upon placing autonomy in the field of values (where it takes on its full meaning, since the search for autonomy is placed inside a logic of values and a quest for meaning), it becomes clear that autonomy is embedded within a "community of values", which makes it, always and in some measure, heteronomous.

If autonomy could be defined as freedom – either social or individual – and self-determination, it would be opposed to constraints or coercion and control, respectively. Thus, the inverse of freedom would be coercion and the inverse of self-determination would be the control exerted by others. This game of oppositions highlights the complexity of talking about work autonomy.

Work autonomy clashes with the philosophical concept of autonomy, for it signifies the control that workers have over their own work situation (and not the control exerted by others) and the realisation of the meaning of this control for the individual. Therefore, work autonomy includes an operational dimension and an identitary dimension.

In concrete terms, work autonomy means: a worker's self-determination, responsibility or freedom to determine many elements of the task, the work method, the stages, procedures, programming, criteria, objectives, place, evaluation, hours, type and amount of work. Autonomy refers to control over these, or some of these, elements.

In theoretical terms, work autonomy is a chimera because it goes against heteronomy and necessity, and the autonomy of an activity marked by necessity is condemned to remain formal. A. Gorz (1988) defines as autonomous those activities which are, of themselves, their own end. Through these actions, the subject demonstrates his sovereignty and fulfils himself as a person. Conceded autonomy imposes a socialisation characterized by a non-coincidence between the individual-subject and his social being; but this coincidence, impossible from now on, is at the origin of individual autonomy and all cultural creation. The individual is condemned to live the duality of being himself (*l'être-soi*) – because he needs to be himself – and, simultaneously, of meeting the work's social requirements demanding "a way of being himself" in the workplace (*le devoir être*). In fact, this duality ends up by keeping him from being himself (*l'être-soi*).

However, in concrete terms, autonomy at work may signify greater responsibility, control and power to determine and decide when certain work elements should be involved.

In this sense, to carry out "independent" or "autonomous" (non-salaried) work means to work without a boss, without being under someone else's control. But how about market control, productivity, quality and customer requirements? To have autonomy in salaried work means either a conceded autonomy – and it is, therefore, a paradoxical injunction – or finding some degree of self-determination and creation in the gap existing between the prescribed work and the real work – which may mean committing an offence. And even this gap tends to disappear in the face of the need for teamwork. "As a result, the part of prescribed work tends to shrink, for the simple reason that giving detailed instructions is no longer possible as, often, though technically feasible, it becomes expensive, not very efficient and, therefore, unprofitable. Autonomy, as paradoxical as it may seem, is therefore imposed, allocated by the organisation or the job, the end mattering more than the means" (Azaïs, 2004: 22).

Informational work, with its immaterial character, would *a priori* contain a greater margin of autonomy since, involving the mobilisation of know-how and the articulation of knowledge, it reduces the possibilities of external control as well as encouraging a greater personal investment and freedom in the execution of the necessary processes for the construction of an immaterial product. Telework and the flexibility that accompanies it seem to be privileged objects in the analysis of autonomy in informational work.

B. Telework

The EcaTT report (Electronic Commerce and Telework Trends: Benchmarking Progress on New Ways of Working and New Forms of Business across Europe) on ten European Union countries, carried out by the German organisation EMPIRICA, defines teleworkers in the following way: "teleworkers are those workers who work in a computerized manner (with a computer), far from their employer's business or from the person who contracts them, and transmit the results of their activity through a telecommunication link".[2] However, telework is a hard category to define. Too many variables (and combinations of variables) open too wide the set of possible definitions. Lacking a precise conceptualisation, teleworking becomes more of an ideological construct of reality or, at most, an attempt to describe the various kinds or modes of telework. It is possible to guarantee that all the different conceptualisations are right, which demonstrates very contradictory ideas. Thus, there are people working at home with their employer's permission so as to avoid commuting, people working at home independently or in telecentres, women working at their own computers because they cannot leave their children; there are some in this situation who find themselves exploited, badly paid and without recognition; there are teleworkers in public and private institutions; there are people working at home who "accidentally" use their computers (it is not the main tool) like architects or translators, while many people who normally work out of the house finish their work at home as overtime. To conclude, with the aid a fax machine, a cellular 'phone, a laptop and the Internet, it is possible to work from almost anywhere. But what interests us here is not its precise definition – which, by the way, is not possible – but the dynamics of its interactions (Huws, 1991).

In a restrictive sense, telework can be defined as distance work using ICTs. In an extensive sense, used by the International Labour Organisation (ILO),[3] telework must be defined according to different variables:

a) place/space of work;

b) schedule/time of work (full time or part time);

c) type of contract (salaried or independent work);

d) required abilities (content of work).

For our part, we shall not take the quantitative element into account; in other words, we shall not consider that the classification of telework depends on the number of hours in a given condition, e.g. those who work at home at least one full day per week.

Combining all these variables, telework can assume a great number of modes or forms, at least theoretically, fully justifying the qualification of "flexible". To uphold the concept, we can identify six categories of telework: 1) home-based work, SOHO (Small Office Home Office), 2) in satellite offices (atomized extensions of a central company, 3) telecenters or telecottages (establishments offering either a workplace to employees of one or more organisations, or telematic services to remote customers; normally regional or near home), 4) mobile work

---

2 See http://www.ecatt.com and http://www.sibis-eu.org.

3 http://www.ilo.org

(outside the home or the main work centre, like business trips, field work or in customer installations), 5) remote or off-shore companies (call-centers or teleservices, through which European and American companies install their satellite offices or subcontract teleservice companies from other zones of the globe with cheaper labour, putting the so-called off-shore telework into practice), 6) informal or mixed telework (arrangement with the employer to work some hours outside the company).[4]

This said, many combinations within these classifications still seem viable: telework can be occasional and not call for a contract change (informal); it can be a kind of alternate work (alternating being at home and in the company); it can be a form of overflow (being connected 24/24hs to professional concerns and interacting with different kinds of requests like e-mails, cell-phone calls, fax, etc.), and there are still other possible combinations, including that of informal with salaried telework (working in the company during the day and doing independent telework outside the company's salaried working hours). In short, if we combine all these possibilities (in terms of place, schedule and socio-professional situation), we can easily see the great quantity of modes or forms that telework can assume, at least theoretically. This fully justifies the qualification of "flexible", generally applied to telework.

Thus, telework cannot simply be defined as distance work, but rather as an element of the strategic organisational changes that point to new forms of flexible work supported by ICTs. Flexibility can be indicated by several elements: time, place, contract, subordination, functional organisation. There is a close relation between the emergence of telework and the notorious flexibility that the organisation needs and demands so as to guarantee competitiveness. For the employer, flexibility means flexible schedules, polyvalence, and an increase or reduction of the number of employees according to demand. It also means several contractual forms: subcontracting, half time, determined time, or home-based work. Telework is one of these options.

In the end, therefore, telework combines with atypical, flexible work, which can be precarious or not. The eventual autonomy is generally associated with working time and schedule flexibility. The teleworker has the autonomy to manage his time, but, paradoxically, he does not have control over his working time, because this is determined by the rules of work volume, i.e. it is always necessary to meet work demands, with no restrictions as to time or availability.

---

4 Definitions proposed by EcaTT (Electronic Commerce and Telework Trends: Benchmarking Progress on New Ways of Working and New Forms of Business across Europe) and Paulo Serra (1995/96), adapted by us.

The practice of telework develops other forms of external control over work, such as the electronic monitoring of results (requirements and achieved goals monitored through the delivery of periodic reports), pre-structured tasks (application of parameters and pre-established actions) and, in some cases, dependent creation (teamwork, final decisions made by the hierarchy).

Telework apologists emphasize the idea that this form of work promotes the integration of disfavoured people and regions, and people with reduced mobility. It also cuts down pollution through reducing commuting, and encourages the projection of new professional perspectives and other fields of work. They also argue in favour of a more impartial distribution of knowledge sources, besides the possibility of combining private life and work through the flexibility telework offers regarding the time and place of work.

However, the practice of telework reveals some difficulties: a substitution of personal and direct human relations with long-distance relations mediated by information and communication technologies (people substituted by their textual, sonorous or visual "image" in the machine), isolation and, in the case of salaried work, work assessment difficulties and the consequent perspectives of career promotion, difficulties in dealing with the lack of clear limits between private and public time and space (which also constitutes and precisely one of the main virtualities of telework), e.g. working at home on Sundays, work invading home privacy, restrictions regarding the use of space and resources by other family members, the common use of the telephone for work and family.

C. Autonomy in Informational Work

The concept of work autonomy raises two issues: 1) its functional, operational requirements, which refer to work organisation; 2) the quest for self-affirmation, freedom, accomplishment, that refers to its dimension of identity. The first question seems relatively well provided for in the case of telework, since its inherent flexibility addresses the demand for greater productivity and smaller costs (telework mobility concerns the flexibility required by organisational methods, so as to react quickly) and, on the worker's side, signifies greater autonomy i.e. a large variety of time, work and place arrangements. When working by projects or objectives, the contractor stipulates deadlines or performances that need to be met and not tasks. This is the combination that telework addresses: stronger pressure for flexibility in the use of the worker's abilities on the one hand, and personal arrangements in the worker's time and working place on the other. "This commitment or contract normally presumes a certain autonomy in the individual organisation of mobility and time of work" (Valenduc and Vendramin, 2001: 251).

From this point on, to question telework autonomy in its operational and identity dimensions proves to be much more complex and hard to answer. Several elements contribute in this direction: 1) the "pure" teleworker (who only teleworks) is a rare phenomenon as many combinations exist: traditionally salaried telework (which includes stability combined with flexibility), or precariousness in a pure state (such as the worker who teleworks because of being unemployed and needing to create alternative forms of income), or high qualifications and independent and unstable telework; 2) even in the case of "the pure" teleworker, if he is independent, he needs to ensure work and sustenance and subjects himself to many things, including working at any time of the day or night so as to meet demands, with no possibility of satisfactorily reconciling work with private life; 3) the various forms of electronic monitoring of the work may restrict the forms of autonomy and self-determination; 4) many tasks connected with ICTs are pre-structured, and that means monotonous, repetitive work with no creativity or initiative, along the moulds of "informational Taylorism".

In this sense, the study of informational work autonomy indicates a strong similarity with post-Fordism inner discussions. The information society does not solely create highly-qualified jobs: although keeping a relational and immaterial essence, this work can also be repetitive, unimaginative and automatized. In activities connected with great explicit control ICTs – such as call centres – there is a simultaneous control of efficiency and attitudes but in real time. The margin of autonomy diminishes and direct control increases. Equally, when work requires higher qualification, the margin of autonomy is generally greater. More qualified and more independent work means indirect control preceding the work itself.

If it is possible to observe a continued increase of qualifications required for work, one should not confuse this with a reduction in the division of labour between those who conceive and those who execute, even in services or intellectual activities. More qualification and ability are not necessarily accompanied by more strategic responsibilisation and work autonomy, even when this appears to be the tendency. Still, if with ICTs there is a diversification of tasks, or an enrichment and versatility, the delegating of responsibilities thus propagated by the "new organizers" only occurs within the procedures and settings unilaterally established by the managers – which corroborates our thesis of conceded autonomy. If in industrial work one encounters a situation of conceded autonomy and appropriation of this autonomy so as to insert the worker's margin of inventiveness in the formal rules, our argument is that ICT work seems to reproduce the industrial model: more qualification equals more autonomy, less qualification means less autonomy.

Continuing the parallel with post-Fordist industrial work, as the individual is submitted to the process of being mobilized for executing the work, one can presume *a priori* that the workers "profit" from the enrichment in content and nature of their work. This gain may be seen through the liberalisation of the work situation that comes to substitute the old, more rigid and authoritarian organisations. However, these transformations are entirely embedded within the register of economic rationality, in spite of the dominant discourse which evokes objectives of a social and/or subjective order. Conceded autonomy evokes the margin of freedom and creation the worker is dispossessed of. The situation is paradoxical: there is a permanent process of searching for real autonomy on the part of the workers, who see themselves, finally, dispossessed by the concession of a pre-defined autonomy. However, its paradoxical dimension goes still further: if conceded autonomy is pseudo-freedom, it is also a symbolic enrichment of work through the increase of real autonomy, creativity and initiative.

The information society transposes this paradox only partially. Based on Castells, our argument is that, whereas in Taylorism the separation was between those who think and those who execute, in the information society one sees the distance separating those who use information to reach objectives defined by themselves (and who therefore have autonomy) from those who suffer the "effects" of the job market and the avalanche of information – and who are reduced to economic and cultural dependence. Apparently the concept of work autonomy can condense both this ambiguity and this paradox, with the same richness that helped understand the reality of the post-Fordist industrial society.

The reality of telework is complex and ambiguous because there are indications of a lasting division between "intelligent" jobs and controlled and repetitive jobs, with their consequent reduction of work autonomy. Moreover, the forms and the contents of work are the most varied: they go from the call-center attendant to the home-based worker, from mobile telework to work in remote companies or offshore firms (such as the call-centre of a French mother company operated by workers in Tunisia). It can, still, combine different work relations: it can be occasional, it can be informal; it can be a form of alternate work (alternating home-based work with ICTs and work in the company); while other possible combinations may also exist, including informal work combined with salaried work.

IV. Final Considerations

Informational work presents such a diversity that any form of universal conclusion becomes impossible. There is, indeed, greater autonomy in the more qualified jobs, as in any work that mobilizes competences, skills and talents more intensely. Repetitive and monotonous work is not an attribute of productive industrial work. If conceded autonomy concerns new forms of control, the electronic monitoring that the ICTs give rise to increases both vigilance and control. Moreover, immaterial work is not synonymous with creative work, as ICTs facilitate the use of pre-structured tasks that only need to be "filled in".

The limitations of individual autonomy in any situation of subordinated work are obvious. In a job situation where the salaried worker offered himself "for rent" (not to say "sold his work force") to an employer in order to execute tasks and reach pre-established objectives, autonomy resides more in the meaning of work than in the determination of one's own objectives (such as method), procedures and/or work programming. One can still add to that a combination of organisational and personal objectives, such as telework, vocational training, flexibility of time and resources to reach the objectives determined by the organisation. Even independent informational work, out of one's own initiative, *a priori* without subordination, ends up subordinated to survival necessities and market impositions. Take the example of an unsalaried, self-employed and highly qualified editor/translator living in a rural zone of Portugal, who always had to respond promptly to translation requests made via the internet from the USA (so as not to lose them to other translators) and was obliged, because of the time difference, to be available practically twenty-four hours a day. One cannot be more independent and less independent, all at the same time.

The central question, however, cannot be diluted in these paradoxes: the quest for autonomy is placed outside economic logic and inside a logic of values and a conquest of meaning, while conceded autonomy (or the autonomy subordinated to survival and market logic) is inscribed in an instrumental logic. Purely operational autonomy, subordinated to instrumental logic, does not imply identity autonomy, in the sense of the realisation of meaning and in the realm of values. Immaterial work (and more specifically telework), producer and consumer of knowledge and information, comes through as flexible work more than as independent work, since the actual autonomy primarily concerns a greater control over time and the working place, but remains subordinated to the demands of flexibility of either the market or economic organisations that pay a salary to, or consume, the informational work. The world of values remains far removed from the world of work.

References

Arendt, H., *A condição humana*. Rio de Janeiro, Forense Universitária, 1991.

Azaïs, Ch., "De-Segmentação do mercado de trabalho e autonomia", in *Caderno de Recursos Humanos*, v.17, No. 41, Salvador, May/Aug, 2004, p. 15-24.

Azaïs, Ch., Corsani, A. and Dieuaide, P., *Vers un capitalisme cognitif; entre mutations du travail et territoires*. Paris, L'Harmattan, 2001.

Brey, Ph., "Worker autonomy and the drama of digital networks in organisations", in *Journal of Business Ethics*, 22, The Netherlands, Kluwer Academic Publishers, 1999, p. 15-25.

Castel, R. and Haroche, C., *Propriété privée, propriété sociale, propriété de soi: entretiens sur la construction de l'individu moderne*. Paris, Fayard, 2001.

Castel, R., *Les métamorphoses de la question sociale*. Paris, Fayard, 1995.

Castells, M., *A sociedade em Rede*. São Paulo, Paz e Terra, 1999.

Dejours, Ch., "Coopération et construction de l'identité en situation de travail", in *Futur Antérieur*, No. 16. Paris, L'Harmattan, 1993/2, p. 41-52.

Durand, J.-P., *La chaîne invisible*. Paris, Seuil, 2004.

Ferrater Mora, J., *Dicionário de Filosofia*. São Paulo, Loyola, 2001.

Friedmann, G., *O trabalho em migalhas*. São Paulo, Perspectiva, 1972.

Gorz, A., *Métamorphoses du travail et quête de sens*. Paris, Galilée, 1988.

Huws, U., "Telework: projections", in *Futures*, Vol. 23, No. 1, Jan./Feb. 1991, p. 19-31.

Kovács, I., *As metamorfoses do emprego; ilusões e problemas da sociedade da informação*. Lisboa, Celta, 2002.

Lazzarato, M., "Le concept de travail immatériel: la grande entreprise", in *Futur Antérieur*, No. 10, Paris, L'Harmattan, 1992/2, p. 54-61.

Martin, D., *Démocratie industrielle*. Paris, PUF, 1994.

Subordination or Autonomy?

The Hybridisation of the Labour Market
The Italian Case

Christian AZAÏS

Senior Lecturer at the Université de Picardie Jules Verne – Amiens, Researcher at IRISSO/Paris Dauphine

Introduction

In the past, the distinction between subordination and autonomy at work was not difficult to make: subordination corresponded to the situation of salaried workers, subjected to an employer from whom they received a salary, a situation in total opposition with that of autonomous labourers. Today, the labour market's flexibilisation means that this situation is not as clearly defined. In many cases, the apparently dependent workers have more autonomy than the autonomous one themselves.

The question of the labour market's flexibility is not new in itself. Already, in the 1980s, French researchers had taken a keen interest in the subject and the works of Boyer (1987), Maruani *et al.* (1989) and Guitton *et al.* (1991) marked this period. In a famous article, Leborgne and Lipietz affirmed that there are two kinds of flexibility in the labour market: a "defensive flexibility" and an "offensive flexibility". The first favours a deregulation of the employment relation and accentuates the division between "creators" and "executors"; it concerns the poorest forms of subcontracting (Leborgne, Lipietz, 1992: 373) and transforms cost-competitiveness into the axis of its direction. In everyday language, this last meaning is predominating when labour flexibility is mentioned; meanwhile firms' flexibility is considered with a milder approach.

The first part of this paper highlights the meaning of subordination and autonomy and stresses the hybridisation that characterizes the labour market, a phenomenon encountered almost universally.

The second part, based on an example of "co.co.co." (*collaborazione coordinata e continuativa*) of the labour market's flexibilisation discusses an insistent – though not so common – tendency in Italy of a dilution of the frontiers between subordination and autonomy. The concept of *parasubordination* corresponds to the existence of a grey zone between subordination and autonomy, characteristic of labour market hybridisation. Regarding the form of employment insertion, the "co.co.co." has consequences in terms of labour rights as, in fact, workers are not totally dependent nor totally autonomous but rather know a combination of both at once. The relative novelty of this situation is that it affects wide sectors of the economy as well as a large variety of professions, independently of sex or age, and, as we will see, in large proportions.

This tendency outlines certain developments of a labour market predestined to flexibilisation, both in developed and developing countries, but subjected to contradictory tendencies. Whereas the phenomena are the same, their interpretation differs according to the context. This fact should mean that the richness of international comparisons surfaces, including those of cases that are apparently extremely contrasting ones.[1] Consequently, this paper attempts to put forth certain basic elements for future comparisons between North and South.

Subordination and Autonomy: Definition

Subordination is based on three normative principles: 1) the exchange of labour and wages; 2) the workers' dependence; 3) the relationship between one specific entrepreneur and one specific work site (Ghera, 2003: 58). To these, one must add the presence of a Welfare State that guarantees the workers' rights arising from their situation as employees, defined by an employment contract. In this context, the employment relation ends up occupying a prominent position: it is the analytical category used to evaluate the workers' degree of subordination, based on the way the labour force is mobilized in the work process, *via* institutional arrangements and a complex legal framework.

In the Marxist approach, labour-power is seen as a particular kind of commodity (Lautier, Tortajada, 1978). Basically, it is consumed before it has been paid for; the workers are subjected to the authority of the capitalist, who hires the labour-power and subordinates his/her possessor. The accompanying rights and obligations are clearly defined by law in an employment contract, each party knowing what it is entitled to. For their part, trade unions exercise a role of control, while professional associations act as a pressure group.

Contrary to independent work, which is ruled by civil and by commercial law, employment law governs salaried work. Instances to

1 A comparative study of two municipalities in France and Brazil, Saint-Denis and Santo André, analyzes the question of insertion from an economic and political viewpoint (Azaïs, 2006).

protect the worker, considered (both legally and socially) as the contract's weak party, regulate this matter, which in a certain way ends up by damaging the specific characteristic of any contract – that is to say the equality of the parties. Hence, legislation modulates the areas of autonomy and tends to protect the worker, so that she/he is in a subordinate position to the entrepreneur (Perulli, 2003: 6; Petit and Thévenot, 2006).

In the Italian Civil Code, subordination is defined by heterodirection:[2] the offer of labour is considered as being under the entrepreneur's direction and depends on him. This means that the offer of labour is made within the enclosed space of a firm, an organisation with a hierarchy, to which the worker submits him/herself.

The subordinate worker depends permanently on the entrepreneur. The dependency or availability of the subcontracted worker *vis-à-vis* the subcontractor is an element that could be considered as resembling disguised subordinate employment, inasmuch as it is totally subjugated to the contractor's orders. Should labour be autonomous, such a situation would not arise. Subordinate employment is defined by the relation subordination-obligation between, on the one hand, a hierarchised firm and, on the other, the protected status of the worker.

The activity of the dependent worker takes place in the context of an organisation, the latter being understood as the place where various productive factors are selected, brought together and used in a coordinated and hierarchised manner. The organisation constitutes an essential legal element in order to differentiate the activity of the firm from that of independent labour. Consequently, today, the organisation criterion cannot stand up to the economy's increasing dematerialisation, teleworking being its most recent form. Furthermore, the outsourcing and tertiarisation of a number of firms' activities further strengthen the difficulty in apprehending what pertains to subordinate employment and not to the independent one.

Should it be true, as suggested by Ghera, that labour law came into existence so as to establish and regulate the labour market and focuses on the workers' supervision, the transformations in the organisations, which result from the gradual expansion of taylorism and fordism in industrial plants, call for a redefinition of conceptual categories such as "subordination" and "work contract" (Ghera, 2003: 47). Indeed, from the moment that workers are increasingly solicited ("body and soul") in the act of producing, the repercussions on the allocation of work time and leisure time are considerable, meaning that the new dividing line

---

2 It is a case of how the salaried worker (the "weak contracting party") is subjected to the employer's power of direction.

becomes "remunerated life"/"non remunerated life" (Bologna and Fumagalli, 1997). Such alterations cause changes in the manner in which the relations of hierarchy and dependency are perceived, when they are not simply found to be out of step with capitalism's development (networking organisations, tertiarisation, etc.), leading to the research instigated by Hall and Solskice, in a first moment, then, Boyer, regarding the existence of various capitalisms (Hall and Solskice, 2001; Boyer, 2004).

Dependent Work and Independent Work: What Differentiates Them?

In order to define the concepts of employment relation and independent labour, European States have adopted two techniques: a) a legislative technique, where the law defines the two general and unitary concepts of salaried work and independent labour; b) a jurisprudential technique, which specifies a series of indicators to determine which category labour comes under, whether salaried or independent.

In its Green Paper, the Commission of the European Communities characterizes the concept of '*economically dependent work*' as the one which

> covers situations which fall between the two established concepts of subordinate employment and independent self-employment. These workers do not have a contract of employment. They may not be covered by labour law since they occupy a 'grey area' between labour law and commercial law. Although formally 'self-employed', they remain economically dependent on a single principal or client/employer for their source of income (Commission of the European Communities, 2006: 11).

The details of the route chosen by each country are not presented here, Perulli does (2003); instead the paper focuses briefly on the Italian and French cases, the latter to a smaller degree.

Dependent Labour, the Subordination in Question

In the case of Italy, judges have introduced a long series of indicators to define heterodirection (and, consequently, salaried work), the most notable being:

the integration into the entrepreneur's organisation,

the absence of economic risk tied to the results of the activity of production,

the methods of payment of the remuneration,

the respect of fixed working hours,

the property of work tools – which must not belong to the employee (Perulli, 2003: 14-15).

In the case of France, the concept of subordination results from a jurisprudential construction. Indeed, the French Civil Code contains no general concept whatsoever of subordination. The work contract is defined as a sub-category of "hiring of work and industry" (*louage d'ouvrage et d'industrie*): "hiring of labour of people who are employed in somebody's service" (Civil Code, art. 1779, 1). In accordance with the French Law of 31.12.1992 (Employment Code, art. L 120-2), which refers to the disciplinary power of the employer, the "salaried worker's subordination must be limited to the strictly necessary". This criterion is also used by jurisprudence to determine whether a person can be affiliated to the employees' general regime of social welfare. Employment law considers that subordination exists when the work is carried out for the benefit of a third party, in the context of an organized structure (Verdier, 1996: 208-209). It comes under the judge to determine the contract's real qualification, which is of a public nature. The judge has also to decide if the subordination is of an economic or of a legal type. It is stipulated that there exists a case of legal subordination, apparent in the nature of the work contract, when the worker is subjected to a managing director and the effective control of his activity. Thus, the workers' place and the hours of work are determined (banning of all and any demands that work or work-related tools be taken home), and their behaviour is controlled, in the same way that they are expected to respect certain rules regarding their attire (though without losing their right of expression). For this to be the case, the worker needs to be integrated in the structure of a firm or of an organised department of an institution (Verdier, 1996: 209).

According to the International Labour Organisation, "the regulation of the worker's protection always differentiates the dependent from the independent workers, the latter being less protected" (ILO, 2000). This institution considers subordination as a situation where there exists "an employment relation, which depends from the simultaneous existence of objective conditions, i.e. the form in which the workers and the employer have marked their respective positions, their rights and obligations, as well as the services actually rendered". Further, the characterisation of dependent or independent does not depend in the least on the interpretation each of the parties attributes to the relation, allowing the "primacy of facts" principle to hold sway. It is for the judge to impose its being respected.

Independent Labour, the Autonomy in Question

Italian employment law usually defines independent work through a negative approach: "labour services executed outside the relation of subordination with the contractor" (art. 2222 of the Italian Civil Code, *Contrato d'opera*).

Independent labour is treated through a contract governed by civil law and, in many cases, by commercial law. In this case, the independent worker is considered as being at the same level of equality as the contractor. In other words, before the law, the independent worker has entered a contract and is treated in the same way as any other individual who has signed a contract. She/he is subjected to the laws of the market.

Labour sociology sees independent labour as being autonomous labour, which does not mean that its status is less ambiguous, especially when it is part of a public policy of labour insertion of individuals in difficulty or when, to a certain measure, it translates the French originality of "assisted contracts" (*contrats aidés*).

Etymologically, *auto-nomy* means "to give oneself one's own (*auto*) law (*nomos*)", and not "to do anything one fancies", nor yet to authorize someone to do whatever they might like. In work situations, the autonomy of workers is required, which in this case is not dissimilar to the idea of responsibility. It is a social issue, therefore part of a context (which is not solely restricted to work situations).

Autonomy is not a recent discovery of flexible production. Until the taylorist or fordist organisation of production, capitalism needed the autonomous worker. "The battle of man against reification was necessary to capitalism", affirmed Castoriadis (1975: 149); it serves as a channel for individuals to express their creativity, which is needed for both the firm's and the system's good working order. Autonomy focuses the mobility individuals need to have in order to organize their own future. It also refers to the tendency towards individualisation encountered in work situations. "A factory where the workers are purely that, simple executors of the management's orders, would come to a grinding halt in fifteen minutes" (*id., ibid.*). Consequently, it is for the individuals to give a meaning to their actions; until heteronomy, the workers are in part the "masters" of the goals of their own work. The subject does not disappear totally. Autonomy is an interiorised obligation; it corresponds to the assertion "to give oneself one's own laws, while being conscious of what one is doing".

According to the *European Foundation for the Improvement of Living Working Conditions* (1996), autonomy refers to "the possibility, for the worker, to control her/his method of work and the order in which the work needs to be executed". This highlights the capacity of defining one's own professional identity and creating one's own performance. Furthermore, it stresses the fact that, because of the incomplete nature of the work rules and norms, the workers must interpret and complete them. It seems that autonomy is more of a consequence resulting from the transformations in labour organisation than the result of individual decisions. The individual becomes the sole person responsible for her/his own destiny and sociability. In a certain manner, autonomy is imposed on workers. Countless work situations of contemporary capitalism illustrate this assertion. For example, in the "Total Quality" programmes, the very act of obliging individuals to write down the details of all operations executed – even those that do not require a great degree of specialisation – is a double-edged knife: at the same time as being considered responsible and acknowledged for the task being executed, the "operator" can be substituted by any other, who will be forced to follow precisely all the steps indicated by her/his predecessor.

The apparent attenuation of hierarchy in firms, or teamwork, calls for individual creativity in resolving technical or organisational problems which are part of this movement. The worker is required to be the seller of her/his talents and abilities. Thus, a gradual sliding from employment law to commercial law takes place. This phenomenon would cause a transformation of abilities, prioritising the task of manipulating symbols to the detriment of the transformation of matter (Boyer, 2001: 4).[3]

In industrial relations, according to Veltz, "efficiency does not depend on labour intensity, which is programmed for the worker, but rather on what occurs among the individuals and work groups, which is beyond any programming" (Veltz, 2008: 17).[4] In a certain manner, efficiency moves from the individual to the group. Yet at the same time, the individual turns to her/his original ability and her/his manner of including these abilities in the group's functioning (Veltz, 2008). Consequently, the worker enjoys a certain degree of liberty. When treating organisational and institutional arrangements and the construction of norms, economic literature highlights the fact that written rules are insufficient without the tacit codes of conduct upheld by the workers (Carleial *et al.*, 2002). Furthermore, in a society where interaction with the customer is important, subjectivity becomes one of the weapons of performance, as the client's behaviour is not easily predictable.

Thus, autonomy reflects the mobility required of the workers so that they may plan their own future under unpredictable circumstances. Autonomy exposes the double tendency of labour situations: on the one hand, the individualisation required of workers so that they might be "entrepreneurs of their own selves", thus separating or distancing them

3 The importance of immaterial capital means that a company such as Renault has adopted the motto "creator of automobiles" and no longer simply producer.

4 "L'efficacité ne dépend plus de l'intensité du travail programmé de chacun, mais de ce qui se passe *entre* les individus et les groupes au travail, et qui échappe en partie à toute programmation" (Veltz, 2008: 17).

from work as part of a collective whole (teleworking, for example)[5] and, on the other, the collective aspect of teamwork.

Nor is it rare for the worker to have to confront situations of paradoxical injunction,[6] which are harmful to her/his health and a source of suffering, sometimes even leading to mental illness. Isolated in her/his work, the worker only has a partial view of the whole – except in the case of a mission which she/he is asked to carry out from beginning to end –, which sporadic reunions do not complete. At the same time, a total and unrestricted engagement is expected of the worker in terms of personality. Here too, it would seem, things differ according to the individuals' level of qualification: the more the individual is master of the totality of the task to be executed, the less likely she/he is to encounter difficulties – allowing for self-esteem to function better – a fact that, in turn, will occasion productivity gains.

The bond of dependency or the state of economic necessity is a typical characteristic of offer on the labour market and is present in both forms of labour, subordinated and autonomous. Reality is full of examples. Thus, in agriculture, the contracts of share croppers combine dependency and autonomy and are at the origin of an industrial entrepreneurship in Emilia-Romagna (Capecchi, 1989: 273); in companies and outside these firms, the emergence of autonomous forms of labour, characterized by offering a personal activity finalized in a work or a result includes a situation of economic dependency for the worker (Ghera, 2003: 60). Consequently, and as already pointed out, legal subordination and economic subordination, though difficult to separate, are far from being one and the same.

Reality is more complex than the simple separation between dependent labour and independent labour. Indeed, when analysing the labour market, the researcher encounters a multiplication of the forms of status, the outstanding fact being their differentiation and the ever-increasing lack of job security.[7] Informalisation reaches the very heart of the employment relation and gives it its hybrid complexion.

5 See Rosenfield's paper (just before).

6 The term "paradoxical injunction" refers to the fact of giving an order that is impossible to execute as it contains of itself, in an undividable manner, an assertion and its denial. It is a case of a self-contradicting proposition which, when repeated, is the source of irritation and mental disturbances for the worker.

7 Respectively, in August 2005 and February 2006, the French government tried to make a new move in the direction of precarious employment by authorising firms of less than 20 employees to hire workers or youths subjected to a two-year trial period, with the possibility for the employer to dismiss the employee from one day to the next within this period. These new types of "work contracts" [*Contrat Nouvelle Embauche* (CNE) and *Contrat Première Embauche* (CPE), respectively, New Hiring Contract and First Hiring Contract] came under the category of CDIs (contracts for

Hybridisation is characterized by the intertwining of different forms of labour insertion and the shifting character of labour relations (Azaïs, 2004). The phenomenon recalls to mind what the analysis on the "informal sector" had brought to the fore regarding individuals' work trajectories in developing countries in the 1980s. Indeed, it was not at all uncommon (and over recent years the movement seems to have spread to the capitals of Latin America), to see the same worker, in the course of the same day, don the clothes of the informal sector, then later on wear those of the formal sector before returning once again to the informal sector at night. Contrary to what held for developing countries, this phenomenon now reaches the very heart of the employment relation and gives it new features. Gone is the time when it was thought that the South would follow the same course as the North and that the employment relation would inevitably spread. Indeed, in the North salaried work has spread and today almost the whole of the working force belongs to this category. In 2002, 87% of men and 92% of women in France were in a employment relation against a proportion of 69% and 79% respectively for men and women in Italy (Maruani and Reynaud, 2004: 53). This proportion has been on the increase over the past 20 years. The European average, in 2002, stood at 81% for men and 89% for women (*id.*, *ibid.*). In all countries, the proportion of female employees is larger than that of males, even in a country such as Greece, which continues to have the lowest level of salaried employment in Europe (58% and 64%, respectively, in 2002, a progression of 8 and 9 percentage points compared to 1983).

The separation between "salaried employment situations" and "independent activities" is becoming ever more tenuous. Everything included in the first category would be protected by the Welfare State; that which is not would be part of a system of non-permanent employment relation. Now, certain salaried activities require that the worker be independent and autonomous, a fact that does not prevent seemingly independent activities, or ones considered as such, from hiding situations of dependency similar to those of formal work contracts, and which Anglo-Saxon literature terms a "disguised employment relation" or "employee-like workers".

This situation is reflected in the variety of juridical labour statuses, visible in the shifting nature of work contracts and in their tendency to

an indeterminate duration), a fact that blurred the differentiating factor between dependent forms and independent forms of labour. After they have been abandoned by the government, one because it was in conflict with the ILO (International Labour Organisation) rules, the other, due to the street pressures, they have been substituted by CDI contracts. The status of *self-entrepreneur*, adopted in January 2009, seems to clarify things by stressing one's own responsibility in employment affairs.

become contracts ruled by commercial, therefore private, law. The use of New Technologies of Information and Communication (NTIC) tends to make former forms of subordination obsolete, and leads jurists to use the expression of "e-collar worker" (Ray, 2001), meaning that the distinction between salaried teleworking and independent teleworking is not in the least obvious.

The increasing individualisation experienced by the salaried population corresponds to the delocalisation of risk, from the employer to the employee. The worker feels compelled to take on part of the risk previously shouldered by the employer.

Moreover, part of the salary received is subject to the worker's performance: commissions, participation in the company's profits, wage cuts and shifting towards a contract with less advantageous conditions for the worker have become commonplace events. The time when the worker received a fixed predetermined salary and which remained the same over the contract's total duration seems to be more and more remote.

By feeling committed to the future and the smooth running of the firm she/he works for, the employee experiences a *continuum* between her/his work space and her/his private space, as proved by the fact that the responsibility for their own condition increasingly rests on the workers' own shoulders. There is a subtle passage from the collective to the individual.

Some Facts Based on the European Reality

On a European level, the percentage of independent workers in relation to the total levels of employment continues to be approximately 15%, in a slight decline compared to the 15.8% of 1992 and 1995, and the 15.7% of 1998. Men, more than women, have an independent activity (17.6% *vs* 10.9% for women in 2000). Over the same period, the proportion is around 17-18% for men and varies between 11 and 12% for women (Perulli, 2003: 36, 39).

	Percentage of independent labour in the European Union in 2000		Percentage of employers in the sector of independent labour*	
Countries		%	Employers*	Independent workers*
1	Greece	44.0	28.8	71.2
2	Portugal	27.5	35.6	64.4
3	Italy	26.2	nd	nd
4	Austria	18.9	68.8	31.2
5	Belgium	17.7	10.3	89.7
6	Ireland	17.0	39.9	60.1
7	Spain	16.6	29.6	70.4
8	The Netherlands	14.3	37.4	62.6
9	United Kingdom	11.8	25.8	74.2
10	Finland	11.2	42.3	57.7
11	Germany	10.2	53.0	47.0
12	France	7.4	49.7	50.3
13	Denmark	6.9	50.1	49.9
14	Luxembourg	6.8	nd	nd
15	Sweden	5.6	41.0	59.0

Sources: Perulli, 2003: 55 and 57 (* = OECD data, 2000, *Employment Outlook*) – elaborated by the author.

The differences among countries in terms of independent labour are important. There appear three large groups of countries:[8]

– in the 1st group, independent labour concerns more than ¼ of the total working population;

– in the 2nd group, it represents between 10 and 20% of the employee population and concerns such diverse countries as Finland and Spain, meaning that one cannot advance the hypothesis of diverging behaviour between the North and the South of Europe, as the countries in the 1st group (Greece, Portugal and Italy) might lead one to believe;

– in the 3rd group, one finds countries with different social systems (such as France, Sweden or Denmark), which at the time (2003) still upheld a certain concept of social protection for employees, with a relatively active welfare State.

The category "independent labour employers" is divided into two sub-categories: independent workers without employees (*own account workers*) – assimilated to micro-employers in OCDE nomenclature – and independent workers with employees (*employers*).[9] Though each country has its own specificity, the proportion of independent workers

8 Based on the analysis of the table's two columns on the left. No more recent data are available today.

9 See the 2 columns on the right in the table above.

without employees – except in the case of Austria – is above or borders upon 50%.

It should be noted that, in Italy, the year 2001 marked a shift compared to what occurred in the immediately previous period. Whereas, between 1997 and 2000, atypical labour (*temping* and *part-time*) increased intensely (26%), full-time dependent labour remained stable (+ 1%). In 2001, full-time dependent employment for an indeterminate period of time increased by 335,000 positions compared to 2000; on the opposite side of the spectrum, atypical forms increased by only 55,000 units. This shows that, in Italy that year, 86% of the increase was due to "typical" employment (Altieri, Oteri, 2003: 1).

Over the same period, the *co.co.co.* contracts represented almost 2,000,000 units, or 9% of employment (+ 29.6% compared to 1999, according to the INPS matriculation records), demonstrating their wide acceptance by the contracting parties, but also highlighting the consolidation of a predominant tendency of a *grey zone* between dependent labour and independent labour.

Economically Dependent, or Parasubordinated, Labour

The *grey zone* between the categories of dependent labour and independent labour refers to:

the zones that present characteristics specific to the two forms of labour, and

are, also, the means of disguising, behind the appearances of independent labour, an employment relation.

Over the past years, the concept of subordination-heterodirection has evolved. The model of subordination-continuity or simple coordination in time and in space, centred around functional cooperation and the insertion of the worker's contribution in the productive organisation, has been consolidated and is preferred to the typical situation observed in the firm hierarchy structure (Ghera, 2003: 66). This method corresponds to a surpassing of the fordist norm of portioned labour division.

Plurality of models: the social typology of the subordinated worker no longer has anything in common with subordination-heterodirection. Nevertheless, the subordinated worker continues to be in an obligated position towards the various productive contexts.

Parasubordinated labour does not deal solely with the worker's personal dependency, which would be equivalent to the worker's past obligation to deliver a product or service within a predefined timeframe or on a specific date. The collaboration, which necessitates labour organisation, ends by being identified with the technical-functional result and becomes an obligation of the worker.

In Europe, from a legal point of view, Italy, Greece and Great Britain define the category of economically dependent worker (or parasubordinated worker). Other States, even though they do not have a legal definition for the subordinated worker, concern themselves with this category; these are Austria, Denmark, Finland, France, Greece, Holland, Ireland, Norway and Portugal. On the other side of the spectrum, in Belgium, Spain, Luxemburg and Sweden, there exists no specific definition and the issue is rarely addressed on the political and social scenes.

Within the first group of countries, Germany and Italy are those that possess a more complete definition of "parasubordinated labour". Our attention will focus on the Italian case as it is one of the most significant and has shaken up the trade-union world. Besides provoking a public debate on the subject, the principal trade union organisations (CGL, CISL, UIL) created specific structures to represent the economically dependent workers (NIDIL-CGL 19, CISL20, UIL20)[10] through collective negotiations, with a view to introducing forms of protection for this type of worker.

Thanks to collective agreements, the individual profiles in relation to work between the economically dependent worker and the firm, as well as the trade union profiles, are considered. The aim is to create a system of stable trade-union relations.

In the specific case of economically dependent labour, collective agreements specify the contract's written form; its duration; the activities, timetable and manner of execution of the task; the remuneration and method of payment; data regarding health and insurance on the job site; permissions (health, accident, family reasons); training; end of relation; worker's obligations; trade union rights (in the majority of cases, economically dependent workers enjoy rights that are compatible with their status and participate in trade-union representation activities within the firm). In other words, these agreements provide a legal framework capable of protecting whoever is involved in atypical forms of labour.

The Collaborazione Coordinata e Continuativa *(co.co.co.), a Hybrid Form of Commitment to Work*

What is the nature of the *co.co.co.* contract? Its main characteristics are summarized in the list below:

– no link of subordination;

– no temporal programming;

---

10 See http://www.cgl.it/nidil; http://www.cisl.it/alai/cocco.htm and http://www.uil.it/cpo, respectively.

– the "*co.co.co.*" collaborator can use the labour of a third party to assist her/him, within a certain proportion provided for by law;

– the services rendered must be unitary and continuous: they must satisfy the contractor's needs;

– the salary is not permanent, therefore it is fixed in advance.

An extreme heterogeneity characterizes the workers (of both the public and private sector) registered with the INPS 10-14% Fund,[11] also known as "*co.co.co.*". The reason of this heterogeneity is to be found basically in the act of its constitution. Indeed, the establishment of the INPS Fund (*Istituto Nazionale della Previdenza Sociale*) was motivated by the need to give social welfare coverage to workers deprived of such coverage, but also in the hope that this might contribute to balancing the Social Security's accounts. Consequently, over and above civil servants, this category includes workers as varied as call-centre operators, firm consultants or company administrators. Despite it being fiscal considerations that predominate for some of them, these workers have in common the need of a guarantee regarding certain direct rights concerning work, such as the assurance of payment for work executed, the possibility of further training, the certainty of social security coverage and the respect of certain universal rights, such as the right to health services and maternity benefits (Altieri *et al.*, 2002).

Heterogeneity, too, characterizes the income of workers registered with the INPS Fund, and which varies between € 10,000 (for 56% of the men and 77% the women) and € 50,000 per annum (for 8% of the men and only 2% of the women). These differences widen by gender: because they find themselves in less protected labour situations, on average women earn half as much as men (Altieri *et al.*, 2002).

Each time that the autonomous workers devote themselves to producing a result, or a sequence of results, integrated in a stable manner into the contractor's productive cycle and organisation (and, consequently, in the socially more significant case of a firm's coordinated autonomous labour), we are in the presence of a social sub-type of *contrato d'opera* presenting the two indispensable principles of autonomy: the freedom of determining the compensation (art. 2225 do CC) and the unilateral rescission of the contract (art. 2227 CC), antinomic with subordinated labour (Ghera, 2003: 83-84).

There is an identity of function between subordinated labour and coordinated (*parasubordinated*) labour; both are the link between the work

11 Name of the Fund established in 1995; the contribution of parasubordinated workers to Social Security, deducted at source, varied between 10 and 13% (Law of August 8, 1995, No. 335). The higher percentage moved to 14% on 1/1/2002. The text of the Law is titled Assimilated income to that of dependent labour.

of the individual and the firm. The sole difference resides in the different relationship between the coordination and temporal continuity of labour. In subordinated labour, there exists a continuity of the worker's activity in both time and space. In coordinated autonomous labour, the continuity is not a specific attribution of the "collaborator", even though it characterizes the subcontractor's interest and through this his relationship with the collaborator: the latter needs to coordinate her/his personal activity and working time so as to produce the one result, or the sequence of results, destined to be integrated into the subcontractor's productive process and organisation (Ghera, 2003: 84).

In brief, the *co.co.co.* contract is amply satisfactory for the entrepreneur, inasmuch as the results of the services rendered are expected to be continuous – therefore avoiding any interruption in the productive process. In this way, the entrepreneur does not need to deal with the coordination or programming, in time or in space, of the activity, which is handled by the worker, a fact that confirms the ambiguous nature of this type of contract. As the supplier of non subordinated labour, the collaborator has, in terms of result, a debt towards the subcontractor even though he is not totally dependent on him but rather on the productive cycle, and therefore is indirectly "part of" the firm (Ghera, 2003: 85).

Therefore, coordinated labour does not belong to any type of contract; it is independent of autonomous and subordinated labour. Thus, labour's *parasubordinated* nature is a process and does not come under the typical protection norms of subordinated labour.

Nevertheless, from a social and economic point of view, the *co.co.co.* worker is in an intermediate position between subordinated and independent labour. This position is uncomfortable and social and fiscal legislation do not clarify it significantly. The income generated from *co.co.co.* labour is considered in the same way as that from dependent labour. It is assimilated to the income of dependent labour that is derived from *co.co.co.* relations, that is to say the income whose object is the execution of an activity carried out without a link of subordination, in the context of a unitary and continuous relation using one's own organisational means with a pre-established periodic payment.

A true *continuum* between the *locatio operis*[12] and the *locatio operarum* (*i.e.* between the new forms of organisation of dependent and

[12] The *contrato d'opera* derives from the *locatio operis*, a category in which Roman law included all types of contracts and relations whose object was the execution of an individual task in exchange of payment. In the case of labour contracts, this means that 1) there is work that needs to be executed; 2) remunerated or indemnified; 3) the contract between parties is reached between persons wishing to sign a contract

independent labour, used by the firm according to criteria of economic functionality to achieve the goal of flexibilising labour), the *co.co.co.* option becomes attractive to those in search of flexibility.

However, in order to limit the use of *co.co.co.*, the Italian government promulgated a reform of the labour market (legislative decree of 10/9/2003, No. 276), introducing the aspect of "labour per project" with a view to keeping in check its abusive use in the private sector, thus safeguarding the collaborator's autonomy.[13]

In the same way, due to the proliferation of *co.co.co.* in the public administration, which in various respects resembles a private firm, the government was forced to legislate. The shift in the administration's organisational approach leads, on the one hand, to the contracting of the dependent worker's employment relation and, on the other, to giving its executives a different role from the one they had until then in terms of human resource management, similar to that of private management.

Three kinds of problems persist. Firstly, those related to the individualisation of the reasons that legitimate resorting to collaboration; secondly, the referents regarding the assessment of the possible supervision which, nevertheless, can be included in individual contracts in accordance with the autonomy contained in the contract signed by the collaborator; and, lastly, those regarding the right rules in the management of fiscal and social security issues.

Co.co.co. relations have been assimilated to dependent labour with respect to their fiscal aspects[14] without, however, any direct impact on the relation's juridical qualification. This said, the law holds that in the public administration *co.co.co.* must only apply to the actions necessitating a high degree of professionalism, consequently, to those where the persons must enjoy a total autonomy. The grounds put forth for this is to avoid harming the public service's hiring regime, i.e. *via* competitive entry examination. One cannot but think that this allows for a lot of leeway, which reinforces the idea of a hybridisation of the labour market.

Conclusion

Taking as its starting point the categories of "dependent labour" (assimilated to subordination) and "independent labour" (presented under the prism of autonomy), the paper focuses on hybridisation, a phenomenon characteristic of the labour market in contemporary capitalism.

(Pothier, Louage, No. 395-403, in www.jusbelli.com/Bouvier/bouvier1856_lin.html – 67k).

13 http://www.governo.it/GovernoInforma/Dossier/cococo/circolare.htm.

14 Art. 34, Law 21/11/2000, No. 342.

Various social sciences have examined the subject. For economic theory, hybridisation covers the shifts noted in the employment relation and highlights the tendency towards a predominance of "atypical" forms of employment relations, pointing out a *continuum* between labour situations, turning more and more inadequate the division subordinated work and autonomous work. For labour sociology, it refers to the individualisation and/or collectivisation of individuals' insertion in the labour market, highlighting the increasing demands made on workers in terms of autonomy and assuming responsibility. Jurists, for their part, use their observations on the employment relation's evolution to concentrate on the nature of the work contract, which leads European countries' law to follow two routes: that of legislation, so as to differentiate dependent labour from independent labour, and that of jurisprudence.

A consensus surrounds the end result: whatever the approach adopted, one notes the presence of a *grey zone*, meaning that, when dealing with labour market insertion, it becomes ever more difficult to differentiate between situations of dependent or independent labour. This is not particular to either developed or developing countries; it concerns all of them in varying proportions, a fact that both invites the comparison of international situations and stresses the importance of political issue, for instance when a government is compelled to withdraw an unpopular measure or even when he tries to implement one. The current focus on the Italian case, considered as being symbolic of what is happening or will occur in other European countries, is, in a certain manner, representative of a situation that is spreading out. Few are the elements that allow to distinguish between, on the one hand, moments where autonomy is predominating and, on the other, times when subordination is prevailing. It seems to be one of the main signs of nowadays employment relations in a globalising world.

References

Altieri, G. and Otieri, C., "Terzo rapporto sul lavoro atipico in Italia: verso la stabilizzazione del precariato?", IRES-CGIL, aprile, http://www.flessibilmente.it/osservatorio/Ricerche/Ricerche, 2003.

Azaïs, Ch., "Dé-segmentation du marché du travail et autonomie", in S. Boutillier, D. Uzunidis (eds.), *Travailler au 21e siècle, Nouveaux modes d'organisation industrielle et spatiale du travail*, Paris, De Boeck Université, Collection "Économie, Société, Région", 2006, p. 113-127.

Azaïs, Ch., "Travail et régulations territoriales: une lecture à partir d'expériences française, italienne et brésilienne", *Innovations, Cahiers d'Économie de l'Innovation*, Paris, L'Harmattan Innoval, No. 24, 2, 2006, p. 115-130.

Bologna, S. and Fumagalli, A., "Dieci tesi per la definizione di uno statuto del lavoro autonomo", in S. Bologna and A. Fumagalli, *Il lavoro autonomo di seconda generazione. Scenari del postfordismo in Italia*, Milano, Feltrinelli, 1997, p. 16-23.

Boyer, R., *Une théorie du capitalisme est-elle possible?*, Paris, Odile Jacob, 2004.

Boyer, R., "Du rapport salarial fordiste à la diversité des relations salariales – une mise en perspective de quelques recherches régulationnistes", CEPREMAP/EHESS/CNRS, No. 14, http://www.cepremap.cnrs.fr/couv_orange/co0114.pdf, 2001.

Boyer, R., *La flexibilité du travail en Europe – une étude comparative des transformations du rapport salarial dans sept pays de 1973 à 1985*, Paris, La Découverte, 1987.

Capecchi, V., "Petite entreprise et économie locale: la flexibilité productive", in M. Maruani, E. Reynaud and C. Romani (eds.), *La flexibilité en Italie*, Paris, Syros/Alternative, 1989, p. 271-286.

Carleial, L., Mezza, M.L. and Neves, L., "Modèles industriels et quelques éléments de la relation salariale dans les firmes réseaux commandées par les constructeurs automobiles dans la Région métropolitaine de Curitiba (Brésil): le cas de Volks-Audi et de Renault", Paris, Actes du *GERPISA*, 9º Rencontre annuelle (CD), 2001.

Castoriadis, C., *L'institution imaginaire de la société*, Paris, Seuil, 1975.

Commission of the European Communities, *Green Paper Modernising labour law to meet the challenges of the 21st century*, Brussels, 22.11.2006, COM(2006) 708 final, 2006.

European Foundation for the Improvement of Living Working Conditions, *Time constraints and autonomy at work in the European Union*, 1996.

Ghera, E., "La subordinazione e i rapporti atipici nel diritto italiano", in Programma Socrates *Collana di diritto comparato e comunitario del lavoro e della sicurezza sociale*, Bari, Cacucci Editore, 2003, p. 47-89.

Guitton, C., Maruani, M. and Reynaud, E. (eds.), *L'emploi en Espagne. Marché du travail et relations professionnelles*, Paris, Syros, 1991.

Hall P.A. and Soskice D. (eds.), "An introduction to Varieties of Capitalism" *Varieties of capitalism: The Institutional Foundations of Comparative Advantage*, Oxford, Oxford University Press, 2001, pp. 1-68.

ILO, *Meeting of Experts on Workers in Situation Needing Protection* (The employment relationship: Scope), Basic technical document, Geneva, 15-19 may, 2000, http://www.ilo.org

Lautier, B. and Tortajada, R., *École, force de travail et salariat*, Grenoble, PUG, 1978.

Leborgne, D. and Lipietz, A., "Flexibilité offensive, flexibilité défensive. Deux stratégies sociales dans la production des nouveaux espaces économiques", in G. Benko and A. Lipietz (eds.), *Les régions qui gagnent. Districts et réseaux: les nouveaux paradigmes de la géographie économique*, "Économie en liberté", Paris, PUF, 1992, p. 347-377.

Maruani, M. and Reynaud, E., *Sociologie de l'emploi*, Paris, La Découverte, Repères, 4th édition, 2004.

Maruani, M., Reynaud, E. and Romani, C. (eds.), *La flexibilité en Italie*, Paris, Syros Alternatives, 1989.

Perulli, A., Travail économiquement dépendant/parasubordination: les aspects juridiques, sociaux et économiques, Rapport pour la Commission européenne, 2003.

Petit, H. and Thévenot, N. (eds.), *Les nouvelles frontières du travail subordonné – Approche pluridisciplinaire*, Paris, La Découverte, Recherches, 2006.

Ray, J.E., *Le droit du travail à l'épreuve des NTIC*, Paris, Éditions Liaisons Sociales, 2001.

Veltz, P., *Le nouveau monde industriel*, Paris, Gallimard, Le débat, édition revue et augmentée, 2008.

Verdier, J.-M., *Droit du travail*, Paris, Mementos Dalloz, Droit privé, 1996.

New Organisational Realities

Individualisation and Atomisation in the Organisations of 'Second Modernity'

Laima SERKSNYTE-SAPPINGTON

Introduction

In the last 20 years together with the emergence and implementation of new information technologies, massive transformations of organisations are taking place. These transformations manifest not only in terms of structural changes, but also in internal revisions of work culture, modifications of work processes, redesign and re-distribution of specialisations. In order to remain viable in a fast-paced economy, organisations take up new opportunities, construct competitive strategies and inevitably encounter risks that force them to find ways to deal with unforeseen effects of their business activities. Various organisational forms, work practices and points of view continue to compete and struggle to coexist.

As volatile market behaviour enters organisational everyday it underscores recurring organisational contradictions in today's business environments between dominant instrumental business rationality that relies on managerial control and command mechanisms and, on the other hand, an increasing demand for autonomous and flexible employees along with more elastic business management approaches. As decentralized internal markets share space with centralized powers and managerial means of control, organisational inconsistencies continue to persist, inadvertently forcing organisations to turn back on their own foundations in search of a new business direction, while responding to impending challenges. This essay offers a conceptual framework to highlight and understand a paradox that characterizes current organisational environments between *individualisation* (as a need for individual autonomy, self-reflexivity, and trust) and increasing *atomisation* (employee exclusion from decision making and a loss of individual initiative). *Atomisation*, an unintended consequence of present-day, efficiency-oriented and market-driven social conditions stands in dire opposition to *individualisation*, a new way of individual relatedness to current socio-economic structure. Both processes conflictingly unfold in organisational everyday thus producing organisational dilemmas that call for a fundamental revision of deep-seated organisational assumptions and new ways of understanding organisational transformation.[1]

Current Organisational Realities: a Paradigmatic Shift

Current political, international and market configurations force organisations to re-structure and globalize. Increasing volatility is brought into organisational life. Global inter-connection of financial markets, information systems, production and communication networks and often unsubstantiated ideas enfold organisations into a state of multi-directional change. Market relations directly enter organisations bringing in unpredictability, competition and uncertainty. Organising of production follows a new logic, where supervisory structure is revised to meet the new requirements. Mechanistic models of organisation such as Taylorism, characterized by control and predictability are no longer effective. Organisational structures are forced to exhibit greater flexibility in modifying work arrangements in accordance to changing demands by giving rise to the late modern form of economy and indeterminacy.

Life in organisations reflects complexities of human interactions that stem from systemic environmental uncertainties caused by emerging global markets and changing cultural perceptions. It is ripe with conflict, risk taking and a need for self-realisation, which can be observed in reference to current political, economic, cultural and socio-psychological conditions. Indeterminacy, frequently experienced in the work environments, lead to qualitatively different ways of co-labouring, task sharing, team cooperation, and flexible work culture. Work is conceived more as tasks and numerous finite projects than as continuous flow of pre-determined activities that require professional commitment and time to perform. Employer-employee relationships increasingly share a common dimension of short-term task fulfilment, part-time work, and limited contractual arrangements that continue to challenge internalized notions of loyalty, commitment, collectivity, responsibility, job security and outcome predictability. New communication patterns emerge between various parts of an organisation and its members. Communicating ideas and strategies represents a big part of working time in dealing with

1 This article is based on organisational research and consultation projects at several Healthcare organisations and IT companies in New York-Connecticut area. Research is focused on the emergence of new forms of work, new conceptions of persons and subjectivity, and changing relationships among organisational members as they adapt to perceptions of competition, new affiliations, and ongoing uncertainty due to constant demands to acquire specialized knowledge. The on-going project grounds social and psychic dynamics within organisational subjects and groups that are affected by increasing technological novelty, erosion of long-term affiliation, and the rise of global markets.

organisational challenges. In organisational everyday communication practices that once were predominantly characterized by face-to-face interactions are now more and more framed by electronic messaging (e-mails, IM, SMS, VoIP) and microblogging (twitter), which arguably tend to downgrade person's capacities for self-expression and learning from others, by creating an illusion of self-control and participation.

Increasingly employees within organisations are no longer given clearly formulated tasks to follow, for which they may be rewarded, thus creating uncertain expectations for one's sense of work and accomplishments. A choice is brought into the place where once was certainty reinforced by an authority. By 'choice' I mean conscious selection of the direction of one's action, in response to uncertain situations, while borrowing from an array of alternatives not necessarily pre-determined by specific role boundaries or worker manuals. As s/he moves in and out of different tasks, an employee is expected repeatedly to take up new organisational tools, quickly adapt to the new techno-social expectations and come up with constructive solutions to problems at hand. However, faced with fluctuating demands, poorly defined tasks and insufficient knowledge about their company status and operations within current market conditions, organisational members experience mounting pressure and unpredictability of their work outcome. One's identity is challenged and one's self-understanding is being recast again and again in light of new experiences and encounters. In order to successfully carry out the tasks that they are presented, employees express an increasing need to access full information pertaining to organisational data and strategies, which for the most part remain exclusively in the hands of their managers, and to invoke non-traditional, non-linear thinking in the execution of those tasks. Hence, noticeably, employees are beginning to relate to their organisation both, internally as well as externally, as whole individuals, who bring into play varied knowledge and a full array of experiences, and not as mere functionaries, attached to their 'job description'.[2]

Such new conditions, which presuppose change as its focal point, signal a shift in societal paradigm, what scholars in the social sciences call the '*second modernity*' (Beck, 2000, 2004) or '*another modernity*' (Lash, 1999).[3] It challenges instrumental rationality of the *first moder-*

---

2 For comparison, *see* Chester Barnard (1938/1968: 16-17), who insisted that an individual has a dual relationship with a cooperative system that is always present. Internally, he or she relates to an organisation in a functional, non-personal way, whereas externally, s/he relates to it as a whole person.

3 The shifts in societal paradigm are widely described in various social science and management literature and signify new direction in organisational thinking (*see*, for example, Westwood & Clegg (eds.), 2003; Biggart, 2002; Guillen, Collins, England, Mayer (eds.), 2002; DiMaggio (ed.), 2001; 'Accounts': a Newsletter of Economic

nity that has dominated economic, political and cultural fields since the turn of the 20th century and was enlisted to predict and control the effects of industrialisation and rationalisation. Systems of labour were conceived to provide material security and, more importantly, integrate individuals into systems of controls and pre-defined meanings. An individual was framed sociologically into a particular social situation, as a part of collectivity with assigned identifications, categorical constraints and pre-set behavioural expectations.

Unlike the *first modernity* of certainty, organisational stability and predictability of scientific and technological knowledge, the *second modernity* operates along the notions of accelerated and flexible technoscientific developments, the ability to adapt to new products and processes, and the capability to shift human perception towards greater and greater task differentiation and training. An individual in an organisation is less and less protected by a strict organisational boundary, but has to engage with the outside processes that pass through organisational environments. No longer can people rely exclusively on traditional models but are forced to confront streaming events and pressing demands, which often carry opposing meanings that have to be translated and harmonized into one's daily existence. Thereby, the person in the paradigm of *second modernity* is expected to become increasingly flexible, somewhat autonomous, trainable, multi-tasking, able to cross diverse knowledge sets and embrace risk, while simultaneously coping with change.

Such individual transformations require re-examination of current organisational structures as well as taken-for-granted assumptions, which frequently act as impediments to change. Industrial age management paradigm built on principles of specialisation, standardisation, hierarchy, control, precise roles, and primacy of shareholders interests[4] simply fails to mobilize human energies and is incapable to align new organisational objectives with the interests and capabilities of its employees, thus producing deep dissatisfaction with the status quo. Unreflectiveness, embedded into taken-for-granted and unconscious assumptions, often continues to drive organisational logic and could, through reflexivity, be brought into transformational processes. However, shifting organisational demands and priorities, various business strategies that organisations undertake in response to unpredictable markets allow neither for internal everyday reflection, bottom-up initiatives, nor for comprehensive calculation of risks to take place. Lack of reflection or awareness at the time of change accompanies numerous attempts of

Sociology, ASA, issues 2005, 2006; Beck, 2004; Kumar, 2005; Sennet, 2006; Sassen, 2006; Touraine, 2007; *Harvard Business Review*, issues 2002-2010).

4 *See* HBR, February 2009 issue.

organisational actors to reconstruct and transform their organisation, resulting into uncertainty of organisational actions and unanticipated side effects of its transformational processes. In fact, it is the unconscious processes of organisational and group dynamics that produce false assumptions and preconceptions, dogmatize organisational foundations and inhibit change. Institutionalized unconscious in the form of organisational defences or resistances (Menzies-Lyth, 1989) often acts as a stumbling block to move innovations ahead.

Organisational Responses to Market Volatility

Organisational resistance to invoke a kind of reflexivity that is required in order to unblock its social defences and resistances to change results into feelings of rupture between one's self-understanding and self-application that often permeate organisational lives, highlighting an observable disconnect between a person and structure, self and other, action and reflection, perception and actuality. One of the responses that the employers and employees undertake to counter such internal turmoil is increasing attempts to combine instrumental work with symbolic orientation within a workplace environment by enlisting religion and spirituality into job-related transactions.[5] Religious values that are brought into the workplace often serve as a buffer against job uncertainty and work intrusion into the private lives of individuals.

What's more, in an attempt to reduce complexity organisations throw multiple resources in perfecting the data, calculating probability of risks and increasing training and information flows. A role of change manag-

5 It may go the other way too, when instituted business models and free market principles guide transcendental institutions in competing for their followers and/or offering religious "products" over the media outlets, as a "church-on-the-go see, for example, Shorto, 2004, p. 42; Casey, 2002 p. 21, pp. 68-194; M. Conlin, "Religion in the Workplace", *Business Week*, November 1999, (http://www.businessweek.com/1999/99_44/b3653001.htm); M. Gunther, "God and Business", *Fortune Magazine*, July 9th, 2001, (http://www.marcgunther.com/god-and-business); D. Grant, K. O'Neil & L. Stephens, "Spirituality in the Workplace: New Empirical Directions in the Study of the Sacred", *Sociology of Religion*, ASA, Fall 2004, pp. 265-83; "Religion at Work is a Bigger Deal", *Work & Family Newsbrief*, October 2005, (http://www.workfamily.com/Search/listLinks.aspx?section=Diversity); G. Haber, "Religion Finding Way into Workplace", in *Deseret News*, August 12th, 2006, (http://www.deseretnews.com/article/645192468/Religion-finding-way-into-workplace.html);
E. Wulfhorst, "Religion Finds Firm Footing in Some Offices", Reuters, December 6th, 2006: http://www.reuters.com/article/idUSN0531418620061206; Bilberman J. and Tishler, L. (2008), *Spirituality in Business: Theory, Practice, and Future Directions*, Pelgrave Macmillan, pp. 1-6; 141-160; p. 216; Nadram, S. and Borden, M. (eds.) (2009), *Spirituality and Business: Exploring Possibilities for a New Management Paradigm*, Springer, pp. 1-33; Lambert III, L., *Spirituality Inc.: Religion in the American Workplace*, NYU Press, pp. 51-79; and numerous other publications, 2009.

ers is often delegated to organisational experts and outside consultants who bring in new strategic suggestions of how to 'control' unpredictability. However, new organisational and leadership models that organisations adopt in order to counter uncertainty and mounting employee stress do not seem to work. They are mostly aimed at internal and external re-structuring, such as internal marketisation, customer orientation, de-layering, downsizing, outsourcing, off-shoring, and others, and focus upon improving economic and financial aspects of an organisational life. They do not seriously consider psychological and sociological dimensions that interpenetrate organisational structures. Moreover, explanations of systemic or structural obstacles in organisational transition are typically carried out with the same conceptual apparatus that created the problems in the first place. Pluralisation of various choices, probabilities and overlapping demands within organisational life, which continue to be cognitively based on the old structural elements (role, position, fixed boundary, etc.) and on categorical imperatives (age, gender, professional, religious, ethnic, educational identifications, etc.) create a distressing working environment. For instance, in order to unleash the creative flow of ideas and production some organisations take on suggestions to dismantle hierarchical structures while in practice continuing to operate within the familiar hierarchical model. However, dismantling hierarchies and purposefully creating horizontal reporting structures does not guarantee better results, and secondly, such an action may become instituted as a business imperative and a diversion from the real organisational objective. A search for the 'right' model often leads to either reification of decentralized structure or reverting back to familiar modes of functioning.[6] Instead of providing clarity, such restructoring attempts result into organisational uncertainties, randomness, disconnected decisions, anxieties and false assumptions that lead to reification of previous hierarchies. Thus, new organisational discourses by and large remain temporary structural solutions to organisational challenges, whereas in stating the problems that exist they fail to address the changing premises of work, individualisation and collective responsibility in an organisation of the *second modernity*.

Customer Orientation

Effects of environmental uncertainty as the major effect of market globalisation are increasingly managed through the response and posi-

6 As an example, General Motors that has been praised for decentralized organisational structure later was blamed for inability to innovate and contemplate change due to ossification of such decentralisation. (R. Kanter, HBR, November 2009). Inversely, an attempt to institute horizontal structures in a health technology company resulted in duplication of tasks and confusion over reporting, which later led to the return of even more rigid hierarchies (from field project).

tion of a "customer". In the last few years 'customer orientation' has become the biggest trend in organisational transition in search of a market advantage.[7] Consumer needs and aspirations have become a part of organisational practices and technologies, where employees are often re-conceptualized from being 'workers' or 'managers' to individuals in search of meaning, with a sense of responsibility, in search of a quality of life (du Gay, 2000: 67). Recent calls to reinvent marketing department as a 'customer department' takes a step further by arguing to focus on a 'two-way', 'individualised communication' rather than 'product profitability' (Rust, Moorman, Bhalia, 2010).[8] By appealing to embedded subjectivity, pre-constructed desires and needs of their customers, organisations engage in what du Gay calls *symbolic expertise*, through which they "make up" new consumers as well as new types of employees for themselves, in order to meet their financial goals. Probing marketing functions, thereby become the major focus of an organisation, what Deleuze calls 'the soul of a corporation' (du Gay 2000: 71-72). What's more, personalised marketing techniques that organisations enlist bring markets into the private worlds of the consumers as well as employees with all the unanticipated consequences of such deregulations.

As conflicting demands, lack of recognition and trust persist, it often leads employees as well as customers to engage in counterproductive behaviour, rumour spread, cheating and disruption of tasks, which compel management professionals to question the ability of employees,

---

7 see, for example, S. Thompke and E. von Hippel, "Customers as Innovators: A New Way to Create Value", *HBR*, April 2002, pp. 74-81; T. Levit, "Marketing Myopia", *HBR*, July-August 2004, pp. 138-149; Thomas J. *et al.*, "Getting the Most of All Your Customers", *HBR*, July-August, 2004, pp. 116-123; G. McGovern *et al.*, "Bringing Customers into the Boardroom", *HBR* November 2004, pp. 70-81; R. T. Rust *et al.*, "Customer-Centered Brand Management", *HBR*, September 2004, pp. 110-120; R. Gulati and J. B. Oldroyd, "The Quest for Customer Focus", *HBR*, April 2005, pp. 92-101; W. McEwen *et al.*, "Inside the Mind of the Chinese Consumer", *HBR*, March 2006, pp. 68-76; J. C. Anderson *et al.*, "Customer Value Propositions in Business Markets", *HBR*, March 2006, pp. 91-99; P. Kreindler and G. Rajguru, "What B2B Customers Really Expect", *HBR*, April 2006, pp. 22-24; P. F. Nunes and W.W. Driggs, "What Serves Customer Best?", *HBR*, October 2006, pp. 37-50; C. Meyer and A. Schwager, "Understanding Customer Experience", *HBR*, February, 2007, pp. 116-126; Harrington R.J. and Tjan A.K., "Transforming Strategy One Customer at a Time", *HBR*, March, 2008, pp. 62-72; N. Howe and W. Strauss, "The Next 20 Years: How Customer and Workforce Attitudes Will Evolve", *HBR*, July-August 2007, pp. 41-60; P. Flatters and W. Willimott, "Understanding the Post-Recession Consumer", *HBR*, July-August 2009, pp. 106-112; E. Janszen, "Selling to the Debt-Averse Consumer", *HBR*, July-August, 2009, p. 113; R. Martin, "The Age of Customer Capitalism", *HBR*, January-February 2010, pp. 58-65; R.T. Rust, C. Moorman and G. Bhalia, "Rethinking Marketing", *HBR*, January-February 2010, pp. 96-101.

8 *HBR*, February 2010.

managers and customers to make logical decisions. In fact, proponents of the burgeoning field of behavioural economics (Ariely, 2009)[9] claim to have found the way to comprehend such conduct as a predominant mode of behaviour in organisational life. They argue for a necessary understanding of irrationality embedded in the fabric of organisations that is said to underlie employees' and customers' actions. The main premise for their assertion of irrationality lies in the discredited belief, according to them, that people (and organisations) acting in their best interest would continue to make rational decisions in any given circumstances. On the contrary, as the argument goes, given an opportunity, they will engage in the irrational behaviours, such as occasional cheating, desire for revenge, sabotaging of tasks, undermining competitors, and so on. However, we maintain, 'understanding of irrationality' would hardly enable organisations to navigate unpredictable business environments if the set neoliberal market orientation and ideologies of self-interest, as conceivably the bedrock of irrationality, continue to be asserted. On the contrary, it most likely would advance further management controls and promote marketing attempts to gain insight into people's 'unconscious cognitive biases' in service of "rational" markets. To make a claim that people are fundamentally irrational would be to engage in further attempts at symbolic and behavioural manipulation of organisational members for the sake of market dominance.

In the past year, there has been a call to understand the 'post-recession' consumer, characterized by 'new thriftiness', 'desire for simplicity' and in search of authenticity (Flatters and Willimott, 2009).[10] Organisational marketing executives are advised to reorganize their business practices in order to accommodate a less confident and debt averse consumer whose needs have shifted from boom time consumption and extreme experience-seeking to focus on value and utility over luxury and brand. Companies are advised to embrace newfound thriftiness as a consumer lifestyle choice rather than a constraint and a shortcoming imposed by the economic downturn. However, sidestepping a call for a radically new economic direction, sole change in marketing focus could hardly be expected to steer companies from a current impasse. Instead of looking reflexively at their own practices, within a specific socio-economic environment, organisations once again place consumers in a position that can be manipulated to either absorb further economic hits or save the company from its future loses.

---

9 *Ibid.* p. 78.

10 *HBR*, July-August, 2009.

Self-Entrepreneurship

Creating decentralized market-like processes within the boundaries of a single organisation and turning their employees into inside entrepreneurs organisations expect to raise efficiency and competitiveness in response to market unpredictability. People are asked to be versatile, quick thinkers, unattached to previous commitments and work in an organisation as if they are running their own business. Project based nature of work propels employees to "sell" themselves to others in order to be accepted to the project team, or to prove to the superiors that he or she 'adds value' to the company. Acting on a self-interest in their positions employees are expected to raise efficiency for the overall functioning of the company. However, individuated performance also means that a person takes on more risks and has to cope with more unforeseen consequences of the decisions that she was forced to make. Such an "enterprising self" is a calculating self that calculates and works upon itself to reach organisational goals based on self-interest (du Gay, 2000: 69). Self-entrepreneurship advocated by an economic organisation points to a rational individual who is given an illusion of independence, powerfulness and self-reliance, while in reality, she or he acts within a framework of tightly pre-determined strategies and economic goals of their firms that are now dependant on the volatile economic conditions. A person who is given a task to perform his job as a self-entrepreneur, in fact is agreeing to self-exploit and self-control by leading a functional, rational goal oriented life for the sake of his or her organisation. As Ulrich Beck puts it, one's life becomes a 'self-chosen life that is conceived of as the business plan of a one-person corporation'...'in conformity with market conditions' (Beck, 2000: 73-74).

Even though entrepreneurial strategy appears to be a current innovation, yet it preserves the established premises of a post-industrial organisation of the *first modernity*, since it does not address the social and economic foundations on which an organisation was built. Turning employees into inside entrepreneurs and transferring to them responsibility for their decision making, in organisations that continue to operate within rational-bureaucratic framework, is an attempt to re-establish but not fundamentally transform the existing management and decision-making structures, division of tasks, firmly established practices of strategic and financial planning, and especially conventional marketing strategies. In fact, organisational reliance on autonomous individuals as inside entrepreneurs who have to take responsibility for the effects of their own actions exposes organisations to increasing environmental uncertainty and brings turmoil into internal working relationships. Moreover, chiselling away emotion and subjectivity from one's own self image in order to meet organisational entrepreneurial expectations leaves one with the same default habits of authoritative certainty to fall onto, which fail to produce results during environmental shifts.

Organisational Contradictions: Control *vs.* Flexibility

Current conditions within today's organisations encompass and reflect organisational and market realities that embrace both, conventional as well as innovative strategies, and habitual as well as ground-breaking modes of reasoning, thus producing extensive contradictions in personal and organisational lives. As uncertainty enters organisational environments employees experience a covert and many times open conflict between several organisational demands, such as new market opportunities, expanding communications networks, new technology initiatives, and, on the other hand, previously established management control structures, entrenched job review and reward patterns, inflexible work roles and rules of subordination.

As our observations in several organisations showed, in face of increasing competition, directional unpredictability, and market volatility managerial control and command mechanisms as well as previously established hierarchical positions tend to be re-enforced in an attempt to eliminate looming ambiguity. Efforts to deal with uncertainty within organisations are often met with more rationalisations, which result in strengthening administrative control apparatus, passing on more directives and increasing supervision that consequently create more uncertainty and ambiguity.

This is a contradictory process, especially apparent at a medical IT firm that is changing its profile from production orientation into a global service oriented organisation. For instance, as new technological initiatives are introduced into organisational processes, they tend to penetrate all layers of the organisation and set an irreversible direction that is transforming the way it perceives its mission, its structure, its roles and role expectations. This forces the company to reflexively re-examine its basic premise and future direction. As they experience impasse and crisis, certain members of an upper management begin to realize that current organisational arrangements no longer work and new forms of work need to be introduced in order to manage the demanding workflows. However, instead of embarking on fundamental change in organisational direction and re-thinking their business model, many senior managers choose to re-enforce the existing business model by preserving previously established hierarchies. In order to control increasing workflows and processes of differentiation they establish new forms of supervision and through new hires add additional layers to organisational hierarchies.

At another healthcare organisation that is presented with a tremendous challenge to integrate new technology vital to its survival, new entrants are requested to possess leadership qualities and psychological capacities that enable them to bring change and help modify the established work pattern in order to accommodate these new technologies with several organisational levels in mind. Their newness to the field, guided by their extensive knowledge of the established occupational experiences, is perceived as an advantage to the organisation rather than a liability that needs to be overcome. However, as such newly hired employees continue taking innovative steps, the upper management often tries to put a stop to their initiatives and demand compliance, all of which points to the management's own resistance to change. Thus, in the conditions that lack transitory mechanisms an individual is forced to rely on and build from her own resources in order to maintain quality of work and integrity of a person, at the same time having to obey conflicting commands.

Such contradictions between empowering employees and making them more autonomous and flexible on the one hand, and setting controls and supervision on the other, is an overwhelming condition in many of today's organisations. Organisations that are slow or unwilling to change their guiding mode of operations and recognize the interdependence of all employees in generating organisational solutions, continue to enlist instrumental business rationality as an operating *raison d'être*. Hence, the dominating rational-bureaucratic framework and ideologies of self-interest remain intact and continue to inform various human resources initiatives and overwhelming number of consulting projects. Efficiency-oriented strategies that organisations undertake fail to address fundamental change dynamics. They tend to atomize employees and erode their sense of craftsmanship and collective responsibility. At the end, such organisations continue to preserve the basis of an existing hierarchical structure with its conventional bureaucratic work practices.

Atomisation, an Unintended Consequence

As volatile market dynamics enters internal functioning of an organisation, it has a defining influence on people's lives and behaviour inside and outside their organisation. While new priorities nationally and globally are given to the economic problems and interests, organisations generally follow the model of operations that is familiar to them, but impose higher expectations and stringent criteria of judgment upon their members. Despite unconventional rhetoric decision makers on the upper levels of an organisation in their practice continuously employ a customary bureaucratic logic and a set point of view that excludes majority of employees from participation in the decision making process. Paradoxically, the majority is asked to quickly implement and adapt to the proposed changes with no time allotted for developing a meaningful rationale for doing so and no clear guidance from the superiors. As a result, people have difficulty in maintaining loyalty to their place of work, which produces anxiety and uncertain expectations. This contributes to the erosion of employee commitment to the organisational ideals and purposes and overwhelming feelings of powerlessness and dependency that many employees experience. On the other hand there are those employees who devote majority of their life to the work requirements and construct their life story in reference to their jobs. But given the nature of uncertain demands and increasing stress of the new economic enterprise such dedicated but mostly unrecognized engagements may eventually strip employees of meaning for their work. For as, the reality of who one is at work and what one does is very different from who one imagines as being and doing (Sennett, 2000).

Thus, whereas some members of an organisation express a desire to actively participate in its transformational processes, many others feel excluded, silenced and left on the sidelines. In most cases, however, people in their organisational lives are not fully aware of the roles they have embraced and do not question the reasons and motivations while carrying out their daily duties. The largest majority of employees develop a capacity to use the codes and behavioural expectations of their workplaces in their private lives, invent overlapping patterns, manipulate course of events and in this way neutralize the internal split between the habitual ways of working and new economic and social expectations that are bestowed upon them. By allowing their selves to be unquestionably absorbed by the cultural and organisational belief systems many of them create internal defences against outer experiences, perceived as threats to their identity, which leaves them unable to take required risks or accept difference. Through subliminal internalisation of market behaviour outside control turns into self-control, which contributes to acceptance and reification of rigid bureaucratic rules while adding to the persistence of organisational hierarchies. Moreover, their resistance to accept difference and unwillingness or inability to embrace diverse experiences further contribute to the employees' atomisation and a loss of initiative, gradually resulting into a persistent feeling of exclusion and ever-increasing sense of personal isolation (*see*, for example, Sennett, 2006).

In theory, organisations seek out and value socially aware individuals who act from the point of view of their own subjectivity, always in relationship to others, and display initiative and creativity in their thinking and acting. However, by embarking on efficiency-oriented strategies and by de-personalizing their members, organisations embrace neoliberal orientation that inhibits change and forces organisational members to preserve the foundations of structural hierarchies and modes of thinking on which their organisations were built. Contrary to the overwhelming demand for a new organisational and social dynamics neoliberal orientation does not support an emergence of self-motivating, self-determining and *self-reflexive individuals*, who are consciously aware of their social conditions and systems of deterministic categorisations of which they are all a part. Authority and leadership that is spread throughout the networked enterprise often fails to provide the necessary recognition, responsibility and follow-up for the work that the employees carry out, which leaves the workers inert or unwilling to move forward. Working in an organisation that is unclear in its authority structures and its strategic direction creates tremendous conflict for employees' self-understanding and self worth that play back onto organisational self-understanding (Sennett, 2000). Moreover, individualized approaches and autonomous decision making in carrying out the tasks are often perceived by the managers as a threat to their authority that have to be managed out of the employees in order to "keep them in line" with the rest of organisational policies. Hence, managerial attempts to reduce complexity and eliminate ambiguity in company's operations eventually lead to the exclusion of the majority of employees from participation in setting an organisational direction and contribute to an erosion of ownership of their work results and subsequent contributions to an organisational life. What follows is a process of atomisation, isolation and an ensuing loss of initiative and certainty that produces insecurity and anxiety among organisational members. Atomized individuals that are requested to participate in neoliberal economic projects increasingly experience exclusion from the strategic decision making processes, fear of slippage and angst of losing the ground on which their economic survival is based. Ironically, this forces people to become even more reliant on market forces and economic deregulations.

Individualism vs. Individualisation

Individualism based on exclusion and self-centeredness, as a characteristic of the *first modernity* has been a predominant pattern in modern society, and continues to have a strong hold in today's organisations, who embrace neoliberal orientation and advocate self-entrepreneurship. Roles as the main component of organisational structure of the *first modernity* not only hold organisations in shape but continue to provide direction to individual lives. To fit into an organisational structure means to successfully role-play various recognizable parts that keep shared institutionalized meanings intact.

Individualism and atomisation point to uprooted, atomized individuals whose existence and survival in the globalised market economy depend on instrumental rationality and ideologies of self-interest. However, the logic of rational self-interest on which individualism is based misses the whole array of references that one's subjectivity relies on. An actor who makes choices from the available options as well as invented alternatives is not necessarily a rational individual who acts on his own self-interest. Individual consciousness, broadly understood as '*being and acting in the world*' (Keen, 1992) entails not only rational, cognitive premise on which instrumental action is based but also affectual and ethical dimensions and regard for the *other* that are enacted in the process of *individualisation*. Thus, as institutionalized meanings and categorical determinants are gradually brought into awareness and challenged by the new realities, structure of *individuation* as the core of the Enlightenment ideology (Lash, 1999) is being challenged in the *second modernity* by dissolving rigid role based practices and questioning pre-given social and economic expectations.

Individualisation and subjectivity that I refer to is characterized by the reference to one's self, always in relation to the *other*, and not to the external demands. Contrary to individualism, conception of *individualisation* (*see*, Beck and Beck-Gernsheim, 2002) that emphasizes a greater self-reliance and self-expression, based on one's individuality and intersubjectivity stands in opposition to the notions of individualism within the established system of traditional roles and pre-determined tasks. Individualisation at work that is marked by a self-conscious, self-organised, and self-realized existence based on a free choice and interrelationship with others, invokes a desire for an active participation in organisational change processes. It stands in opposition to a controlling, rationalising subject of the Enlightenment. When economic and cultural globalisation begins to shake the taken-for-granted individual and institutional convictions and assurances, desire for individualisation comes as a response to failed search for certainty that was so indefatigably promised by neo-liberal and communitarian ideologies. Such shifting dynamics, it seems to me, is a sign of the current times where failed promise for certainty is confronted with a need to 'make peace' with uncertain realities. Hence, it is not *individuation* of the Enlightenment period, but *individualisation* as the outcome of reflexive processes of the *second modernity* that becomes the basis for an epistemological, moral, conscious self, which emerges as a result of stripping away categorical impositions and, through greater awareness of itself and the other, is capable to confront conflicting outside pressures. One of such systemic pressures, described above, is an overwhelming demand for employees to become "enterprising" individuals for the company's sake. Although such a request appears to place the focus on one's individual capabilities to manage oneself in a role, it is, however, based on a preset, rigid idea of individualism and preconceived notions of rational, individual needs and self-interests. In this way, a person would be considered a passive organism whose corporate subjectivity ('soul') and self ('ego') can be packaged and manipulated by the external market dynamics and strategic organisational projects. In such employee/consumer "construction" process there is no place for ethics or higher levels of awareness, nor there is a place for a common sense logic. Moreover, attempting to understand 'embedded irrationality' (Ariely, 2009) as well as engaging in 'symbolic expertise' (du Gay, 2000), mentioned above, which are exercised by the organisational experts, could go only so far as the consumer and the employee, both are willing to respond in pre-calculated and pre-determined ways to market manoeuvrings. Paradoxically, the side effect of such "manipulations" may be an increase in levels of individual awareness and a desire for a conscious living, free of imposed categorical constraints that stifle creativity. The skills of becoming a 'sovereign' consumer or a 'sovereign' employee may not bring ultimate fulfilment to an individual who lives her life reflexively and makes her choices through reference to one's self. Instead of becoming an economized or "economically corrupted" individual, one may choose an ethical life and engage into the process of creating new ways of working that contribute to the common good. Similarly, an organisation could begin to recognize its employees as well as consumers and clients not as fixed ego driven subjects but as reflexive agents, capable of tolerating competing interpretations, who in their responses combine typical as well as arbitrary, irregular as well as habitual, rational as well as unreasonable behaviours that cannot be managed into typified responses but have to be approached in complex and creative ways.

Individualisation and Atomisation – a Contradictory Coexistence

Paradigmatic shift from the *first* to the *second modernity* is not an evolutionary transition from one stage of development to the next one, but a mutually inclusive socio-economic transformation. Conceptually, it embraces both, old and new types of action and patterns of thinking that remain intertwined on different levels of social life (Beck, 2004: 30-32). Both, individualized and collective, uncertain and predictable modes of existence and work are a part of the new paradigm of the *second modernity* organisation. Thus, to pursue Ulrich Beck's insight, *individualisation* as a process of liberation from traditional role and task constraints continues to be dependent on the pre-existing institutional arrangements and employment market that require consistent typified behaviour and standardisation of roles and positions. This creates a contested space for contradictory social dynamics that could proceed either way – by reifying control and command mechanisms and contributing to employee atomisation on the one hand, or opening space for innovative and individualized work processes, on the other.

Volatile market behaviour has placed new demands on organisations that, as successful practices show, can be best met by enlisting employee initiative and creativity that are based on individualized responses and trust. However, managerial answer to the new impending challenges frequently comes from customary work practices, inflexible business structures and habitual modes of thinking that no longer produce desired results.

Recent calls for companies to re-engage their people and to rethink both management and leadership needs, and promote the atmosphere of trust and initiative has been loud and clear.[11] Research in present day organisations shows that individualisation as an emergent characteristic of current organisational and social realities does not threaten organisational collaboration, team work and collective responsibility in organisations that open themselves to new challenges and embrace risk as an ingredient of new economic reality. More so, people seek out workplaces where they can exercise their creativity, contribute to positive changes while being flexible, working remotely but also being able to deeply connect with their colleagues. *Adaptive* leadership (Heifetz *et al.*, 2009) that embraces disequilibrium and uncertainty as a part of changing and challenging business world is considered much better equipped to mobilize people's creativity, commitment and trust in their own and organisational capacities. Loyalty to an organisation is not replaced or discarded, but is supplemented by a desire for individual learning and individualisation, belonging and self-reliance that an organisation embraces as part of its new robust culture. The *old* is not replace by the *new* but embraces both to create a new socio-economic reality. Hence, an answer to contemporaneous challenges often lies not in pursuing new results with the old tools but having the courage to risk new solutions to the old problems.

Conclusion: "New" Organisational Employee

The new conditions of a connected world require creative response and understanding not just of macro processes but of how mentalities are shaped and cultivated. Changing organisational *modus operandi* from the production oriented industrial pattern to service and technological orientation bring fundamental changes not only in the internal functioning of organisations, but also in the social consciousness of its

---

[11] *HBR*, July-August, 2009.

participants who are required to have new cognitive and emotional skills to deal with the fluctuating market demands in day-to-day situations. Awareness applies not only to individuals but also to collectivities. Organisations as collective entities can no longer respond inertly to the outside influences, but have to exercise innovation and reflexivity to weigh opportunities and threats. In the new social and economic conditions, no longer normative structures, rigid expectations or taken-for-granted assumptions are able to provide behavioural guidance that produces desired results. Only situational negotiation and acceptance of difference as a constitutive part of one's subjectivity enable one to make sense of surrounding confusion. The basis of organisational work becomes conscious reciprocal coordination of various duties, perspectives and tasks among its members. In thinking about the organisations there needs to be a change in understanding that brings to awareness a shift from reification and embeddedness to uncertainty and reflexivity, from bounded social organisation to change in the nature of social, conceptual and natural boundaries.

Empirical realities demonstrate that organisations of today operate with revisable rules open to interpretation and modification, requiring people to have flexible orientations. Hence, there is a rising need for new conceptual models of understanding as well as for practical tools in managing change that draws from various social science and managerial disciplines. When decisions are made and passed on using the fixed rule-based categorical framework, at the time when a new interpenetrating logic is in demand, validation for the impending changes comes in the form of directives and their execution is based on subconsciously concealed fear of losing a job or even a life purpose. Powerlessness and dependency are direct consequences of unquestioned and unreflexive actions of the members of an organisation that threaten the basis for one's subjectivity.

The challenge for organisations is to create a framework of predictability but leave space for self-organisation, where employers and employees are expected to exercise their creativity and feel ownership in organisational outcomes. Hence, we may suggest, that the *second modernity* gives rise to an organisational 'person', 'self-referential subject' (Touraine, 2000) that is asked to operate independently, with multiple knowledge sets, emphasize knowledge flows instead of specialisation, and develop a new kind of psychic structure that brings to awareness an embedded organisational resistance to change, and enables qualitatively new relationships and interactions among economic agents, that are based on trust, respect and ethics of choice.[12] In this respect, organisational collaboration and collective responsibility is not an opposite to individualisation and subjectivity but a combined state of individualised working and acting that emerges as a logical outcome of a symbiotic, ontological relationship between subject and object, self and other, and is based on interdependence of individualised projects.

We may further propose that a new form of individual agency, based on subjectivity and claims of individualisation is attempting to take form within organisations, which poses a challenge to the existing institutional and organisational imperatives. Choosing to make sense of social ambiguity is choosing to participate in the process of individualisation and structural transformation. This means, that increasingly people in organisations are relying less on what is ascribed to them and is expected of them, but instead are building upon their own unique subjecthood, identities and self-referentiality that includes recognition of the other. This self-referentiality overturns notions that individual agency and one's place in the world is constituted of and dependent on a web of complex technologies, subjugations and normative behaviour. It redirects our attention to sociology of subjectivity in organisational life that emerges through and is rife with role conflicts, flexible demands on workers, and continual interplay of old skills, new technology, innovation and knowledge. Moreover, in relationship to the conditions of reconfigured modernity emergence of a *"new" employee* puts pressure on organisations, forcing them to become reflexive. To what extent organisations are able to create the space for self-reflexive agents or 'self-referential subjects' will very much account for the identity and direction of an impending organisational dynamics. The type of business logic (or logics) that an organisation develops in order to deal with its challenges will essentially define its future role and a degree of influence that an organisation will have in the global marketplace.

References

Amabile, T. and Kramer, S., "Inner work Life. Understanding the Subtext of Business Performance", in *Harvard Business Review*, May, 2007, pp. 72-83.

Ariely, D., "The End of Rational Economics", in *Harvard Business Review*, July-August, 2009, pp. 78-83.

Barnard, I. C., *The Functions of the Executive*, Cambridge, Mass. & London, England, Harvard University Press, (1938) 1968.

Bauman, Z., *The Individualized Society*, Cambridge, UK, Blackwell, 2001.

---

[12] See, for example, Amabile, T. and Kramer S., *HBR*, 5:2007; Gardner, H., *HBR*, 3:2007; Rooke and Torbert, *HBR*, 4:2005; also Leonard and Swap, *HBR*, 9:2004; Heifetz, *et al.*; Hewlett, *et. al.*, *HBR*, 7-8:2009.

Beck, U., Giddens, A. and Lash S., *Reflexive Modernisation: Politics, Tradition and Aesthetics in the Modern Social Order*, Stanford, CA, Stanford University Press, 1994.

Beck, U., *The Brave New World of Work*, Cambridge, Polity Press, 2000.

Beck, U. and Beck-Gernsheim, E., *Individualisation. Institutionalized Individualism and its Social and Political Consequences*, London, Thousand Oaks and New Delhi, Sage Publications, 2002.

Beck, U. and Willms, J., *Conversations with Ulrich Beck*, Cambridge, UK, Polity Press, 2004.

Case, P., "From Objectivity to Subjectivity: Pursuing *Subjective Authenticity* in Organisational Research", in R. Westwood and S. Clegg, (eds.), *Debating Organisation. Point-Counterpoint in Organisational Studies*, Oxford, Blackwell Publishing, 2003, pp. 156-180.

Casey, C., *Critical Analysis of Organisations, Theory, Practice, Revitalisation*, London, Thousand Oaks, New Delhi, Sage Publications, 2002.

Castells, M., *The Rise of the Network Society*. Vol. 1 of *The Information Age: Economy, Society and Culture*, Blackwell Publishers, 1996.

DiMaggio, P. (ed.), *The Twenty-First-Century Firm: Changing Economic Organisation in International Perspective*, Princeton, New Jersey, Princeton University Press, 2001.

Gardner, H., "The Ethical Mind", in *Harvard Business Review*, March, 2007, pp. 51-56.

du Gay, P., "Markets and Meanings: Re-Imagining Organisational Life", in M. Schultz, M. Jo Hatch, and M. Holten Larsen (eds.), *The Expressive Organisation. Linking Identity, Reputation, and Corporate Bond*, Oxford U. Press, 2000, pp. 66-74.Guillen, M. F., Randall C., England P. and Meyer M. (eds.), *The New Economic Sociology: Developments in an Emerging Field*, New York, Russell Sage Foundation, 2002.

Heifetz, R., *et al.*, "Leadership in a (Permanent) Crisis", in *Harvard Business Review*, July-August, 2009.

Keen, E., "Being Conscious is Being-in-the-World", in F. S. Kessel, P. M. Cole and D. L. Johnson (eds.), *Self and Consciousness. Multiple Perspectives*. Hove and London, Lawrence Erlbaum Associates, 1992, pp. 45-63.

Kumar, K., *From post-Industrial to Post-Modern Society: New Theories of the Contemporary World*, Second Edition, Oxford, UK, Blackwell Publishing, 2005.

Lash, S., *Another Modernity a Different Rationality*, Oxford, Blackwell, 1999.

Lash, S., *Critique of Information*, London-Thousand Oaks-New Delhi, Sage Publications, 2002.

Leonard, D. and Swap, W. "Deep Smarts", in *Harvard Business Review*, September 2004, pp. 88-97.

Levit, T., "Marketing Myopia", in *Harvard Business Review*, July-August 2004, pp. 138-149.

McGovern, G., *et al.*, "Bringing Customers into the Boardroom", in *Harvard Business Review*, November, 2004, pp. 70-81.

Mead, G. H., *Mind, Self and Society: From the Standpoint of Social Behaviorist*, Chicago and London, The University of Chicago Press, 1934.

Menzies-Lyth, I., *The Dynamics of the Social*, London, Free Association Books, 1989.

Meyer, C. and Schwager, A., "Understanding Customer Experience", in *Harvard Business Review*, February, 2007, pp. 126.

O'Reilly III, C. and M.L. Tushman, "The Ambidextrous Organisation", in *Harvard Business Review*, April 2004.

Palmisano, S.J., "The HBR Interview: Leading Change When Business is Good", in *Harvard Business Review*, December 2004, pp. 59-70.

Powell, W. W. and P. J. DiMaggio (eds.), *The New Institutionalism in Organisational Analysis.* Chicago and London, The University of Chicago Press, 1991.

Rooke, D. and W.R. Torbert, "Seven Transformations of Leadership", in *Harvard Business Review*, April 2005, pp. 67-76.

Rust, T.R., *et al.*, "Customer-Centered Brand Management", in *Harvard Business Review*, September, 2004, pp. 110-120.

Sassen, S., *Territory, Authority, Rights. From Medieval to Global Assemblages*, Princeton and Oxford, Princeton University Press, 2006.

Schultz, M., Hatch, M.J. and Larsen, M.H. (eds.), *The Expressive Organisation. Linking Identity, Reputation, and Corporate Bond*, Oxford U. Press, 2000.

Sennett, R., *The Corrosion of Character: The Personal Consequences of Work in the New Capitalism*, New York and London, W.W. Norton & Company, Inc., 2000 (1998).

Sennett, R., *The Culture of the New Capitalism*, New Haven & London, Yale University Press, 2006.

Shorto, R., "With God at Our Desks. The Rise of Religion and Evangelism in the American Workplace", in *The New York Times Magazine*, October 31: 2004, p. 42.

Thomas W. M., "Bringing the Market Inside", in *Harvard Business Review*, April 2004, pp. 106-115.

Thomas J., *et al.*, "Getting the Most of All Your Customers", in *Harvard Business Review*, July-August, 2004, pp. 116-123.

Thomke, S. and von Hippel, E., "Customers as Innovators: a New Way to Create Value", in *Harvard Business Review*, April 2002, pp. 74-81.

Touraine, A., *Can We Live Together? Equality and Difference*, Stanford, California, Stanford University Press, 2000.

Touraine, A., *New Paradigm for Understanding Today's World*, Cambridge, UK and Maden, MA, Polity Press, 2007.

Westwood, R. and Clegg S. (eds.), *Debating Organisation. Point-Counterpoint in Organisation Studies*, Blackwell Publishing, Ltd, 2003.

PART III. B

AUTONOMY AND CAPITALISM

Limits of Fulfilment in an Age of Flexibility

Changes in Management Semantics and the Critique of Capitalism

Christoph HENNING

University of St. Gallen (CH), Philosophy Department[1]

In recent years various trends (such as the globalisation of financial markets, the triumph of the shareholder value approach in management or the economic impact of the internet) have significantly changed the social organisation of labour worldwide. But capitalism has not only changed its face; it has also grown in strength: the Nation-State has lost or withdrawn from many of its regulating capacities, the political and economic power of large corporations has increased, and in many Western countries alternatives to market capitalism (e.g. the welfare state as a major provider for alternative ways of living, or labour unions as an effort of increasing the "voice" of workers) are shrinking. The resent crisis demonstrated this invigorated power of global capitalism, only in an unpleasant way. All of this is well known. Now, one could have expected that these changes would lead to an increase in critical perspectives on modern society, both politically and theoretically. And there are, indeed, new critical voices, as the annual meetings of the World Social Forum demonstrate.[2] But compared to the *dimensions* of change and the resulting economic hardships for so many people, the level of criticism is relatively low, both in size and in its theoretical prominence. In the United States, for example, where the welfare reforms were among the harshest worldwide, they met comparatively little resistance from the population concerned.

According to Boltanski and Chiapello (2007: 36), who analysed the changes in management semantics in great detail, in order to transform

---

1 This paper is based on a presentation held in Stockholm in 2005. Much has been written on this topic since, but I believe my conceptual approach is not redundant yet.

2 See www.forumsocialmundial.org.br or www.weltsozialforum.de or journals like www.redpepper.org.uk.

feelings of indignation into an effectual social criticism a theoretical framework is needed. And for them the most important theoretical frameworks for criticism have suffered several defeats in the 1990s. They distinguish two families of criticism: a "social critique", demanding more equality and mainly driven by the labour movement, and an "artistic critique" (2007: 38), demanding more autonomy and mainly driven by intellectuals and bohemians. Moreover, they diagnose a "neutralisation"-crisis in *both* families. Though this observation is true, I disagree with the reasons they give. Neither has "artistic" critique become obsolete because of its seeming actualisation in the new spirit of capitalism (as they suggest at times, 2007: 419; or at least as some sympathetic readers interpreted the argument), nor does "social" critique need to be completely overhauled due to fundamental structural changes, as Boltanski/Chiapello indicate at times (2007: 346f., e.g.) – at least not if that implies the replacement of key concepts. I want to claim that even in the face of the enormous changes in the labour world the older vocabulary of the critical tradition does not need to be abandoned. The paper aims to demonstrate this. Once these terms are reinstated the two separate streams of criticism can also be reunited.

Is the Restructuring of Labour the End for Artistic Criticism?

What is the argument for the – almost Hegelian – thesis of an 'realisation' of the earlier social criticism from the artistic standpoint in modern management approaches?[3] This criticism was based on the perfectionist idea of self-realisation, an actualisation of all human potentials; an idea developed in the renaissance and enlightenment (e.g. Rousseau and Condorcet), later found in early Socialist writings (e.g. William Godwin and Charles Fourier) and 19th century Romanticism (e.g. Carlyle, Ruskin and William Morris), and maintained by various generations of *avant-garde* thereafter. Industrial labor of the 19th century and the typical Fordist job on an assembly line in the early 20th century had very little in common with this idea indeed, so this criticism was very relevant most of the time. Sometimes such ideas even came from a management perspective, as classically described by Reinhard Bendix.[4] However, several changes occurred in the nature of jobs and in the organisation of work in recent decades, allowing for more self-realisation *within* the job. A standard term for this trend is "flexibility" (Sennett, 1998), meaning that workers have to be able to constantly

3 "As for the artistic critique, its crisis was, rather, the result of its seeming success and the ease with which it found itself recuperated and exploited by capitalism" (Boltanski/Chiapello, 2007, 326).

4 Bendix, 1956, later on repackaged by Illouz, 2007. Also see Cometta, 2009.

adapt to new tasks and situations. In order to make the argument of a institutional 'realisation' of a pre-existing concept, the work-related flexibility found in current conditions needs to sufficiently resemble the former demands for autonomy made by the artistic critical approach. At a closer look, that does not prove to be the case.

The turn to flexibility implies several things: First, technology has developed. New production technologies involve an increasing amount of computer technology so that, unsurprisingly, some companies shifted towards producing and selling knowledge-related services (the so-called 'knowledge economy'). Jobs in these sectors call for more creativity than the traditional jobs on the assembly line.[5] As, secondly, the service sector's share in the economy increased sharply in the 20th century, this trend has become dominant. Even in the industrial sector, we now find a growing demand for more individualistic and creative forms of work, though to a lower degree.[6] In addition, the average level of education amongst workers has increased since the 1960s, so that today more people have the *ability* to work on different parts, and also wish to be more creative on the job.[7] This "normative subjectivation" (Baethge, 1991) means that employees themselves ask for more responsibility. So we have a shift in sectors, new technologies, a demand for "new labour" and an increased supply of employable persons with higher education. If we add the crisis in profitability since the 1970s (Brenner, 2002), which called for an increase in the rate of exploitation, we have mentioned the major conditions that allowed for the 'new' management techniques which became so widespread since the early 1980s, inspired from Japanese lean production models and Silicon Valley philosophies.

The effects were twofold. First, most types of labour are increasingly individualised as modern management techniques appreciate individual talents and workers' 'tacit knowledge' to a much greater extent and therefore try to *incorporate* them. Workers are involved in broader parts of the production process (this is called process management, management by objectives, empowerment strategies, human capital approach, etc.). In other words, it is no longer only *a part* of the person that is meant to be employed, but companies are now "employing the whole man" (Drucker, 1954: 227ff.), including her/his feelings and an ever larger share of her/his private life. Workers today are asked to take over

---

5 Reich, 1991; Pettinger, 2005, or, much earlier, Riesman, 1950 and Whyte, 1956. For Germany see Schmiede, 1996; Konrad/Schumm, 1999 or Menez/Töpsch, 2003.

6 See Moldaschl 2003 or, much earlier, Hillmann, 1970 and Friedman, 1977.

7 See the "changing values"-thesis 40 years ago (Inglehart, 1971). More recent studies showed that the new, supposedly "post-materialistic" elites aimed to work *more*, not less (Heidenreich, 1996). It is an effect of getting paid more that money counts less (the marginal utility falls), so in the effect, this is no clear-cut "post-materialism".

more responsibility, not only in their jobs, but also outside them, for example by taking precautions for their pension schemes or in case of illness.[8] This higher responsibility of every single working unit in turn also leads to a recombination of organisational tools – new, informal forms of co-operation (the 'network') have often taken over the part of the formal organisation. Teams are created that work together for a limited time and which are responsible not only for part(s) of a product, but for a whole product itself, while more than one profit centres work competitively *within* one company. In this way, personal relations (with team members, customers or superiors) count a lot more than before. Yet another dimension of the worker's personality, namely her/his ability to socialise, is subsumed under the labour process to a much larger degree than before. These are the first set of changes that motivated the idea of an end of artistic criticism: the incorporation of autonomy, authenticity, creativity – and even emancipation – into the working life seemed to leave pretty little to 'actualise', so this criticism no longer seemed relevant (cf. Honneth, 2002). The first question is: can this critique nevertheless be maintained, and if so, how?

The Hegemony of the Management Discourse in the Workplace

Up to now, we have not used any particular social theory; we only described the changes from the perspective of everyday life, without judging them either morally or theoretically. There is a reason for this theoretical abstinence: a lot is lost, in terms of theory, if we move from simple descriptions to the level of theory too quickly. If we look at the explanations and answers that social and economic theory can offer, we no longer find many critical contributions at the theoretical level, for the reason mentioned above. We do find descriptions of these processes, as well as *value judgements*, i.e. whether somebody approves or disapproves of what is happening. But that alone does not constitute a critical theory of labour market restructuring. Herein lies the persisting weakness of current critical theories from the artistic tradition: many of the old critical concepts (like autonomy) only seem to duplicate in theoretical terms what is happening in practice anyway. New critical concepts are still lacking.[9] There are various explanations for this weakness. One is the assumption that in some respects the world is really getting better

[8] The 'end of welfare as we knew it' in the USA came with a personal responsibility act in 1996. See Goodin/Schmitz, 1998 or Gilbert, 2004.

[9] This weakness concerns post-Marxist and Foucauldian traditions alike. The latter has theoretical difficulties legitimizing a criticism of what they describe as "subjectivation". If taken seriously, this approach does not allow for a non-socialized residue within the subject that could resist (Moldaschl, 2003; cf. Honneth, 1985).

and that the critical *habitus* has consequently lost its relevance.[10] Even though this may not seem likely in general, there is a kernel of truth in this claim.

Another possibility would be that high gloss management theories are not the best source for judging real-world practices in the workplace itself. Management theory is instrumental from the start. It is not a pure "description", but it carries a clear interest. Hence the first objection to the actualisation thesis: instrumentalised autonomy is not autonomy proper.[11] But what *is* the interest in this case? Can we ascribe a social function to modern management? From the perspective of the owners of capital, as presupposed in the principal-agent theory, the picture is clear: higher returns on direct investment – be it machines, offices or a multitude of employees – suppose either investing in better equipment, or convincing workers that they should either work for less, work extra shifts or work more intensely. The latter is the easier way, as one cannot bargain with machines – one can only buy or improve them, both for a lot of money. If one therefore chooses to extract more from the hired labour power, one might either provide workers with better resources (be it machines like a computer), a better working environment or more time, all of which is expensive once again. Alternatively, one may try to get all of this *without* increasing one's own costs. Marx called this the "intensification of labour".[12] How does this work? The improvement of machines necessitates scientists and technicians (and indeed this field is growing, too). For its part, the improvement of working conditions calls for the advice of a psychologist.

So what is the function of management? What management does in relation to labour is at least twofold: it organizes the hired employees in such a way that in the end they work more efficiently at any given time, and it extracts more labour time out of the individual labour power that is bought. So in order to increase returns on investments, one hires a management that is able (or at least claims to be able) to do that.[13]

Where does this miraculous ability come from? One element of many optimizing strategies is surely to sublimely increase the pressure on workers' performance (the 'stick'). As a last instance, employees

---

10 An illustration may be found in Jonathan Franzen's novel: *The Corrections* (2001). Arguing from such assumptions, the end of critical theory was proclaimed by Sloterdijk, 1999; Bolz, 1999; Horx, 2001 or Schulze, 2003.

11 See the criticism in Wolf, 2004: 228; cf. Pongratz/Voss, 1997.

12 Karl Marx, *Capital*, London, 1887 (MEGA II.9, Berlin, 1990), 357.

13 This raises the question whether management itself is "productive". It helps extract more surplus labour time (see the labour process debate), or it provides images for the financial market that in the future this will be so, but in a strict sense this is not "productive labour", as it only increases the productivity of the work of others.

must be in fear of the ultimate choice, even if it is not explicit: either you follow, or you are fired. There are many ways to do that, even within fixed contracts – this is what business students actually study. Currently, workers' political rights and legal protections (designed to counterbalance exactly such situations, where their weakness can be exploited) are under attack in many countries, which clearly increases the power of management in the workplace. The higher the unemployment rate, the more serious this threat becomes – and in Europe, for instance, the rate oscillates around 8.5%,[14] so the pure *threat* of being laid off is already a very powerful weapon in the hands of business executives. In fact, executives often executed this threat over the last two decades: many companies laid off labour in enormous numbers. This initiated a fashion amongst professionals (success was sometimes measured in the number of layoffs), even if this fashion was instantly naturalised as 'competitiveness'.[15]

The tricky thing with employees is that they are neither things nor machines – this is why the economic term 'human capital' is so cynical: it reifies persons into disposable items. The human capital of a worker is initially considered as being nil, so long as no 'upgrading' measures are taken.[16] So management runs the risk of inducing *resistance* if it downsizes too aggressively. The second dimension management needs to organize, in parallel, results from this risk of scaring the staff too thoroughly: a major task is to manufacture consent (Buroway, 1979). Even if, or especially if layoffs are planned, executives need to organise *compliance* amongst employees and workers. Thus as far as management is not only concerned with technical issues, this implies a large degree of rhetoric (Kieser, 1996). Management needs to develop and establish a new world-view (the 'carrot'), according to which workers and politicians may believe that what happens is not only best for their company, let alone owners and shareholders, but is at some point good for the employed, too. In Althusserian terms, management theories function here as an ideological apparatus. This often works in isolated cases of corporations, yet it is also effective on a much broader political scale (Resch, 2005). As a famous myth goes, if 'the economy' as a whole needs to recover, in order to serve the nation workers need to

14 According to www.wko.at/statistik/eu/europa-arbeitslosenquoten.pdf.

15 This has unintended side effects: when in a boom phase more labour is needed, there might be a shortage of *qualified* labour if "free labour" has not been able to keep track of technical changes. So the "breathing" (i.e. hire and fire) company may prove to be quite inflexible. As a result, companies will try to externalise the costs of educational training to the community (an exploitation of public funds for private gain; cf. Bollier, 2002). For the culture of lay-off see the movie *Up in the* Air (2009).

16 This was elected the bad-taste term of the year ("Unwort des Jahres") 2004 by high officials of the cultural sector in Germany.

discipline themselves and work for less. This has become the dominant view in the media in many countries. Management has won a position of hegemony not only in the workplace, but on a social level too. The exceedingly high management salaries may well be a result of this.

Of course the new management theory did not *create* the new situation. The new technologies, the new qualifications and pretensions of the working population and the profit crises obviously were there before. What the new management 'managed' was to find new approaches in the *organisation* of labour and to win a position of hegemony in political thinking. Following this semantic, nowadays the individuality of a worker is included in the workplace, and the responsibility for shortcomings is also increasingly shifted to the individual. But is this really a 'realisation' of the earlier humanism and hippie utopia? Social theory can only interpret the changes if it takes into account the dialectics between ideology and social processes. The social effects of this change in semantics are not as clearly cut. The actualisation thesis may very well capture semantics only, without catching the real social costs. Does this linguistic game not mantle reality? And why does social theory often tend to overlook this gap? A possible answer could be that the social hegemony of the management discourse has also managed to affect social theory.

The Hegemony of the Management Discourse in Social Theory

Obviously, if – and only if – one takes liberation management (Peters, 1992) at face value, a critical semantic relying on the same conceptual sources as these management theories seems *prima facie* to be useless. Bearing in mind the mentioned crisis of the artistic critical theory, could these semantic changes have had such an impact on social theory? Could this 'buying into' the semantics of management be a reason for the crisis? How are we to understand the mechanisms?

A first consideration concerns the transfer mechanism. What allows for this transfer from shifts in management semantics to social theory? Basically there are two ways that could permit this transfer of Trojan concepts from management to social theory. One aspect that might explain the missing distance is the career path of some consultants: young sociology researchers of management trends may well end up in the management business themselves, or at least intend doing this, so too much 'distance' (which is the lifeblood of sociology) would clearly send out the wrong signals. Given the possibility of transforming the cultural capital of investigating society's prestigious spheres (management, financial markets, business consultancies, brokers, etc.; see Minssen, 2006: 196ff.) into the social capital of networks and eventually into the economic capital of 'getting a job' (to cite Mark Granovetter) in these same prestigious spheres, it is no wonder that a researcher might have little reason to overtly object semantic trends in these spheres. (And of course it becomes more attractive to study the behaviour of bankers in Hongkong than to study workers, say, in India.) This is an argument *ad hominem* only, yet for a self-reflexive sociology of knowledge in the tradition of Karl Mannheim this factor has to be considered, as it may explain emotional bindings of world-views.

Another way to explain this transfer of world-views from management to social sciences is a certain poverty of theory when it comes to social structures. Various influential post-Marxist approaches have replaced the seeming objectivism of some Marxist traditions (which, for example, reduced many phenomena to anonymous functions of capital or class struggle) with an inverted approach, which in effect lost sight of objective structures. British cultural studies, for example, concentrated on the media (Fiske, 1987), French post-structuralism often confined itself to analyzing texts or discourses, and German systems theory turned from social structures to "semantics" as the new field of research (Luhmann, 1980). What remains unclear in these academic fashions is the relation of changes in *semantics* to the changes in the real world. It is easy to see why it has become unfashionable to probe in this way – what seems to lurk in the background is an all too simplistic 'objectivism' of base and superstructure that undercuts the cultural turn. But classical Marxism had more in store than reductionist approaches – the theory of ideology, for instance, was intended to explain such tensions between theoretical utopias and real world miseries. When we fail to draw a distinction *between* discursive and structural changes, the alternative trap is an equally simplistic idealism that confounds theoretical or semantic changes with structural ones. The very possibility of an ideological function of management theory can only be considered if we do not exclude structures from the start, due to preliminary conceptual predefinitions. This does not necessarily lead to an objectivist simplification: on the contrary, it opens up new interpretations of the changes in semantics that Boltanski and Chiapello so saliently described.

To recapitulate: if social theory basically shares concepts that are applied in business re-engineering, they are likely to have fewer objections to what happens there.[17] Critical objections to such a transfer are not based on moral or aesthetic judgements, but on a theoretical consideration. Due to their different guiding interest, management approaches *cannot* serve as a basis for social theory. Management strategies have a

17 To the "network" or "knowledge society", to human and social capital theory or other loans from the dominant economic discourse (Fine, 2010).

practical intention, located on a particular level: their aim is to lead a business (which in the last instance translates into making money, or, more precisely, to extract *more* money out of a given process in order to satisfy shareholders) and to find the best "tools" to do this (Peter, 2005). Social theory has a different and more contemplative aim: it has to explain how these strategies work, and investigate their conditions and effects – not only (and not primarily) for the business records, but for society in general, which also includes, for example, workers and their families and environments.

Social Effects of the new Management Discourse

In order to assess the social effects of this new semantics, we need to leave the management textbooks and look at the situation of those who are directly affected. The higher degree of 'individuality' in many workplaces means that the employee has to adopt the company's viewpoint as her/his own viewpoint ('corporate identity'). Here management has a direct impact on society, and per implication also on the social sciences as a part of society. Following Marx, every new class has to illustrate its own particular interest as the *common* interest – this is the core of ideology. But post-modern philosophy has told us that a plurality of interests is not reducible to a common, 'one-size-fits-all' world-view. So what happens here? In the economy especially there is an irreducible plurality of interests. Many people need a job in order to feed their family; this is a matter of necessity. Every concession they make translates into a direct drawback in their lives. The concessions capital sometimes has to make are drawbacks in rates, a fact that often refers to the degree of *additional* income for the owning classes. Whether this is a necessity is debatable. What we would usually expect here is a bargaining process, and this is what the social organisation of "welfare capitalism" had, in fact, institutionalised. Social democracy, as the term already indicates, was not only about economic redistribution; it was also about participation as an active form of citizenship. Both sides in this bargain had their rights and obligations.

What current management asks for is, at the first glance, only another concession in this bargaining process. The demand, taken to its extreme, ideal-typically is:

> 'Work more, work longer, constantly re-educate yourself and drop all your rights in the workplace'.

Usually, one would expect a response like:

> 'Wait, what do you have to offer in return?'

The answer in this case is:

'Nothing; you just have to',

and then comes some well-known t.i.n.a.-narrative ('there is no alternative') of competitiveness, market pressures, globalisation, etc. (Henning, 2006a). So the concession in this case is a different issue. It really amounts to the accepting *not to formulate one's own interests any more*, at least as far as they are different from the company's interests. This no longer is a case of negotiation, it is the breakdown of communication and co-operation and the beginning of a clear-cut dominance; in other words: an exit from voice.[18] In order to avoid the impression of direct force,[19] which if applied too openly could lead to political resistance (as during the summer of 2005 when mass demonstrations against the politics of welfare reform were held in many European countries), two things need to be reinterpreted by a new rhetoric: force has to be dressed like a natural necessity ('naturalisation'), and the plurality of interests needs to be levelled into but one national or public economic interest ('harmonisation'). In these hegemonic language games, we are asked to acknowledge but *one* interest, the interest of the owners and bosses. Miraculously, it is identical to that of the nation, even if the profits are parked in an offshore tax haven. In this narrative, the workers' interest is not opposed to this, but is basically the same – or it is not there. This is the new management techniques' *functional message*, and this is ideology at its best.[20] In terms of philosophy, this resembles a metaphysics of identity that falls way behind the post-modern critiques of idealism, let alone modern pluralism.

One example for this construction of identity runs as follows: we are told that work as we knew it is gone (Rifkin, 1995), and that workers today are in fact *entrepreneurs*.[21] An entrepreneur has no use for a union that protects him, at least not in economic theory or in the management discourse (in fact many corporations *do* have very influential organisations, which Adam Smith already mentioned as a major inequality between capital and labour). An entrepreneur does not have regulated and fixed labour times; instead they are willing to work as long as it takes, without knowing whether they will get a 'return on investment'. They are responsible for what they do; and needs their creativity and individuality in order to be successful. And above all, entrepreneurs

[18] Laclau (2005) re-established the concept of political "demands": they are essential in the political process; yet labour is increasingly losing its "voice" (Hirschman, 1970).

[19] See the force-based theory of exploitation in Reiman 1987.

[20] Following Slavoj Zizek and others, ideologies are best recognized by their claim that they are the only worldview possible and that they therefore hold for everybody.

[21] Cf. the notorious German "Ich-AG" (which means "myself & Co"). See Pinchot,1988; Priddat, 2000; Pongratz/Voss, 2003.

have to accumulate their capital. And this is, we are told, what 'new labour' looks like: it is, itself, capital. The value of a worker is their use value for capital and nothing else – they only have to understand themselves in this way; otherwise they are essentially wrong and need to be educated or 'activated'. Interestingly the activation does not come along as an overriding of interests, but as the creation of autonomy – as if there *was* no such thing as workers' own interest any longer. In effect this is meant to reduce tensions between capital and labour, which in turn reduces transaction costs for investors.

In the management sphere such a perspective has to be expected. Trying to minimise the other part's interest translates into maximising one's own interests, which is just the usual way of thinking in business. Some professionals may even believe, or pretend to believe, that this perspective is the only *possible* one. But to call this a theory of society is going a step too far. Such a statement cannot be the task of management textbooks themselves (no sentence can attribute truth to itself; *cf.* Wittgenstein, 1922: 3, 332). It has to be left to an impartial spectator.[22] So what do social sciences have to say in this respect? How do they evaluate the impact of management?

My impression is that social theory today rightly pays attention to new management strategies;[23] but it endangers its own legitimacy if it *takes over* management concepts too quickly, even where it rejects them on moral grounds. This happens if the management idiom is read as a description, not as an interpellation driven by certain interests. As it is no longer politically correct to use terms such as ideology, class struggle, property relations, alienation, exploitation or emancipation, new concepts are treated more openly than these old ones. Though at the time this theoretical promiscuity was a positive development against dogmatic petrifactions, today this is an open door through which the management perspective happily influences the social sciences. Let me give an example. Let us take the following sentence:

'Every worker should understand her/himself as an entrepreneur'

This sentence openly contains an appellative subtext: because if they obey, they will be more likely to accept the massive cutbacks, and as a useful side effect they will not claim social benefits. Clearly it would be a mistake to translate this normative sentence into the following descriptive sentence that claims to be empirically valid:

---

22 Another irony of these changes is that nowadays consultant companies are undertaking, or at least financing, research – for example, they are evaluating universities (instead of being evaluated by them).

23 See Rose, 1991; Townley, 1994; McKinlay/Starkey, 1997; Willmott, 1997; Bröckling, 2000, e.g., or – as mentioned already – Bendix, 1956.

'Today workers are entrepreneurs'.

This would be a normativist fallacy, the reversal of the naturalistic fallacy. If some groups in society claim something should be the case, this does not mean that this is the case, even if the groups in question are very powerful. Even though most sociologists would reject the notion that they convey a management perspective, the lack of critical perspectives might have to do with a certain carelessness in the use of such ambivalent terms. Once such terms are commonly used, it is most likely that the hegemonic perspective will overwhelm any form of resistance in the symbolic struggles about how to interpret it. All that is left from the critical perspective would then be cynicism.

Reviving a Critical Perspective

As we have seen, the struggles for the possibility of a critical perspective start at the conceptual level already. If concepts from a management perspective are used, this has an effect on the theoretical conclusions drawn. Buying into hegemonic sociolects comes at the risk of swallowing a lot of the world-view involved, even if unnoticed or denied. The following lines want to demonstrate that the same phenomena can also be described with traditional theoretical concepts, which keep the door to a critical perspective open without losing touch with the rapidly changing realities.

Though many things have changed in society (and will continue to change in the future, especially concerning conventions in the economy), in a Hegelian sense these changes on the labour market and at the workplace are on a particular level. This does not imply that we cannot use the classical formal terms any longer, since they are located on a general level. Production is production, whether one produces needles, cars or semiconductors. Likewise one sells one's labour power, whether one works in a small company, a huge Fordist assembly line, in a post-Fordist team or during the night as a security officer. Such terms may be unpopular, but this aesthetic judgement does not imply that they no longer fit. In other words, intellectual fashions are not arguments. As long as classical terms grasp more than their equivalents, social theory should use them. It may sound dialectical: in order to be able to understand and criticize the present, we need to turn back to some of the classical terminologies. In the following I will give further examples.

The real-world changes that occurred over the last two decades are obvious: competition has increased on many markets, between companies as well as within companies, and even between nations. The changes on the labour market have a decisive trend. Local labour markets opened up their restrictions and the contract is in the process of being expunged. Labour mobility increased the competition among workers from different countries, within and between countries, i.e. when capital chooses to "exit" and build its plants in other countries (Sassen, 1988). Both variants put a pressure on wages that already squeezes the middle classes. I see no reason why this should not be called an increase in the rate of *exploitation*, as at the same time profits and management revenues are piling up tremendously. For a rising rate of exploitation simply means: profits rise faster than wages.

As many new jobs (e.g. telework) are highly individualised, so is the organisation of labour. As a result in many countries labour unions, which relied on a broad homogeneity of labour, are continuously shrinking, and with them real wages fall further. The new McJobs in the service sector are often low-paid jobs (Ehrenreich, 2001). With Marx, we may call this a *re-commodification* of labour (Candeias, 2004; Henning, 2007). This economic tendency is accompanied by a politics of retrenchment, a reduced public provision of decommodifying unemployment benefits. The welfare state declines: many areas which were formerly protected (like public transport, health and education), are privatised; they are then taken over by companies which are doomed to "profit or perish", much to the disadvantage of the weakest members of society: the elderly, families, students, the un- or under-employed and cultural or ethnic minorities (Hays, 2003). In most countries, the welfare state reforms explicitly intended to "end welfare as we knew it", in favour of underpaid jobs ('active labour market politics'). The cutbacks of the welfare state force the majority of the population back onto the labour market, willingly or not. In many cases the exit option (which is not really a way out of, but rather into, the ruthlessness of the market) is to commodify oneself as a thing called 'labour power' (or human capital) and try to sell oneself on the market, like any other commodity.

A third and related example is the seemingly outdated term of *alienation*. According to Boltanski and Chiapello, today it is almost useless to criticize modern capitalism by claiming that work is 'alienating', as the new management techniques mostly allow for self-expression and self-realisation. This comes down to saying that if one demands emancipation today, one must go to work – in other words, the language of authenticity can no longer be used against the economy. I think this argument is wrong (and Boltanski and Chiapello did not want to suggest this), for several reasons. First, there is a *class* bias involved: jobs requiring a much higher qualification and an ability to motivate and organize oneself (reflexivity)[24] are not available for everybody. Higher qualification has its price, especially when universities are privatised. The necessary resources for the forming of soft skills and 'self control'

[24] This term, made prominent by Beck, 1986, already appeared in Gouldner, 1970: 488.

are far from being distributed equally: they can be viewed as a cultural capital mainly of the middle and higher classes, formerly known as 'bourgeoisie'.[25] At the same time, whereas many jobs disappear, it is mostly at the very bottom of the ladder that new jobs are created. Low-paid jobs and workfare are meant to fill up the gaps of unemployment. So inequality is clearly rising.[26] In lower echelon jobs, one is permanently threatened by a lack of perspectives, as one's very means of existence could be at stake at any moment. I see no theoretical reason why the term "*class*" should be avoided here. The upward tendencies in but a few areas are built upon a widespread casualisation for a large share of the population. So the actualisation thesis is not an argument against a criticism of alienation for a large share of the jobs offered.

Jobs in knowledge-related industries (which include marketing, advertising, journalism, all kinds of organizing or consulting services, etc.) might be more rewarding in some cases, but they do not solve the problem on a social level – first, because of the mentioned inequality of resources; secondly, because they cannot provide the same number of jobs as those lost in traditional sectors; and, thirdly, because the lucky employees experience similar trends here. In many of these sectors, there is very little security: contracts are limited, competition is even stiffer, so sometimes one may find oneself working for free – on a prolonged internship – or as a temporary worker on a much lower salary. So in jobs for the higher educated, alienation is not abolished either; rather it is displaced. It is not so much the contradiction between stupid work and a meaningful life on the side that marks the difference here, but a fine line between private self and company self that may induce feelings of alienation. If employees have to sell themselves totally, this can very well lead to an increase in commodification.

Even if no feelings of alienation from the workplace arise because one is allowed to work more individually, the main argument of the theory of alienation still holds: a main cause for experiences of alienation are *property relations*. As long as one does not decide what to produce in the first place and one does not own one's products at the end, one might very well feel alienated from one's own activity. Of course, this is not visible in management theories, but that does not mean it is not there. Eventually we have to ask people (see Bourdieu, 1993; Schultheis/Schulz, 2005).

If we look at the increase in the total hours worked in the new sectors of the economy, we can even add another point. Many working situations increasingly involve emotional labour. In many cases one needs to

[25] See Bourdieu, 1989; Sklair, 2001; Hartmann, 2002.

[26] On this subject, see Alderson/Nielsen, 2002; Noll/Lemel, 2002; UN, 2005.

co-operate with others at a much closer level: one needs to be in a good mood at almost all times, and one needs to "deep-act" positive vibrations towards customers, colleagues and superiors (Hochschild, 1983). Maybe we are no longer alienated that much from our workplace, but from our own lives instead – from our families and partners, including cultural recreation which can only be reproduced outside economic compulsions.[27] The result is a growing interdependence of work and free time and a moral devaluation of free time and private life in general. Most likely the demographic problems of our times can be approached from this perspective, too. To recapitulate the point on alienation: it is not by chance that emotional disorders are increasing *both* at the top and at the bottom. A contemporary theory of alienation has to take into account the pathological tendencies that may follow from too much work – depression, nervous breakdown, burnout, etc. Clearly, working conditions have an impact on mental health.[28]

All of these phenomena constitute systematic limits of fulfilment, quite contrary to the actualisation thesis. It is good to have a more pleasant workplace, yet it would be futile to seek fulfilment in the workplace only. The economy's *raison d'être* is still that of making money. This is valid under the 'new management', too. So in the case of a conflict between a person and the economic imperative of making money, the person is still very likely to lose.[29] Instead, the re-creation of personality depends on satisfying resources of free time and enough money to spend, and the dominant tendency for many in the working population is that *both*, i.e. free time and disposable money, are shrinking. The changes in semantics need to be dialectically correlated to all this.

Conclusion and Prospects

I have argued that there is no *theoretical* problem that would cause a crisis in critical theory, neither in the artistic nor in the economic tradition – in fact they can hardly be separated. My examples were the terms

---

[27] See Riesman, 1950; Hochschild, 1997; Sennett, 1998 or Gottschall/Voß, 2003. Marx called free time "time for human creation, for mental and spiritual progress, for the satisfaction of social needs, for socialising, for a free play of physical and spiritual desires" (*Capital I*, MEW 23, 280; my translation). Only outside of work "lies the human potential that is an end in itself, the realm of liberty, which nevertheless has to be build upon the realm of necessity" (*Capital III*, MEW 25: 828).

[28] For depression see Ehrenberg, 1998; Dooley, 2000; Ahlers/Brussig, 2004 and Henning, 2006b. Unlike Israel 1972 and Weber 2006, Jaeggi 2005 no longer deals with labour.

[29] In advanced industrial economies, work is not designed for the purpose of conveying internal goods. It is designed, of course, for productivity and profit (Muirhead, 2004: 157).

exploitation class, inequality alienation, commodification and insecurity, all of which name endogenous social costs of capitalism. The underlying question for the applicability of these terms therefore is: may we still call the present socio-economic condition 'capitalism'? If we assume that the prior condition, which in many Western countries was a social democratic compromise (welfare states with relatively high employment, rising wages and an expanding social security, but also limited financial markets), was already capitalism proper, then we have to find a new name for the new situation. We have to say what precisely is *new* in the new condition, and we have to formulate theories that can name the driving force behind this change and explain its mechanisms. In other words, theories of historical 'stages' come into play (for example of financial capitalism, post-Fordism, turbo-capitalism, the era of globalisation or the knowledge economy). The problem with these conceptualisations is the implicit assumption that a different *logic* is at work at each of these stages. The anti-metaphysical intention of modern social theory usually tries to confine itself to mere 'descriptions', without trying to explain everything by a grand narrative. Yet sometimes, maybe unnoticed, these descriptions are taken as explanations – changes in semantics are wrongly interpreted as changes in social structure. Ironically, what happens here is the opposite: these descriptions-turned-explanations carry even *more* metaphysical baggage concerning the underlying philosophy of history. The theory of stages implies an underlying logic of society which miraculously changes rapidly – if we follow academic fashions, then this happens almost every other year: from the industrial to the post-industrial to the network society, to the information society, to 'post-neo-liberalism' and so on.

But as I argued, this is not the only way of looking at the situation. One might also claim that after World War II, most countries had a 'mixed economy' with a relatively high level of state intervention. Keynesianism dominated for decades and the welfare state did not allow for "real" markets in many fields (education, the health sector, social security, etc.). In other words, we did not have "full" capitalism before. From this perspective, what we experience now is a *return* of capitalism proper. If that is so, why should we not use the classical vocabulary, which intended a critical theory exactly for conditions like these?

Despite all the recent spectacular shifts in semantics when it comes to descriptions, I want to suggest that the theoretical and critical concepts we had at hand before, in particular the ones from the tradition of critical theory, are still applicable today. Yet this is possible only if we do not wrongly understand them as 'descriptions', as has often been the case (as if the term 'labour', for example, were only applicable for low-paid industrial workers with a high degree of unionisation). They are meant to be formal terms. If we use them to explain a certain situation, we need to adjust them theoretically and fill them empirically in order to combine theoretical and empirical approaches. This is evident if we look at Hempel and Oppenheim's (1948) definition of explanation: it needs both general laws *and* antecedent conditions in order to formulate a theoretical explanation. New empirical trends do not have to substitute older theories; they can also be combined with them. This is where I see the future of critical theory.

References

Ahlers, E., Brussig, M., "Gesundheitsbelastungen und Prävention am Arbeitsplatz: WSI-Betriebsrätebefragung 2004", *WSI-Mitteilungen* 11, 2004, p. 617-624.

Alderson, A. S., Nielsen, Fr., "Globalisation and the Great U-turn: Income Inequality Trends in 16 OECD countries", *American Journal of Sociology* 107.5, March, 2002, 1244-1299.

Baethge, M., "Arbeit, Vergesellschaftung, Identität. Zur zunehmenden normativen Subjektivierung von Arbeit", *Soziale Welt* 42, 1991, p. 6-19.

Beck, U., *Risikogesellschaft. Auf dem Weg in eine andere Moderne*, Frankfurt/Main, Suhrkamp, 1986.

Bendix, R., *Work and Authority: Managerial Ideologies in the course of Industrialisation* (1956), New Brunswick, Transaction, 2001

Bollier, D., *Silent Theft. The Private Plunder of Our Common Wealth*, New York, Routledge, 2003.

Boltanski, L., Chiapello, E., *The new Spirit of Capitalism* (1999), London, Verso, 2007.

Bolz, N., *Konformisten des Andersseins. Ende der Kritik*, München, Fink, 1999.

Bourdieu, P., *La noblesse d'État. Grandes Écoles et esprit de corps*, Paris, Minuit, 1989.

Bourdieu, P. *et al.*, *La misère du monde*, Paris, Seuil, 1993.

Brenner, R., *The Boom and the Bubble. The US in the World Economy*, London, Verso, 2002.

Broeckling, U. *et al.* (eds.), *Gouvernementalität der Gegenwart. Studien zur Ökonomisierung des Sozialen*, Frankfurt/Main, Suhrkamp, 2000.

Burawoy, M., *Manufacturing Consent. Changes in the Labour Process under Monopoly Capitalism*, University of Chicago Press, 1979.

Candeias, M., "Erziehung der Arbeitskräfte. Rekommodifizierung der Arbeit im neoliberalen Workfare State", *Utopie kreativ* 165/166, 2004, p. 589-601.

Cometta, Cl., "Unternehmerische Subjektivität und Arbeit. Historische und Aktuelle Perspektiven am Beispiel ausgewählter Organisations- und Managementkonzepte", Dissertation St. Gallen, 2009.

Dooley, D. *et al.*, "Underemployment and Depression: Longitudinal Relations", *Journal of Health and Social Behaviour* 41.4, 2000, p. 421-436.

Drucker, P.F., *The Practice of Management*, New York, Harper & Row, 1954 (Reprint 2007).

Ehrenberg, A., *La fatigue d'être soi*, Paris, 1998.

Ehrenreich, B., *Nickel and Dimed. On (not) Getting by in America*, New York, Metropolitan, 2001.

Fine, B., *Theories of Social Capital. Researchers behaving badly*, London, Pluto, 2010.

Fiske, J., *Television Culture*, London/New York, Routledge, 1987.

Friedman, A.L., "Responsible Autonomy *versus* Direct Control over the Labour Process", *Capital and Class* 1, 1977, p. 34-57.

Gilbert, N., *Transformation of the Welfare State. The Silent Surrender of Public Responsibility*, Oxford University Press, 2004.

Goodin, R.E., Schmitz, D., *Social Welfare and Individual Responsibility*, Cambridge University Press, 1998.

Gottschall, K., Voss, G.G. (eds.), *Entgrenzung von Arbeit und Leben. Zum Wandel der Beziehung von Erwerbstätigkeit und Privatsphäre im Alltag*, München, Hampp, 2003.

Gouldner, A., *The Coming Crisis of Western Sociology*, New York, Basic Books, 1970.

Hartmann, M., *Der Mythos von den Leistungseliten. Spitzenkarrieren und soziale Herkunft in Wirtschaft, Politik, Justiz und Wissenschaft*, Frankfurt/Main, New York, Campus 2002.

Hays, S., *Flat, Broke, with Children. Women in the Age of Welfare Reform*, Oxford University Press, 2003.

Heidenreich, M., "Die subjektive Modernisierung fortgeschrittener Arbeitsgesellschaften", *Soziale Welt* 47.1, 1996, p. 24-43.

Hempel, C.G., Oppenheim, P., *Studies in the Logic of Explanation* (1948), *Aspects of Scientific Explanation*, London, 1970, p. 245-296.

Henning, Chr., *Narrative der Globalisierung*, Trier, Karl-Marx-Haus, 2006(a).

Henning, Chr., "Depression", in *Marxglossar*, ed. Christoph Henning, Berlin, Freitag, 2006(b), p. 69-76.

Henning, Chr., "Verdinglichung: Ein Schlüsselbegriff Kritischer Theorie", *Berliner Debatte Initial* 6, 2007, p. 98-114.

Hillmann, G., *Die Befreiung der Arbeit. Die Entwicklung kooperativer Selbstorganisation und die Auflösung bürokratisch-hierarchischer Herrschaft, Reinbek*, Rowohlt, 1970.

Hirschman, A.O., *Exit, Voice and Loyalty. Responses to Decline in Firms, Organisations and States*, Cambridge/MA, Harvard University Press, 1970.

Hochschild, A.R., *The Managed Heart. Commercialisation of Human Feeling*, Berkeley, University of California Press, 1983.

Hochschild, A.R., *The Time Bind. When Work becomes Home and Home becomes Work*, New York, Metropolitan, 1997.

Honneth, A., *Kritik der Macht. Reflexionsstufen einer kritischen Gesellschaftstheorie*, Frankfurt/Main, Suhrkamp, 1985.

Honneth, A. (ed.), *Befreiung aus der Mündigkeit. Paradoxien des gegenwärtigen Kapitalismus*, Frankfurt/Main, New York, Campus 2002.

Horx, M., *Smart Capitalism. Das Ende der Ausbeutung*, Frankfurt/Main, Eichborn, 2001.

Illouz, E., *Cold Intimacies. The Making of Emotional Capitalism*, Cambridge, Polity, 2007.

Inglehart, R., "The Silent Revolution in Europe: Intergenerational Change in Post-Industrial Societies", *The American Political Science Review* 65.4 (1971), pp. 991-1017.

Israel, J., *Entfremdung*, Reinbek, Rowohlt, 1972.

Jaeggi, R., *Entfremdung. Zur Aktualität eines sozialphilosophischen Problems*, Frankfurt/Main, New York, Campus 2005.

Kieser, A., "Moden & Mythen des Organisierens", *Die Betriebswirtschaft* 56 (1996), p. 21-39.

Konrad, W., Schumm, W. (eds.), *Wissen und Arbeit. Neue Konturen von Wissensarbeit*, Münster, Westfälisches Dampfboot, 1999.

Laclau, E., *On Populist Reason*, London, Verso, 2005.

Luhmann, N., *Gesellschaftsstruktur und Semantik*, 4 Vls., Frankfurt/Main, Suhrkamp, 1980-1995.

Marx, K., *Capital*, London 1887, MEGA II.9, Berlin, Akademie, 1990.

McKinlay, A., Starkey, K. (eds.), *Foucault, Management and Organisation Theory: From Panopticon to Technologies of the Self*, London, Sage, 1997.

Menez, R., Töpsch, K., "Arbeitsregulation in der IT-Branche: Organisationsbedarf und Organisationsfähigkeit aus gewerkschaftlicher Sicht", *Arbeitsbericht Nr.* 231, Akademie für Technikfolgenabschätzung in Baden-Württemberg, März 2003.

Meschnig, A., Stuhr, M. (eds.), *Arbeit als Lebensstil*, Frankfurt/Main, Suhrkamp, 2003.

Minssen, H., *Arbeits- und Industriesoziologie. Eine Einführung*, Frankfurt/M., Campus, 2006.

Moldaschl, M., "Foucaults Brille. Eine Möglichkeit, die Subjektivierung von Arbeit zu verstehen?", in *idem*/Guenther G. Voss (eds.), *Subjektivierung von Arbeit*, München, Hampp, 2003, p. 135-176.

Muirhead, R., *Just Work*, Harvard College, 2004.

Noll, H.-H., Lemel, Y. (eds.), *Changing Structures of Inequality: A Comparative Perspective*, Montreal, McGill University Press, 2002.

Peter, L., 'Der neue Geist des Kapitalismus'. Stärken und Schwächen eines Erklärungsversuchs, *Z: Zeitschrift für Marxistische Erneuerung* 62 (06/2005), p. 7-24.

Peters, T., *Liberation Management. Necessary Disorganisation for the Nanosecond Nineties*, New York, Knopf, 1992.

Pettinger, L. *et al.* (eds.), *A New Sociology of Work?* Malden, Blackwell, 2005.

Pinchot, G., *Intrapreneuring – Mitarbeiter als Unternehmer*, Wiesbaden, Gabler, 1988.

Pongratz, H., Voss, G., "Fremdorganisierte Selbstorganisation: Eine soziologische Diskussion aktueller Managementkonzepte", *Zeitschrift für Personalforschung* 11 (1997), pp. 30-53.

Pongratz, H., Voss, G.G., *Arbeitskraftunternehmer. Erwerbsorien-tierungen in entgrenzten Arbeitsformen*, Berlin, Sigma, 2003.

Priddat, B., *Arbeit an der Arbeit. Verschiedene Zukünfte der Arbeit*, Marburg, Metropolis, 2000.

Priddat, B., "Human Capital", in Chr. Henning (ed.), *Marxglossar*, Berlin, Freitag, 2006, p. 133-142.

Reich, R.B., *The Work of Nations*, New York, Knopf, 1991.

Reiman, J., "Exploitation, Force, and the Moral Assessment of Capitalism: Thoughts on Roemer and Cohen", *Philosophy and Public Affairs* 16.1 (Winter 1987), p. 3-41.

Resch, Chr., *Berater-Kapitalismus oder Wissensgesellschaft? Zur Kritik der neoliberalen Produktionsweise*, Münster, 2005.

Riesman, D. *et al.*, *The Lonely Crowd. A Study of the Changing American Character* (1950), Reprint, Yale University Press, 2001.

Rifkin, J., *The End of Work. The Decline of the global Labor Force and the Dawn of the Post-Market Era*, New York, Tarcher, 1995.

Rose, N., *Governing the Soul. The Shaping of the Private Self*, London, Routledge, 1991.

Sassen, S., *The Mobility of Labour and Capital*, Cambridge University Press, 1988.

Schmiede, R. (ed.), *Virtuelle Arbeitswelten. Arbeit, Produktion und Subjekt in der Informationsgesellschaft*, Berlin, Sigma, 1996.

Schultheis, Fr., Schulz, Kr., *Gesellschaft mit begrenzter Haftung. Zumutungen und Leiden im deutschen Alltag*, Konstanz, UVK, 2005.

Schulze, G., *Die Beste aller Welten. Wohin bewegt sich die Gesellschaft im 21. Jahrhundert?*, München/Wien, Hanser, 2003.

Sennett, R., *The Corrosion of Character. The Personal Consequences of Work in the New Capitalism*, London/New York, Norton, 1998.

Sklair, L., *The Transnational Capitalist Class*, Oxford, Blackwell, 2001.

Sloterdijk, P., "Die Kritische Theorie ist tot", *Die Zeit* 37, 1999.

Townley, B., *Reframing Human Resource Management: Power, Ethics and the Subject at Work*, London, Sage, 1994.

United Nations, *The Inequality Predicament. Report on the World Social Situation*, New York, United Nations, 2005.

Weber, W.G., "Added Value statt menschlichen Werten? Zur Genese von sozialer Entfremdung in Arbeit und Interaktion", *Journal für Psychologie* 14 (2006), p. 120-147.

Whyte, W.H., *The Organization Man*, New York, Simon & Shuster, 1956.

Willmott, H., "Rethinking Management and Managerial Work: Capitalism, Control, and Subjectivity", *Human Relations* 50.11, 1997, p. 1329-1359.

Wittgenstein, L., *Tractatus logico-philosophicus*, London, Kegan, 1922.

Wolf, H., *Arbeit und Autonomie. Ein Versuch über Widersprüche und Metamorphosen kapitalistischer Produktion*, Münster, Dampfboot, 1999.

Wolf, H., "Arbeit, Autonomie, Kritik", in J. Beerhorst *et al.* (eds.), *Kritische Theorie im gesellschaftlichen Strukturwandel*, Frankfurt/Main, Suhrkamp, 2004, p. 227-242.

Ideology Down Under and the Shifting Sands of Individualism

Georgina MURRAY and David PEETZ

School of Arts and Griffith Business School respectively, Griffith University, Brisbane, Australia

I. Introduction

The capitalist corporation faces many challenges, one of which is to promote an ideology that is conducive to the generation of profit. This requires an adroit balancing of apparent contradictions. While individual corporations may attempt to create organisational "cultures" that emphasise the primacy of corporate interests, such attempts often fail because employees are subject to external ideological influences that expose the contradiction between the image it projects of its values and the practice of capitalist management (Willmott, 1993).

So corporations need to engage in collective action that promotes sympathetic popular ideologies and minimises the dissonance between internal and external ideology. At least as importantly, they need to encourage policy makers to enact laws and adopt practices that will facilitate profit growth.

As the schisms between political parties in many countries are at least in part class-based, the optimal situation is one in which "conservative" political parties, representing the interests of the capitalist class, hold government. Even when parties purporting to represent the working class are in government, suitable policy outcomes can be achieved if a beneficial ideology is sufficiently pervasive amongst the policy-making elite. Over the past three decades, this policy ideology has come to be known by various names, including "neo-liberalism" (Rudd, 2008), "economic rationalism" (Pusey, 1992), "economic fundamentalism" (Argy, 1998), "economic liberalism" (Stilwell, 2002) and "market liberalism" (Quiggin, 2010). For consistency we use the term "economic liberalism".

Our chapter examines one country and its experience with the propagation at popular and elite levels of a core aspect of market liberal ideology. We consider Australia, notable because of its experiment with radical changes in work and employment law in 2005, promoted under the banner of "individualism" by the conservative government of John Howard and by business lobby groups and think tanks. Their newly imagined "enterprise worker" was individualistic, focused on being rewarded for their own hard work and eschewed collectivism (Howard, 2005). Yet in 2007 those enterprise workers threw the government out of office and the legislative edifice created in their honour was largely but not completely dismantled.

The process by which the labour movement organised to defeat this legislation has been covered elsewhere and is beyond the scope of this chapter (Muir, 2008). Our interest here is on the ideological disconnect that led to it – between popular ideology about individualism and collectivism, and elite ideology – and the interests that have promoted the ideology of individualism. While the Australian legal regime is unique, arguments about the new orthodoxy of individualisation (or as Beck (1992) described it, "individuation") are common through many developed countries. We show how, "down under", parts of the Australian capitalist class initiated and entrenched an individualist coup with the help of formal and informal networks; through top business directors and their interlocking board directorates key employers, employer associations and think tanks. Although our focus is on the workers' response and elite businesses dissemination of, the dominant ideology, we do not suggest that business networks are exclusively responsible for it. Other institutions such as top state bureaucracies (Pusey, 1992) and key elements within universities (Readings, 1996) are relevant but again are beyond the scope of this paper.

II. Market Liberalism and Individualism

Economic liberalism is the idea that only markets, not governments, laws or bureaucracies, can be efficient (Pusey, 1992). Economic liberal roots can be traced back beyond classical economics to the anti mercantilist, non-state interventionism of Dudley North in his work *Discourses on Trade* (1691) and the selfish-is-good theories of Bernard Mandeville in the *Fable of the Bees* (1704). Adam Smith in *An Inquiry in to the Nature and Causes of the Wealth of Nations* (1776) brought these ideas together to focus on the virtue of private property and free market competition. Smith's eclectic vision gave rise to classical economics, which in turn gave rise to the economic liberalism we see today. The global financial crisis discredited the core of market liberalism, including a number of key economic propositions such as the efficient markets hypothesis, the benefits of privatisation, and the idea of 'trickle down' (policies that advantage the rich will also advantage the poor). Its demise was exemplified by Prime Minister Rudd's disparaging description of how the Australian people were 'left in the wake of this most spectacular failure of the entire neo-liberal orthodoxy' (Rudd, 2008). No coherent alternative, however, has been broadly articulated to take the place of neoliberalism, and so these ideas still underlie the thinking of policy makers. They are, as Quiggin (2010) argues, like zombies – 'neither alive nor dead'.

The individual is central to understanding liberal theory. Stilwell (2002) suggested that economic liberalism has four interrelated assumptions which are: individualism, whereby the individual is regarded as the basic unit of society to the extent that no claims can be made for an aggregation of individual interests; hedonism, centring on individual drive to seek pleasure and avoid pain; rationality, which involves weighing up cost and benefit assessments of the most advantageous outcomes; and inertia, whereby people are lazy unless motivated to act by the promise of personal gain (Stilwell, 2002: 71).

Our interest is the first of these four assumptions – individualism – and its role in relation to the shift in workplace industrial relations. Individualism, in industrial relations commonly refers to "individual contracting", the antithesis of collective bargaining. Sometimes this is referred to as "procedural individualisation". Brown *et al.* (1998: i) defined this as the "removal of collective mechanisms for determining terms and conditions of employment" and their replacement by individual employment contracts, which employees sign and which set their pay and conditions.

The Howard Government vigorously promoted this procedural individualisation, first through the Workplace Relations Act 1996 by introducing statutory individual contracts that could weaken collective employment standards. Its second phase of legislation, known as 'WorkChoices' and taking effect from March 2006, even more actively promoted individual contracts (known as "Australian Workplace Agreements or AWAs), allowing them greater capacity to undercut collective standards, while hampering collective bargaining through restrictions on union rights and rights to undertake industrial action. Within months of the defeat of the Howard government in November 2007, the Rudd Labor government introduced the first phase of legislation to overturn that legislation, abolishing that capacity to make statutory individual contracts. Later changes, under the banner of the "Fair Work Act", overturned more but not all of the Howard agenda. Did these shifts towards, and away from, individualisation in employment relations reflect the shifting sands of popular ideology? Or did these radical policy changes occur *despite* popular ideology?

III. Ideology and Economic Liberalism

Although there are several different meanings to "ideology", the term can be defined as "beliefs, attitudes and opinions which form a set, whether tightly or loosely related" (Abercrombie, Hill and Turner, 1984: 206). Ideology was a concept first associated with Georg Hegel (1770-1831) and his understanding that ideas generate action, which was then famously turned on its head by Karl Marx's (1818-1883) argument that "ideas can never lead beyond an old world order but only beyond the ideas of the old world order" (Marx *et al.*, 1975: 4.119) as ideas mask class interests through being held as a "false consciousness" (Marx *et al.*, 1965: 459). We distinguish between what we call "popular ideology" – the beliefs, attitudes and opinions of the population at large, described variously as "working class", "middle class" or "battlers" – and "elite ideology" – that is, the self-serving beliefs, attitudes and opinions of the capitalist class. There is Australian evidence of the elite shaping popular ideology documented by R.W. Connell's (1977) in the classic *Ruling Class, Ruling Culture*. It remains, however, a continual challenge for that elite to present its interests as common sense wielded for the common good.

During this period of intense economic liberalism that commenced in the mid 1980s and peaked under the Howard government, Australian polity was reshaped. Tariffs were cut or abolished, major government enterprises corporatised or privatised, and whole areas of state activity opened up to private sector competition through "competitive tendering". Yet while the "economic liberal" ideology is faithfully reproduced in media discourse, the public was slow to fully catch on. For example, reflecting concern for jobs, a 1999 poll showed 80 per cent of Australian electors thought there should be import quotas on certain imported goods – an increase from 64 per cent in 1962 (Roy Morgan, 1999; see also Roy Morgan, 1997). Similarly in 2005 some 70 per cent of Australians opposed the imminent sale of the 51 per cent of communications giant Telstra that remained publicly owned – a mere 16 per cent supported it (Newspoll, 2005). And when a recently re-elected state Labor government announced the privatisation of several major assets in breach of election commitments, its popularity plummeted to levels from which it appeared unable to recover (Steel, 2010).

While the private appropriation of public assets has been a key feature of the shifting polity, arguably the most important change for workers has been the shift from collectivist to individualistic patterns of industrial relations, as this directly affects their power and working conditions. Union membership declined from a half to a fifth of the workforce in just twenty-five years, centralised wage fixation through the Australian Industrial Relations Commission was abandoned and the pay of over one third of employees is now determined by individual agreements of one form or another (ABS, 2009). These trends, we were told, reflected the growing individualism of Australians, and their discarding of collectivist values (e.g. BCA, 1989; Pearson, 2002). Close examination, however, reveals that individualistic shifts in popular ideology are weak or non-existent and, to the extent that any exist, they follow rather than lead the institutional changes that the capitalist class has brought about.

IV. Popular Ideology on Individualism

We first examine popular ideology: to what extent does it reflect a growing acceptance of the individualistic discourse? The evidence is mixed but broadly suggests that individualism is not inherently favoured over collectivism and, if anything, the shift has been away from, not towards individualism. In 1979 the Australian Political Attitudes Survey found that, given a choice, 59 per cent of Australians thought that government should reduce taxes, whereas only 36 per cent thought it should spend more on social services – a gap of 23 percentage points (Aitkin, 1982: 385). Nearly three decades later, the Australian Election Study showed a very different finding – in 2007 only 34 per cent favoured cutting taxes, while 47 per cent favoured spending more on social services (McAllister and Clark, 2008: 29). This hardly indicated a shift away from collectivist towards individualist sentiments, particularly as taxes were no lower in 2007 than in 1979. Moreover, in 2001, 58 per cent agreed that Australia should be "a unified body pursuing a common goal", while just 19 per cent thought it should be a "collection of people independently pursuing their own goals" (AES, 2001). Similarly, in 2003, only 30 per cent favoured the statement 'living standards in Australia would be best improved if each individual looked after his or her own interests first' while 49 per cent preferred the opposite view: 'living standards in Australia would be best improved if we looked after the community's interests first' (ASSA, 2003). Other surveys found that majorities considered that the rich are getting richer and the poor are getting poorer, the distribution of wealth across Australian society has become less fair, and a smaller gap would be preferred (Newspoll, 2000, 2003).

The evidence of any shift to individualism is no stronger if we look specifically at attitudes towards industrial relations. As discussed later, the Business Council of Australia (BCA) led the charge for the shift to individualism, in particular through a 1989 Study Commission report Enterprise-Based Bargaining Units (BCA, 1989). The BCA claimed employee values and preferences were changing to an individualistic, enterprise focus, as Australians were: increasingly seeking a society in which individual talent is rewarded, and becoming less concerned with uniformity and equality (BCA, 1989: part 1: 19-21, 27-28). Each of these claims was challenged due to lack of evidence, or refuted (Frenkel and Peetz, 1990: 75-6). National opinion surveys showed not decreasing but increasing support for the redistribution of income and wealth, with the net margin in favour of redistribution growing from 7 percentage points to 31 percentage points between 1990 and 2004 (McAllister and Clark, 2007: 29). Australia in this regard is no different to most other countries, which show no systematic trend in public ideology towards individualism and away from collectivism (Peetz, 2010).

A better way to examine attitudes towards collectivism is by explicitly examining opinion poll data on ideology regarding trade unions, measured through attitudes to such questions as whether unions have too much power, have been a good thing for the country, should be subject to tighter controls, and are doing a good job. Shifts in union sympathy do not suggest a consistent shift towards individualism. Indeed, following a slow decline in union sympathy between the 1940s and the 1960s (probably attributable to anti-communism's association with anti-unionism) and a sharp deterioration during the early 1970s (associated with a significant rise in industrial conflict), union sympathy recovered slowly from the early to mid 1980s. For example, the proportion of Australians saying unions were doing a "fairly good", "very good" or "excellent" job rose gradually from around 35 per cent in the mid 1980s to 50 per cent in the mid 1990s (Peetz, 2002b), while the proportion saying unions had too much power more than halved between 1979 and 2007 as concern about the excessive power of big business grew (McAllister and Clark, 2008: 27). Newspoll data also shows attitudes to unions becoming more favourable between 1996 and 2004 (Bearfield, 2003; Robertson, 2005).

Translated into policy outcomes, the shift to individualism was epitomised by the federal government's "WorkChoices" legislation. The WorkChoices legislation was hurriedly drafted and rushed through Parliament to maximise the length of time before the next election, in the expectation that, in a tight labour market, the combination of benign impacts of the law and an expensive, sophisticated campaign would offset any initial adverse political impact the announcement of the new law would have. The conservative government spent USD 110 million of public funds on advertising and other activities promoting the WorkChoices legislation. Yet numerous surveys showed strong public opposition to it, and it was the biggest single factor explaining why voters swung from the conservative government to the Labor opposition party in the lead up to the 2007 election (eg Essential Research, 2007; Roy Morgan Research, 2005; Lyons, 2010). This opposition was consistent from the time the policy was announced (Lyons, 2010). Contrary to the effect of WorkChoices, some 85 per cent of voters said they supported "laws that would allow workers to have a collective agreement if that is what a majority of employees in a workplace want" (Essential Research, 2007), while 69 per cent agreed (just 24 per cent disagreed) that "individual contracts give too much power to the employer" (Essential Media Communications, 2007).

The rejection of WorkChoices took place despite concerted fear campaigns about the implications of the alternatives to WorkChoices, undertaken: by business lobbyists including the Business Council of Australia, individual Ministers and backbenchers, who did not hesitate to personally attack academics or others who criticised aspects of WorkChoices (Buchanan, 2007), and the governing Liberal Party, whose advertising during the 2007 election campaign focused on the threat of union domination of the alternative government. The unions' campaign against the legislation was described by the Workplace Relations Minister as 'the most sophisticated and political campaign in the history of this country' (Coorey and Davis, 2007). WorkChoices and the campaign it elicited sealed the fate of the eleven year old Howard government despite its presiding over a sustained period of economic prosperity.

In substance, the shift to individualism, in as much as it is meant to encapsulate changes in popular ideology, was a mirage. There were no major shifts towards, and then against, individualism as an ideology. Rather policy, driven by elites, stepped so far away from what popular ideology was willing to tolerate that the government was removed from office. Certainly, "individualism" dominated the institutional arrangements in Australia that shaped wages and conditions for over a decade. But this reflected an ideological offensive aimed not so much as changing popular opinion as it was at changing elite opinion – amongst policy makers, commentators, editors, theorists, and most importantly amongst the policy making cadre in the capitalist class – the boards and senior executives of large companies. We turn to this now.

V. Elite Ideology and Corporate Ties

The change in capitalist ideology did not take place overnight; it required effective transmission belts of ideas. In the rest of this chapter we focus on those transmission belts: think tanks, employer association lobby groups, consultants, interlocking directors and movement and communication amongst senior executives themselves. The central movers and shakers in this story are the company that invented deunionisation and the procedural individualisation of employment: CRA (now Rio Tinto), the BCA, and John Ralph, who straddled these two worlds. The emergence of new, procedurally individualist employment relations model was seen initially in the operations of companies in the CRA/Rio Tinto group (Hearn Mackinnon, 2007), but it is also now evident in varying ways in the behaviour of other employers, such as BHP Iron Ore, Telstra, the Commonwealth Bank and Optus (Peetz, 2002a).

In the late 1970s and early 1980s Australian employers showed little interest in "doing away with unions" (Niland and Turner, 1982; also Spillane, 1980). By the mid 1990s the picture had dramatically changed, with employer values (Hilmer *et al.*, 1993; Geare, 1990) and strategies decidedly more aggressively anti-union (e.g. Waring, 1999). While changing market circumstances were obviously important, so too was the way in which transmission of information about employment relations strategies and ideologies took place.

The most direct formal exchanges of information between members of the capitalist class occur through directors sitting on multiple boards, executives sitting on boards of other companies, and executives moving between companies and taking their ideas and strategies with them. Many of the Australian companies known for adopting anti-union individualistic approaches had links to each other and to CRA/Rio Tinto through management personnel and directorships (Murray, 2006: 106, 109, 111). Employer associations and management consultants reproduced the ideas and tools of procedural individualism. For example, Telstra, CRA, Optus, BHP Billiton and the Commonwealth Bank were linked to each other through interlocking directorates. Widely known management consultant firm World Competitive Practices included former senior members of the BCA Employee Relations Study Commission on enterprise bargaining, a body that provided much of the impetus to non-union work arrangements, and former senior executives in CRA and Rio Tinto (Peetz, 2002a; WCP, 2001). Each of the above-mentioned companies had sought to introduce individual contracts to some or all of its employees.

While these patterns are evident now, to understand the earlier spread of the procedurally individualistic ideal we should go back to the early 1990s, when CRA was embarking on the early, more successful phase of its strategy and the Liberal Party was embracing, at state and national levels, the most radical version of individualism – that exemplified by New Zealand's Employment Contracts Act 1991. Figure 1 shows 1992 Australian "interlock" data – that is, it shows interlocking positions on boards of major corporations between either chairpersons or executives.[1]

Figure 1 illustrates CRA's significance in 1992. It had links through several directors, including the CEO John Ralph, to other major compa-

1 This information has appeared in Murray, 2001 and 2006.

nies. By 1998 Ralph had left CRA but his position to the network had become pivotal. The distribution of 1998 interlocks (see Murray, 2006: 109) indicate that John Ralph then became the political centre of top business, while journalists recognised he "worked as a link man between the Federal government and the Alliance of business groups, the Business Coalition for Tax Reforms" (Gluyas, 1999: 32). Ralph had also played a key role in the shift to an "enterprise-based" industrial relations system and, through CRA, the decollectivisation of one of Australia's largest companies. In an interview a director put it this way:

> There was a study commission set up by the BCA that worked through a period of about five years [from 1983], from which time it developed the ideas of enterprise bargaining. Enterprise bargaining was, I won't say our greatest success, but it is a really good example. Enterprise bargaining was an anathema when the stake was put in the ground. Now the words are used commonly sometimes to mean something quite different but at least it's in most agendas and things have moved (Murray, 2006: 108).

Figure 1: 1992 Directional Interlocks in the Top 30 Companies

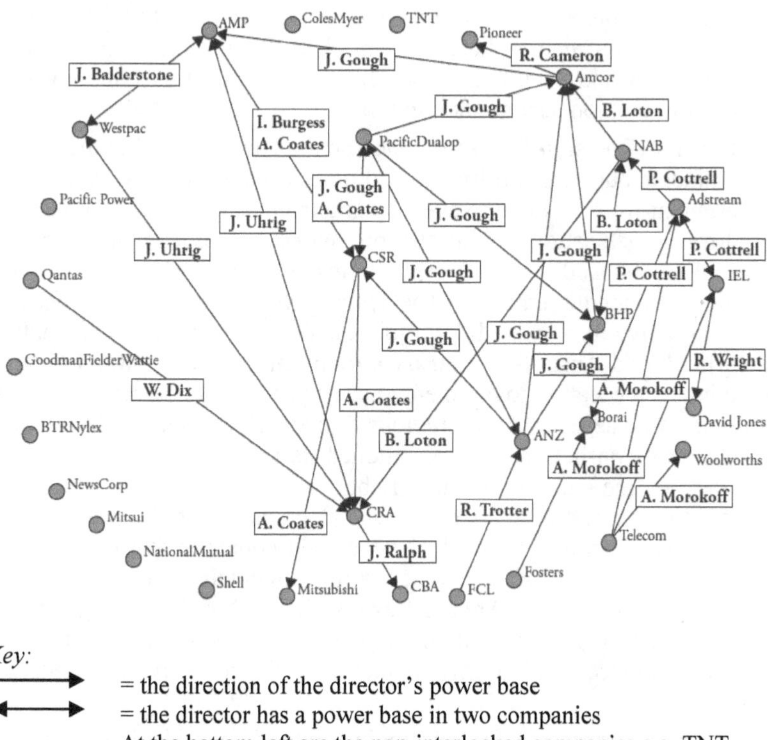

Key:

→ = the direction of the director's power base

↔ = the director has a power base in two companies

At the bottom left are the non-interlocked companies e.g. TNT

Source: Annual Reports 1992 http://www.connect4.com.au; Murray (2006).

Key directors, such as Ralph, integrate the class and reassure them as to the value of the innovations they propose. As Higley *et al.*'s (1979) work suggests, the interlocks run parallel to positions of power in the lobby groups; specifically the BCA, of which Ralph was President from 1992 to 1994.

VI. Lobby Groups and Think Tanks

Lobby groups and think tanks are crucial to the development and spread of ideas or ideologies. The BCA was pivotal in (though not solely responsible for) the Australian government's shift away from centralised wage fixation to enterprise-based employment relations and individual contracting. The BCA was established in the Hawke Labor government's corporatist climate of 1983 as a merger between the old pro-tariff Australian Industries Development Association and the pro-free market Business Roundtable (Hywood, 1997). It represented, and continues to represent, big business – originally the 80 largest companies in Australia. By 1997 the BCA was amongst the wealthiest lobby groups or think tanks with an operating budget of $4.9 million. It had a staff of 14 people and 95 corporate members, who are CEOs or managing directors. Its reports were influential in shaping media debate and CEO opinion and facilitating the shift in the business elite towards opposition to union accommodation.

The BCA had significant influence on the Hawke and Keating Labor governments but its authority reached a peak under the Howard Liberal government from 1996. However, its alignment (along with many other employer organisations) with the pro-WorkChoices campaign in the lead up to the 2007 federal election lost it some influence with the incoming Labor government. The latter gave its ear more to the one major employer body that did not join the political campaign, the manufacturing-based Australian Industry Group. Still, the BCA was far from impotent as the Labor government kept its promises to employer groups to retain some aspects of the previous framework particularly in relation to industrial conflict. The BCA softened its rhetoric after the election, but despite the success of the Labor government's neo-Keynesian intervention in response to the financial crisis (Australia was consequently one of only a handful of developed countries that did not fall into recession), the BCA retained a fundamentally economic-liberal positioning. In its 2009 Annual Review, BCA President Greig Gailey (2009) called for government, amongst other things, to build and maintain 'a workplace relations environment that fosters workplace collaboration'.

Other key processes for reinforcing individualist ideological structures were exercised by the informal ties of associates loosely grouped in "think tanks". Think tanks are organisations that produce information and research relevant to particular issues or interests. Although some are non-partisan (e.g. the Australian Institute of International Affairs, the oldest Australian think tank and a forum for discussing foreign policy issues) they are most commonly tied to a particular ideological agenda through their funding. While thinks tanks, like business lobbyists, are normally funded by corporations, they are distinguished from lobbyists by their claimed "independence" and "research" functions in the "public interest". Think tank members are frequently ideologues of the right who are dependent on private (usually) corporate financiers who expect a single (market liberalist) paradigm sympathetic to the politics of the sponsors. Through the late 1980s and 1990s the individualist agenda was championed by a number of think tanks, including the Institute of Public Affairs (IPA), the Centre for Independent Studies (CIS) and the HR Nicholls Society (Coghill, 1987).

The first think tank created with a specifically ideological agenda was the IPA, established in 1942 by the Victorian Chamber of Manufacturers to fill the void created by the collapse of the conservative United Australia Party Coalition Government in 1942 and to "combat socialism". Its long run political objective was "to endeavour to combine all the anti-socialist parties into one united body", though of course at the time (and ever since) it maintained it was "non-political" and "owed no allegiance to any political party" (Crisp, 1973).

In the last two decades Australian think tanks have proliferated with their numbers estimated at 80 to 90 (Herd, 1999; Marsh, 1994). Marsh estimated that Australian think tanks had a collective budget of $130 million; they employed 1,600 people, published 900 reports and discussion papers and held almost 600 conferences and *symposia* each year (Marsh, 1994). Corporate contribution and personal wealth are the biggest source of funding to the budgets of pro-market research think tanks. In a challenge to unions, some think tanks now like to call themselves the "fifth estate", whereas previously unions were referred to as the fifth estate (Da Silva, 2002).

As Cahill (2002) and Da Silva (2002) in different ways articulate "it's hard to overestimate the influence that conservative think tanks have had on the political agenda in Australia" (Da Silva, 2002: 73-77). Or as conservative Malcolm Turnbull, later a leading federal politician, put it: "Information is to public policy debate what gasoline is to a motor car... You need to have facts, information and comparisons with other countries. That's where think tanks can be very useful... The era of winning government with political spin, or waiting for the other side to crash, is coming to a close" (Turnbull, *in* Da Silva, 2002: 23).

Funding for think tanks comes through a variety of sources (Da Silva, 1996; NIRA, 1996): corporate and individual donations and endowments, publications and conferences. The government was a source of funds for economic liberal think tanks. For example the Menzies Foundation in 1997 received a $100,000 Liberal government grant. This meant that the Liberal Party could "undertake this 'intellectual' branch of their work without eating into their funds that they can use for other work" (Grattan, 1997). According to Grattan, this was money reallocated by the government from the Evatt Foundation (a left leaning think tank). Greg Lindsay (CEO of the CIS) admitted it received its big financial break from Hugh Morgan, the conservative CEO of Western Mining, and his corporate allies who generated $200,000 for the CIS (Da Silva, 1996). From the start Lindsay saw the CIS's role as influencing policy-making:

We set out to influence the general ideas environment… but as I went on I realized that there was more to achieving change than dreaming up what a Liberal Party future might be. For instance… If you felt that shopping hours should be deregulated, it was not just a matter of putting it on to paper and feeling confident that your brilliant statement would win the day (Lindsay, 1996).

Probably the best known of the narrowly focused think tanks is the H R Nicholls society, established in the mid 1980s as an avowedly anti-union organisation. Its explicit aim is to "support the reform of Australian industrial relations with the aim of promoting… the right of individuals to freely contract for the supply and engagement of their labour" (H R Nicholls 2003) and its extensive publication agenda reflects this. The H R Nicholls Society's purpose is so avowedly policy-focused and ideologically driven that it sits somewhat awkwardly between lobby groups and think tanks, having many characteristics of both.

Think tank board members came from positions of power on corporate boards and state boards. For example on the board of the CIS were leading members of the corporate class: Robert Champion de Crespigny, (Chairman of Normandy Poseidon Ltd a major gold producer, who later led leading the push for an Australian nuclear power industry), Marco Belgiorno-Zegna (director of Transfields Corp. and personally credited with a $80 million fortune by the financial magazine *BRW*, on its 2002 'Rich 200 List', Donald Morley (a long-time finance director at Western Mining) and M. John Phillips, also a WMC board member and a former deputy governor of the Reserve Bank. Richard Charlton, ex-Shell Oil CEO and presently a Coles Myer director is on the CIS board. Carnavon Petroleum's Michael Darling has also been also on the CIS board. Hugh Morgan (WMC CEO), another key advocate for nuclear power, was ubiquitous as the "primary contender for the title of the ideological father of the New Right" (Da Silva, 1996: 6), and was also on the board of a number of think tanks. Morgan was a member of the IPA board from 1981, was on the board of the Liberal Party's private company Vapold Pty for over ten years, and was a one third shareholder of the Cormack Trust Foundation, which donated $800,000 to the Liberal Party. Morgan is a founding member of the H R Nicholls Society. Other examples of class ties are those shown in the Tasman Institute's backing by businessmen such as the late Richard Pratt, Rupert Murdoch, Will Bailey, Hugh Morgan and Ballieu Myer (BRW 2002; Da Silva, 2002). Through these ties, the consistency between the agenda of the think tanks and their class sponsors is ensured.

The major think tanks, but especially the IPA and HR Nicholls Society, aligned themselves strongly with the WorkChoices agenda. Indeed, one of the major embarrassments for the Howard government occurred when a senior minister proclaimed to what he thought was a closed meeting of the HR Nicholls Society that there was still more to be done in the area of workplace reform (Workplace Express, 2006). Although after that government's defeat they expended resources arguing against Labor's 'Fair Work' regime, several (most notably the IPA) have redirected their efforts to derailing the Rudd Labor government's climate change policies.

VII. Conclusion

One of the pillars of economic liberal ideology is the doctrine of individualism, and in many countries the rise of market-based policies has been sometimes excused as an almost unavoidable consequence of the rise of individualism in western societies. It has been particularly potent in justifying policies that undermine collectivism and promote non-union arrangements and, in Australia's case, individual contracting. Australia is an important case study because in the recent decade it was the country with the most radical policy shift towards individual contracting of any developed country, and one where the government and employers directed enormous resources towards promoting acceptance of individualistic policies and rhetoric and attacking those who dissented.

Yet in that country, the reasons for the decollectivisation of employment relations prior to 2007 cannot be found in the changing ideologies of workers. Australians showed no major shift towards individualistic ideology. They continued to exhibit a combination of collectivist and individualistic attitudes and behaviours. Indeed, Australian workers showed scepticism about the benefits of market liberalism in general.

To understand the reasons for transformation of the regulation of work we instead must focus on wider developments in elite ideology and behaviour. A key to understanding the transmission of these ideas is the network links that members of the capitalist class had through interlocking directorates, executive mobility, lobby groups and think tanks, and the role that the latter bodies play in shaping the ideologies accepted by commentators, editorialists, and governments. An example was the anti-collectivist strategy that started in the metalliferous mining sector with CRA/Rio Tinto and spread to many other large corporations. Rio Tinto and its lawyers in turn helped shape the WorkChoices legislation.

The revolution in workplace regulation – epitomised in 2006 by WorkChoices – was an adaptation to the re-creation of elite ideology, not of popular ideology. As a result, it was a highly disputed arena at the workplace and in the body politic, the semantic irony of 'work choices' arousing so much ire that for a while the term WorkChoices was dropped from all official lexicon. So contested was this terrain that it cost the party that was legislatively promoting individualisation its position at the reins of government. Now in Opposition, the conservative parties have found themselves in a difficult position, simultaneously denouncing WorkChoices and supporting the abolition of AWAs, while proposing their return under a different guise if re-elected. The compromise represented by Labor's 'Forward with Fairness' seems likely to provide the basis for a more stable and consensual framework for industrial relations policy over coming years. The fate of WorkChoices and the government that begat it has demonstrated the folly of those who would believe their own rhetoric about the individualisation of society. What seemed like a rock-solid foundation for the restructuring of work and society turned out to be built on shifting sands. Yet for the conservative parties, major business lobbyists such as the BCA and quasi-lobbyists like the IPA, the doctrine of individualism (and antipathy to unionism) is so deeply embedded that it is difficult to imagine them stepping away from it.

The success of the campaign against the individualisation of employment relations shows that, despite a halving of union density over two decades, the labour movement still has enormous mobilising potential that can exceed that of the state and corporate lobbyists. It has, as yet, failed to articulate a broader, effective alternative to the general economic liberal model. There is no doubt that the ideology of economic liberalism has been fundamentally undermined by the failures so starkly exposed through the global financial crisis. Yet in the absence of consensus amongst over a viable alternative, its ideas continue to underpin much of policy-making. Mobilising *against* individualisation is one thing; but mobilising *for* an alternative vision of economy and society, and developing something resembling a consensus around that, is quite another.

References

Abercrombie, N., Hill, S. and Turner, B. S., *Dictionary of Sociology*, London, Penguin, 1984.

Argy, F., *Australia at the CrossRoads: Radical Free Market or a Progressive Liberalism*, Sydney, Allen and Unwin, 1998.

Aitkin, D., *Stability and Change in Australian Politics*, Canberra, ANU Press, 1982.

Australian Bureau of Statistics (ABS), *Employee Earnings and Hours, Australia, May 2008*, Canberra, Cat No. 6306.0, 2009.

Australian Election Study (AES), User's guide for the machine-readable data file, Australian Social Science Data Archive, Australian National University, 2002, http: //assda.anu.edu.au/codebooks/aes2001/contents.html.

Australian Survey of Social Attitudes (ASSA), on-line computer file, ACSPRI Centre for Social Research, Australian National University, Canberra, 2003 <http: //assda224–110.anu. edu.au/nesstarlight/index.jsp>

Bearfield, S., "Australian Employees' Attitudes Towards Unions", Working Paper No. 82, ACIRRT, University of Sydney, March, 2003.

Beck, U., *Risk society: towards a new modernity*, London, Sage, 1992.

Brown, W. A., S. Deakin, M. Hudson, C. Pratten, and P. Ryan, *The Individualisation of Employment Contracts in Britain*, Employment Relations Research Series No. 4, Department of Trade and Industry, London, 1998.

Buchanan, J. 'Values, research and industrial relations policy: recent controversies and implications for the future', *Dialogue*, Speech to NTEU, UWA forum on academic Freedom Forum, 22 November, 2007.

Business Council of Australia (BCA), Enterprise-based Based Bargaining Units: A Better Way Of Working, BCA, Melbourne, Part 1, 1989.

Business Review Weekly (BRW), Rich 200 List, http: //brw.com.au/businesslists/businesslists.asp, 2002.

Cahill, D., "Funding the Ideological Struggle", *Overlander*, No. 168, 2002, pp. 21-26.

Crisp, L. F., *Australian National Government*, Melbourne, Longman, 1973.

Coghill, K. (ed.), *The New Right's Australian Fantasy*, Ringwood, Penguin, 1987.

Connell, R. W., *Ruling Class, Ruling Culture*, Cambridge, Cambridge University Press, 1977.

Coorey, P. & Davis, M., "Qantas joins war on Labor over AWAs", *Sydney Morning Herald*, 18 May 2007.

Da Silva, W., "The New Social Focus", *The Australian Financial Review Magazine*, June, 1996, pp. 18-28.

Da Silva, W., "Signal Drivers", *Australian Financial Review Magazine*, 22 June 2002, pp. 23-28.

Essential Media Communications, "Memo: ACTU Research Findings", mimeo, EMC, Melbourne, 26 March 2007.

Essential Research, "National Opinion Poll: Summary Report", conducted for Australian Council of Trade Unions, Melbourne, July 2007.

Frenkel, S. J. and Peetz, D., "Enterprise Bargaining: The BCA's Report on Industrial Relations Reform", *Journal of Industrial Relations*, 32(1), March, 1990, pp. 69-99.

Gailey, G., "Annual Review: many connections, one focus", *Business Council of Australia*,elbourne, acc 24/3/10, http://www.bca.com.au/content/100825.aspx, 2009.

Geare, A. J., "Do Bosses Still Love the Closed Shop?", *Employee Relations*, 12(6), 1990, pp. 17-23.

Gluyas, R., "Utopian Agendas", *The Australian*, January 22, 1999, p. 32.

Grattan, M., "The Dirty Trail of a Think Tank Grant", *Australian Financial Review*, April 21, 1997, pp. 25-31.

Hearn MacKinnon, B., *Behind WorkChoices: How one Company Changed Australia's Industrial Relations*, Melbourne, Heidelberg Press, 2007.

Herd, B., "The Left's Failure to Counter Economic Rationalism in Australia: Classical Economists Legacy to Government, Bureaucracy, Think Tank and the Union Movement", thesis, Doctorate of Philosophy, Griffith University, 1999.

Higley, J., Deacon, D. and Smart, D., *Elites in Australia*, London, Routledge, 1979.

Hilmer, F., Angwin, M., Layt, J. E., Dudley, G., Barratt, P. & McLaughlin, P. A., *Working Relations: A Fresh Start for Australian Enterprises*, Melbourne, Employee Relations Study Commission, Business Council of Australia, 1993.

Howard, J., "Workplace Relations Reform: The next logical step", Address to the Sydney Institute, Sydney, 11 July 2005.

H.R. Nicolls Society, "Application Form and Aims", 1998, http: //venue.exhibit.com.au/~nicolls/introthl.htm.

Hywood, G., "BCA Needs New Energy" Editorial *Australian Financial Review*, February 13, 1997, p. 14.

Lindsay, G., "Greg Lindsay Speaks Out about the Early CIS", interviewed by Andrew Norton, *Policy*, Winter, 1996, also http: //www.cis.org.au/glint.htm.

Lyons, M., "Industrial Relations Policy, Polled Opinion and the Howard Government", in Barnes, A., Balnave, N. & Lafferty, G. (eds.), *Work in Progress: Crises, Choices and Continuity. Proceedings of the 24th AIRAANZ Conference*, Sydney, Association of Industrial Relations Academics of Australia and New Zealand [CD], 2010.

Marsh, I., The Development and Impact of Australia's 'Think tanks', *Australian Journal of Management*, December, 1994, pp. 177-20.

Marx, K and Engels, F., *Selected Correspondence*, London, Lawrence and Wishart, 1965.

Marx, K and Engels, F., *Collected Works*, London, Lawrence and Wishart, 1975.

McAllister, I and Clark, J., *Trends in Australian Political Opinion: Results from the Australian Election Study, 1987-2007*, Australian Social Science Data Archive, Australian National University, Canberra, 2008.

Muir, K., *Worth fighting for: Inside the Your Rights at Work Campaign*, Sydney, University of NSW Press, 2008.

Murray, G., "Interlocking Directorates: What do they tell us about Corporate Power in Australia?", *Journal of Australian Political Economy*, June, No. 47, 2001, pp. 5-27.

Murray, G., *Capitalist Networks and Social Power in Australia and New Zealand*, Aldershot, Ashgate, 2006.

Newspoll, National telephone survey of 1200 adults, 14-16 January, Sydney, 2000, http: //newspoll.com.au/image_uploads/cgi-lib.13778.1.0101quality_of_life.pdf.

Newspoll, National telephone survey, 12-14 August, Sydney, 2005, http: //newspoll.com.au/cgi-bin/polling/display_poll_data.pl.

Newspoll, "Newspoll Polling for ACTU Congress 2003", ACTU, Melbourne, 2003, www.actu.asn.au/public/news/files/newspoll.pdf.

Niland, J and Turner, D., *Control, Consensus or Chaos? Managers and Industrial Relations Reform*, George Allen and Unwin/Industrial Relations Research Centre (University of New South Wales), Sydney, 1985.

Nira World Directory of Think tanks (1996) http: //www.nira.go.jp/ice/tt-info/nwdtt96/1050.html.

Pearson, N., Fifth Annual Hawke Lecture, Adelaide, 3 November, 2002, www.capeyorkpartnerships.com.

Peetz, D., "Decollectivist Strategies in Oceania", *Relations Industrielles/Industrial Relations*, 57(2), 2002a, p. 252-281, Printemps/Spring.

Peetz, D., "Sympathy for the Devil? Attitudes to Australian Unions", *Australian Journal of Political Science*, 37(1), March 2002, 2002b, p. 57-80.

Peetz, D., "Are Individualistic Attitudes Killing Collectivism?", *Transfer*, 16, 2010.

Pusey, M., *Economic Rationalism in Canberra: a Nation-building State changes its Mind*, Cambridge University Press, Melbourne, 1992.

Quiggin, J., *Zombie Economics*, Princeton University Press, New Jersey, 2010.

Readings, B., *The University in Ruins*, Cambridge, Mass., 1996.

Robertson, J., 'State of the Union', *Workers Online* <http://workers.labor.net.au/features/200504/b_tradeunion_auspoll.html.>, April, 2005.

Roy Morgan Research Centre, "Almost Three-Quarters of Electors Believe Jobs More Important Than Reducing Tariffs", Finding No. 3021, Melbourne, 23 September, 1997.

Roy Morgan Research Centre, "Most Australians Favour Import Quotas", Finding No. 3210, Melbourne, 27 July, 1999.

Roy Morgan Research Centre, "Opinions Unchanged After Massive Publicity and Debate On Industrial Relations Reforms – Only 10% Say They'll Be Better Off", Finding No. 3909, Melbourne, 18 October 2005.

Rudd, K., "The Global Financial Crisis", *The Monthly*, February, 42, 2009 http://www.themonthly.com.au/monthly-essays-kevin-rudd-global-financial-crisis--1421 (acc 1.4.2010).

Smith, A., *An Inquiry in to the Nature and Causes of the Wealth of Nations, Wakefield*, London, 1776.

Spillane, R., "Attitudes of Business Executives and Union Leaders to Industrial Relations: 23 Years Later", *Journal of Industrial Relations*, 22(3), September, 1980, p. 317-25.

Steel, S. "More on that leaked Qld polling", *Pollytics*, Crikey, Melbourne, acc 25/3/10, http://blogs.crikey.com.au/pollytics/2010/03/15/more-on-that-leaked-qld-polling/#more-7380, 15 March 2010.

Stilwell, F., *Political Economy: the contest of Economic Ideas*, Oxford University Press, South Melbourne, 2002.

Waring, P., "The Rise of Individualism in Australian Industrial Relations", *New Zealand Journal of Industrial Relations*, 24(3), 1999, p. 291-318.

Willmott, H., "Strength is ignorance; slavery is freedom: Managing culture in modern organizations", *Journal of Management Studies*, 30(4), 1993, p. 515-552.

Workplace Express, "Howard Government should seek mandate for third wave, says Minchin", *Workplace Express*, Sydney, acc 8/3/06, http://www.workplaceexpress.com.au/nl06_news_selected.php?selkey=31206, 4 March, 2006.

Public Sectors Becoming a Flexible Labour World

Consequences for the Employees

Kerstin WÜSTNER

Professor in Psychology – Berlin School of Economics

The Flexible Labour World

Numerous authors agree that the labour world has become increasingly flexible. This is partly due to globalisation, technological progress, socio-demographic changes and changes in value patterns. Indications of the flexible labour world are to be found, among others, in the increasing number of non-permanent employments, of part-time workers, or of outsourcing and downsizing (European Commission, 1998, 2000).

The change of the work system does not only affect the private sector, but also the public one. In particular, the so-called "new public management" calls for more flexible structures in public administrations, etc. (Bogumil, 2001; Hood, 1991; Barzelay & Füchtner, 2003; Davidson, 2002; Durant & Wilson, 2001; Osborne & Gaebler, 1992). In general, certain recurring social representations (Moscovici, 2001) are observed in the underlying discussion (see figure 1).

Figure 1: Recurring social representations concerning new public management

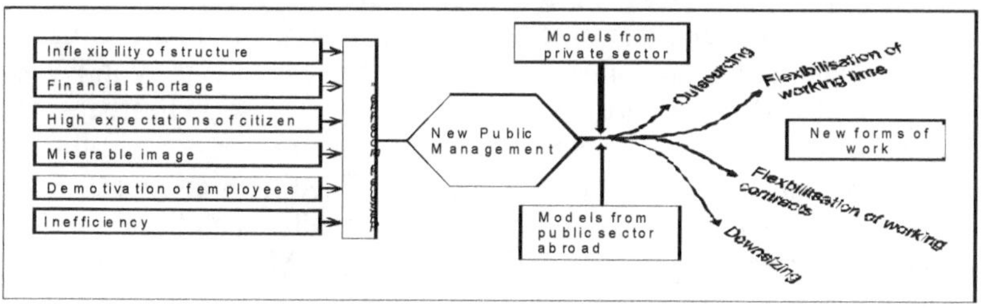

The public sector is said to be characterized by the inflexibility of its structure, demotivated employees and inefficient procedures. It has to cope with financial shortages and live up to citizens' increasing expectations. Further, it is said to have a miserable image. Due to this, the pressure rises to modernize this "antiquated" type of organisation. When trying to determine exactly how the changes should be carried out, supporters of new public management refer to models derived from the private sector and from public organisations abroad. Some of these important "new" strategies are the flexibilisation of working contracts (more and more employees should get short-term and/or part-time contracts), or outsourcing and downsizing (see also European Commission, 1998, 2000). The underlying aim is to become lean, concentrated on main tasks and to employ only the strictly necessary number of staff.

Although this argumentation seems to persist, it might present more social representations than reality as, to our knowledge, there are no representative data verifying all the stated suppositions. For example, it is questionable whether people working in public organisations are truly less motivated than their counterparts in the private sector, or whether the practised structures are more inflexible than those in a private organisation of the same size.

Irrespective of this, the public sector seems to develop further in the direction of private organisations. Hence, one could argue that the differences between both forms of organisations have become appreciably marginal. Both try to become as flexible as possible.

The question interesting us, is what this means to employees. First of all, we shall refer to the mentioned new forms of work and consult empirical studies. What are the consequences of non-permanent jobs, of part-time employment, outsourcing or downsizing? In this section we shall include studies conducted in the private and public sectors. In a next step, we shall turn to our case study where possible consequences are analyzed in a German city council.

Consequences of Non-permanent Jobs

Several studies analyze the effects non-permanent employment could have on employees. For example, van Dyne and Ang describe how employees with fixed-term contracts show weaker organisational citizenship behaviour than their colleagues with indefinite contracts (Van Dyne & Ang, 1998). Other authors reach converse results, e.g. Feather and Rauter (2004) or Parker *et al.* (2002), who found stronger organisational citizenship behaviour among employees with fixed-term contracts. It is possible that people with fixed-term contracts exhibit such behaviour or attitudes in order to get a permanent position. More consistent are results of other studies setting forth the higher exposition to hazardous sources and increased health problems of employees with fixed-term contracts (Letourneux, 1997; Platt, 1997; Benach & Benavides, 1999;

Goudswaard & Andries, 2002). This is (partly) confirmed by data of the European Foundation for the Improvement of Working and Living Conditions (2002):

Figure 2: Working contract and expositions (in%)

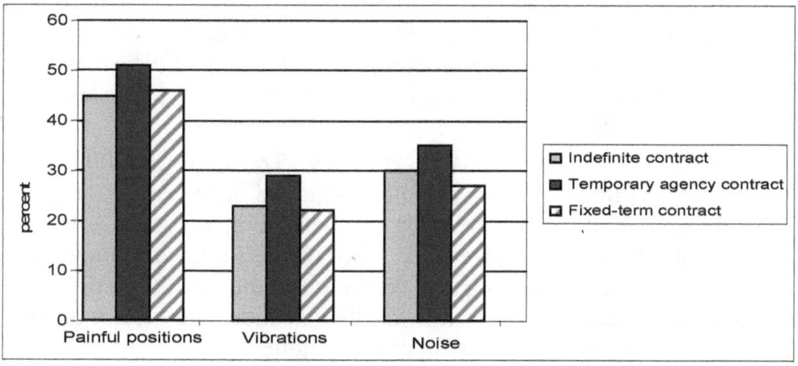

The figure above shows that employees with indefinite contracts are the ones with the lowest level of painful working positions. The group with the worst working conditions holds a temporary agency contract. Employees with a fixed-term contract have almost the same working conditions as their colleagues with permanent contracts. In the case of vibrations and noise, they are even less exposed.

When examining time pressure, monotony and control, the three groups differ once again (European Foundation for the Improvement of Working and Living Conditions, 2002):

Figure 3: Working contract and expositions (in%)

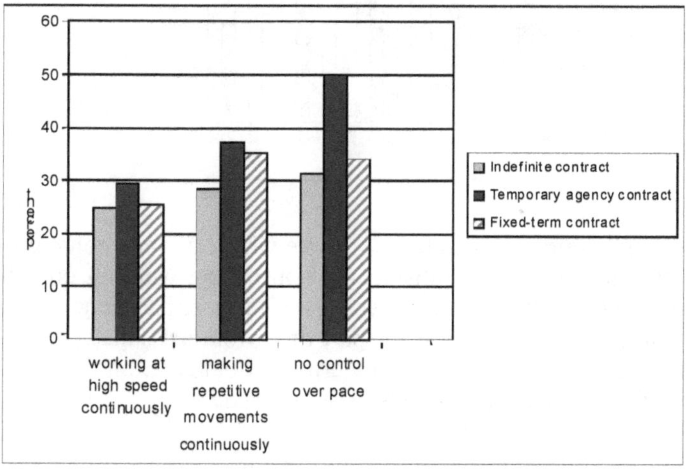

Working Conditions, 2002). This is especially the case for German workers. This hints at the fact that the flexibilisation of working hours serves organisational interests more than it represents individual autonomy.

Certain studies demonstrate that a lot of full-time employees would prefer to work fewer hours (National Study of the Changing Workforce, Bond; Galinsky & Schanberg, 1998), while people with part-time contracts would like to work more (Fagan, 2001; Lilja, 2001). Hence, it is important whether part-time workers voluntarily work fewer hours or not (Keil *et al.*, 2000).

On the basis of his meta-analytical review, Thorsteinson (2003) concludes that full-time workers are more satisfied with pay, interaction with colleagues and work contents. Also, their job involvement is higher than that of part-time employees. A study of the European Foundation for the Improvement of Living and Working Conditions (2003) differentiates between work status and time on the one side, and certain dimensions of work experience on the other side (figure 4).

Figure 4: Working contract and time – and work experience (in%)

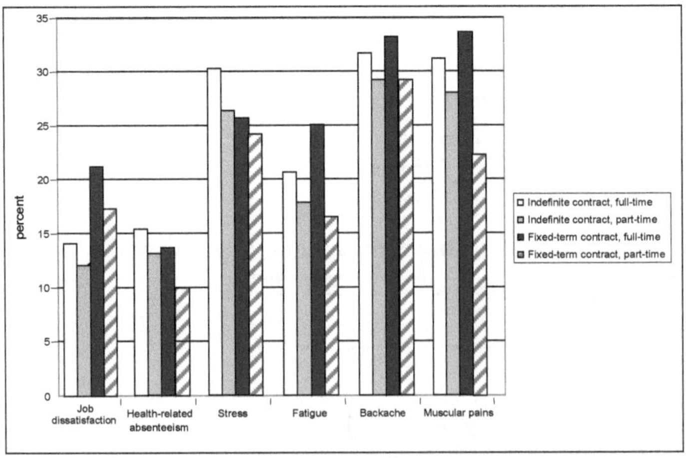

We can therefore conclude that people with indefinite contracts have a significantly higher job satisfaction than people working on a fixed-term contract. Health-related absenteeism, fatigue, backache, and muscular pains are always lowest for part-time workers. Thus, people who have a reduced working contract in terms of hours are, on the one hand, less satisfied but, on the other, also less strained.

Consequences of Outsourcing

Only a few studies analyze the effects of outsourcing empirically. This might be partly due to methodological problems. Some organisations might be reluctant to ask for their employees' opinions after outsourcing was undertaken. If they do consent to carry out a survey, only those who "survived" outsourcing are questioned. There are more difficulties to ask "victims" of outsourcing procedures about their opinions. One study in a public organisation by Nelson and others (1995) examines the long-term effects of outsourcing. The authors conclude that job satisfaction was reduced and that psychological problems (e.g. depression, anxieties, and lower self-esteem) were higher or had become worse. Kennedy and others (2002) reach similar conclusions. Negative effects could be observed (lower job satisfaction, stronger wish to leave the organisation) even if people did not lose their jobs, but were "only" asked to work in a different organisational unit.

Consequences of Downsizing

Downsizing seems to have become one of the – if not *the* – most important strategy for an organisation wishing to become more "flexible". If the number of orders has decreased, if new technological devices are implemented, a certain number of employees is labelled as being "dispensable". Therefore, organisations try to get rid of the superfluous group by either dismissing them or by resorting to so-called "natural fluctuation". Most empirical studies on downsizing show up negative effects on the "surviving" employees. For example, according to Dougherty and Bowman (1995), entrepreneurial networking dissolves and innovation potentials dwindle away. People who observe downsizing going on in their organisation lose confidence and become risk averse (Bommer & Jalajas, 1999). They develop more health problems, which in turn leads to higher absenteeism (Kivimäki *et al.*, 2000). Littler (2000) compared post-downsizing human resource outcomes in three countries (figures 5 and 6).

In all three countries, employees' morale, motivation and organisational commitment, as well as perceived promotional opportunities, declined after downsizing – in Australia and South Africa a lot more than in New Zealand, where downsizing does seem to be accompanied by as many negative effects. Looking at the development of job dissatisfaction and concern regarding job security, results are even more alarming:

Figure 5: Post-downsizing human resource outcomes in three countries I (1993-1996, n=1,703, Littler, 2000)

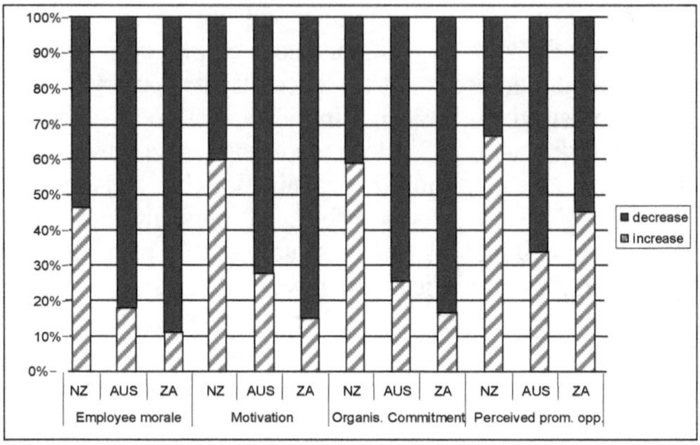

Figure 6: Post-downsizing human resource outcomes in three countries II (1993-1996, n=1,703, Littler, 2000)

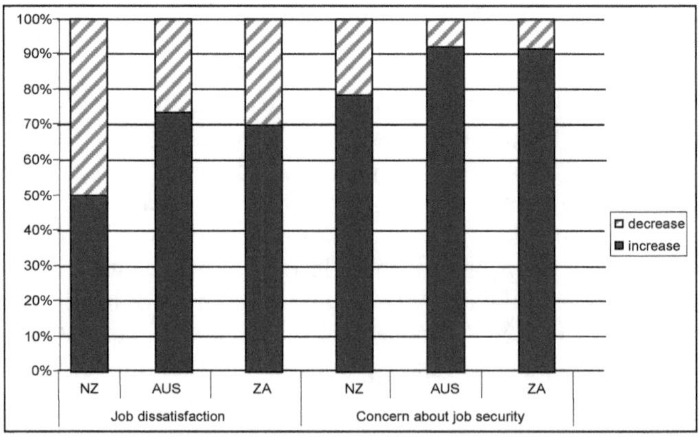

In Australia and South Africa especially, employees become a lot more dissatisfied with their jobs and employees of all three countries develop concerns about job security.

Returning to our central question of the consequences a flexible labour world could have for employees, we can conclude:

- People with indefinite contracts have better working conditions, experience less time pressure and monotony, and have more control over pace. However, if only permanent and fixed-term employees are compared (i.e. if temporary agency workers are left out) the differences are not very big.

- Having a part-time job is accompanied by lower job satisfaction, but also by fewer health problems.
- Outsourcing and downsizing clearly have negative effects on the survivors' work experience.

The mentioned studies were conducted in different countries and based on organisations of either the public or the private sector. In the following section we shall turn to our case study, which narrows the perspective to one organisation of the German public sector.

Case Study: a City Council as a Flexible Labour Environment – Consequences for the Employees

The public sector is still a very important part of the German economy. About 4.7 million employees work in the public sector. Several organisational changes have been taking place for some years. They include a tendency to make public organisations flexible, by offering more and more fixed-term contracts, part-time contracts, outsourcing and downsizing.

The Organisation: a City Council

The city council where we carried out our study occupies around 5,000 employees. It is structured in several departments and includes, for example, refuse disposal, a slaughter-house, a botanical garden, public baths, public homes for the elderly, public day-care centres for children, public schools, theatres, museums, traffic control, a registry office and so on. Several attempts had already been made to modernise and reorganise the city council over previous years, including, for example, outsourcing, downsizing and restructuring.

In relation with reorganisation attempts, several surveys were carried out and project groups were implemented to figure out how structures and processes could best be changed. All in all, this process dragged on over a time span of about four years. Many employees had been enthusiastically engaged. Yet, not much happened afterwards: changes concerned minor issues and only a very few of the elaborated ideas were implemented, leading to extreme dissatisfaction and frustration. After the Burgomaster changed, the new one made another attempt to introduce reforms. One aspect of this reform, besides many others, was to ask employees about their opinions.

Questionnaire

The survey used in this study was developed over a time period of two years. For the two previous projects, the questionnaire had been constructed to ask employees in general about working conditions and experience, so it did not take into consideration the public sector's special working conditions. Before starting our project in the city council, we carried out 13 qualitative interviews to ensure that the questionnaire covered all the a public administration's important aspects as well as the specificities of a public administration. The questionnaire's final version consists of 12 pages and 208 items. For the greater part, we used a six-point scale, with 1 for "not at all" and 6 "very strong", for example.

Response Rate

All in all, 2,395 people returned their questionnaire, corresponding to a response rate of 48%. Yet, we needed to exclude those questionnaires with too many missing values. The final data set consists of 2,294 questionnaires, or a response rate of 46%. The response rate needs to be seen with respect to the organisation's history mentioned before: It is highly likely that some employees did not feel like participating in our survey because of their experiences with the previous actions. Only about every fourth blue-collar worker took part in the study. The low response rate could be due to the relatively high number of workers whose mother tongue is not German and who might therefore have been overwhelmed by the questionnaire. The response rate of white-collar workers and public servants is almost identical (around 50%). With reference to the departments, the response rate differed a lot. For example, it was highest for the department of general administration (72%), and lowest for the department of cultural affairs, where only every fourth person took part in the study.

Respondents

Of the total, 1,248 respondents are female (55%) and 1,022 male (45%); the missing ones did not state their sex. The age of the respondents is as follows: 8% are younger than 25 years, 34% are between 26 and 40 years, 45% are between 41 and 55 years and 13% are older than 55 years. 61% are married, a further 19% have a steady partner and 13% are single. 60% have children, 5% are single parents.

97.5% of the respondents are German, 0.8% hail from another European Union country and 1.7% are of another nationality.

6.4% are disabled.

17% are blue-collar workers, 52% white-collar workers, 28% are civil servants. 20% are executives – while 4% (n = 85) do not know whether they are executives or not.

6% do not have any kind of educational certificate (yet), 26% have a degree from a secondary modern school (Hauptschule), 33% have a degree from a secondary school (Realschule), and 9% have some kind of "Abitur" degree. 26% of the interviewees hold university degrees.

About 36% of our sample are administrative officers, 12% are teachers, 9% work in a day-care centre for children, 8% are technicians or engineers, a further 8% are indoor workers (e.g. cleaning personnel), 6% are outdoor workers (e.g. refuse workers, street cleaners, gardeners), 6% are health-care personnel for the elderly, 3% are firemen and 1.5% are artists.

Finally, for our purposes, it is important to have a look at working contracts: 67.6% have a permanent contract and 24.2% a fixed-term contract (the rest did not answer this question). Furthermore, 22% work part-time, all of the others holding a full-time position.

Perceived Organisational Changes

Approximately 75% report on having some form of quality management in their department, 56% state that their organisational unit has outsourced certain tasks. About 40% explain that there are continuous reorganisation processes and implementation of new working methods and techniques. One fourth states that there are high fluctuations in their units, 43% mention downsizing. As stated before, this paper analyzes the consequences of the city council's flexibilisation for employees by focusing on the following aspects:

temporary contracts,

part-time work,

outsourcing, and

downsizing.

This leads to the last item we shall examine:

anxiety that the department is closing down.

The last aspect is something quite new for a public organisation that had been stable for so long.

Data Analysis

First of all, we made a factor analysis for each thematic block. The questions elucidating how people might experience their work resulted in five dimensions (Varimax Rotation with Kaiser-Normalisation, KMO: 0.91; factor loadings are annotated in brackets):

Box 1: Dimensions of Work Experience

Factor 1 (explained variance: 15.43%): "*Job satisfaction*"

- My tasks are interesting challenges (0.767).
- Knowledge is very important in my work (0.737).
- My work is psychologically challenging (0.734).
- I can identify with my work (0.583).
- There is no variation in my work, but only always the same routine (-0.538).
- I am assigned to tasks adequate to my qualifications (0.537).
- I am able to contribute my own ideas (0.506).
- I am satisfied with my work (0.493).
- Often, I feel underchallenged (-0.430).
- I am proud of working in this department (0.411).

Factor 2 (explained variance: 14.40%): "*Burnout*"

- More and more, I feel indifferent towards my superior (0.675).
- I do not feel like engaging much in my work (0.669).
- More and more, I feel indifferent towards my colleagues (0.663).
- Since first starting work in this job, I have realized that high ideals end in disappointment (0.602).
- My work has exhausted my feelings (0.551).
- I am satisfied with my work (-0.547).
- I am proud of working in this department (-0.515).
- More and more, I feel indifferent towards my clients (0.410).

Factor 3 (explained variance: 9.65%): "*Distress*"

- Often, I have to leave tasks unfinished, because I have not enough time (0.831).
- Often, I am under deadline pressure (0.778).
- I am not able to concentrate on important things, because I have too many unimportant things to do (0.683).
- Often, I feel overstrained (0.452).

Factor 4 (explained variance: 8.52%): "*Autonomy*"

- I can influence which tasks I have to do (0.787).
- I am free to choose the way in which I carry out my work (0.747).
- I am able to contribute my own ideas (0.583).
- I am assigned to tasks adequate to my qualifications (0.476).

Factor 5 (explained variance: 8.52%): "*Eustress*"

- When there is stress at work, I usually feel inspired (0.669).
- Often, I feel overstrained (-0.550).
- I feel full of energy (0.594).
- I feel burned out (-0.543).
- Often, I feel underchallenged (0.501).

For our analysis, we shall also cover health problems, by using an index including common cold, headache, gastrointestinal ailments, backache, cardiovascular disease, fatigue, physical exhaustion and sleeping disorders. People were asked how often they suffered from the mentioned health problems.

Work Experience – a Question of Having a Permanent Working Contract?

First of all, we shall compare employees with both permanent and non-permanent contracts with respect to their work experience (the significance of differences was checked by using t-tests):

Figure 7: Means of work experience – permanent and non-permanent contract

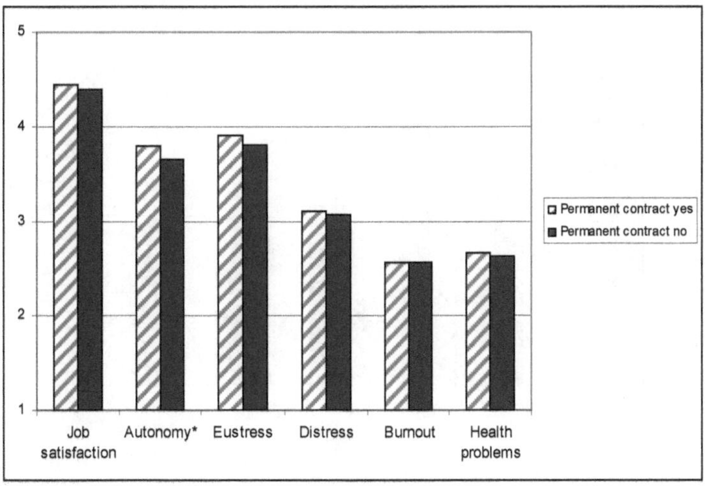

* $p \leq 0.1$

The only significant difference is that people with permanent contracts experience slightly higher autonomy than the others ($p = 0{,}051$). Employees with indefinite contracts probably bear more responsibility and hence experience more autonomy than employees who work at the city council only for a given time.

As this questionnaire did not test for organisational citizenship behaviour, the results are not comparable with the empirical studies mentioned above. Yet, with respect to health problems, those of the employees of our city council employed on a fixed-term contract do not present more health problems than their colleagues. This is different in the studies quoted above.

All in all, the work experience of both groups does not differ much. Therefore, the city council can expect that not many changes will intervene in its employees' work experience should it employ an increasing number of personnel on a non-permanent basis – at least in a short-term perspective and initially leaving out other aspects.

Work Experience – a Question of Working Hours?

The second distinction that needs to be examined concerns *part-time jobs*, which have become more established not only in the private, but also in the public sector.

Figure 8: Means of work experience – full time and part time workers

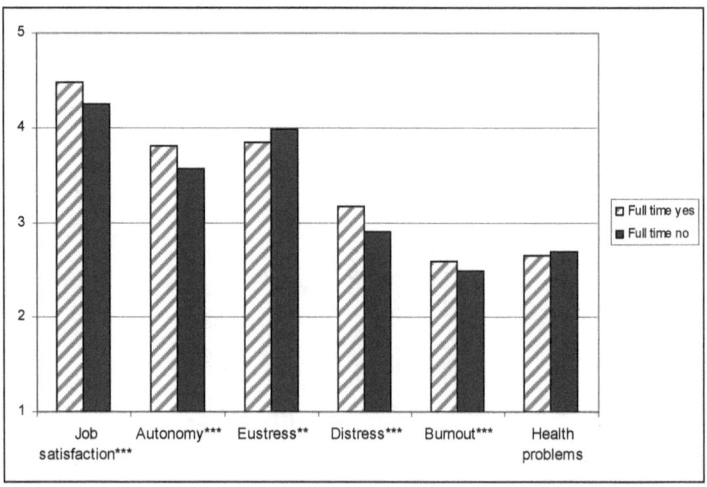

* $p \leq 0.1$, ** $p \leq 0.05$, *** $p \leq 0.01$

Differences of means are obviously not extreme, but significant: job satisfaction of full-time workers is higher than that of part-time employees. This result is commensurate with Thorsteinson's (2003) conclusions, as well as with the results of the European Foundation for the

Improvement of Living and Working Conditions (2003) quoted above. Part-time workers experience less autonomy, but are not as distressed or burnt out as full-time employees; they even experience more eustress. One specific feature needs to be mentioned: whereas other studies report more health problems among full-time workers, in our study there exists no significant difference between full- and part-time employees.

Work Experience – a Question of Outsourcing?

The third aspect we would like to analyze is whether people who watched outsourcing definitely going on in their department ($x = 6$) experience their work differently from those who did not ($x = 1$).

Figure 9: Means of work experience and outsourcing

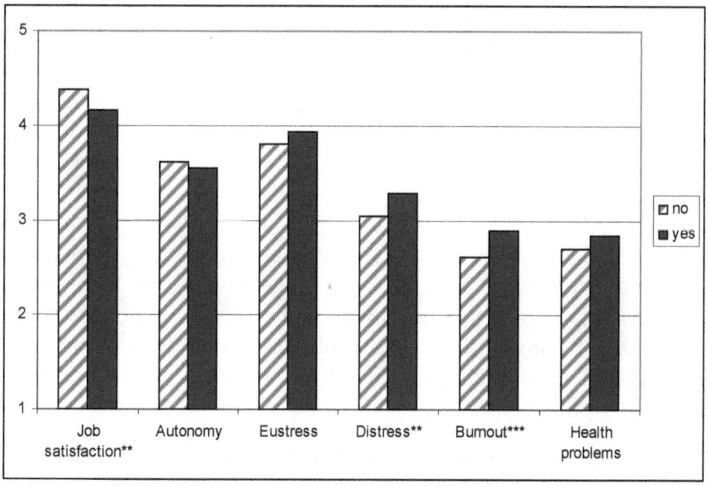

$p \leq 0.1$, ** $p \leq 0.05$, *** $p \leq 0.01$

The results present a clear tendency: employees working in departments that use outsourcing are less satisfied with their job, and feel more distressed and burnt out. This is coherent with the results presented by Nelson *et al.* (1995) or Kennedy *et al.* (2002). Interestingly, there are no significant differences regarding autonomy, eustress and health problems.

Work Experience – a Question of Continuous Downsizing?

Another question is whether employees who watch extreme continuous downsizing going on in their department experience work differently from those where the situation is stable. Again, only those groups are compared where the respondents spoke of extreme downsizing (x = 6), or where they answered "not at all" (x = 1).

Figure 10: Means of work experience and continuous downsizing

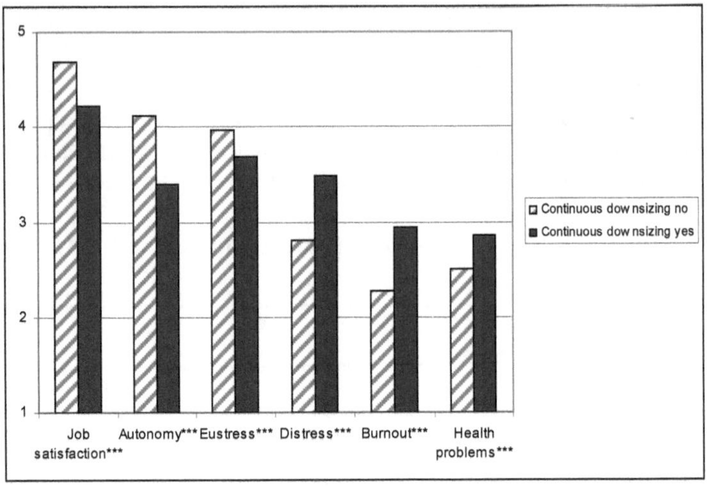

* $p \leq 0.1$, ** $p \leq 0.05$, *** $p \leq 0.01$

The differences between both groups are all highly significant and distinct: employees who observe continuous downsizing have lower job satisfaction, experience less autonomy and eustress, while also reporting more distress, burnout, and health problems. The unambiguously negative effects of downsizing on the "survivors" described above, are confirmed by our study as well.

Work Experience – a Question of Being Afraid of the Department's Closure?

The last aspect we would like to address is whether working experience is influenced by concern regarding what employees perceive to be an impending closure of the department they work in.

Figure 11: Means of work experience and anxiety of closure of department

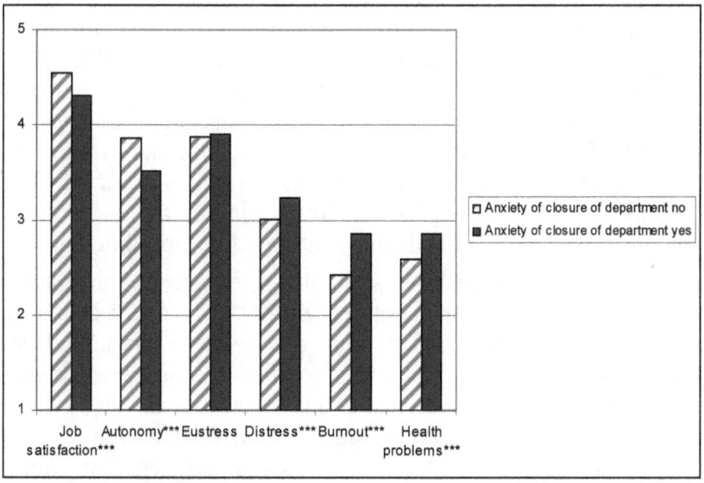

* p ≤ 0.1, ** p ≤ 0.05, *** p ≤ 0.01

If employees are afraid that their department might close (for example, due to outsourcing or reorganisation), this has an important impact on their work experiences. They are less satisfied and experience less autonomy, while distress, burnout and health problems are significantly higher. Only in the case of eustress is there a lack of significant differences.

Summary and Conclusion

If we summarize the results of our case study, it comes up to the following (table 1):

Table 1: Work experience and various organisational strategies

	Job satisfaction	Autonomy	Eu-stress	Distress	Burnout	Health problems
Temporary contract		□				
Part time	□	□	□	□	□	
Outsourcing	□			□	□	
Downsizing	□	□	□	□	□	□
Anxiety of closure	□	□		□	□	□

Job satisfaction is influenced by all organisational flexibilisation strategies in a negative way, with one exception: fixed-term contracts show no significant effect. Autonomy decreases when the aforementioned strategies are followed. Only outsourcing does not seem to be of great importance on this subject. New flexibilisation strategies appear to have the weakest effects on eustress, which is only higher for part-time workers and lower if the organisation resorts to downsizing. Distress and burnout are not higher for employees with temporary contracts and lower for part-time workers. Both dimensions are higher if outsourcing and/or downsizing are carried out and people become worried about their department's future. Health problems are only significantly higher when employees witness continuous downsizing going on around them and develop concerns that the department could be closed down.

If we focus on organisational strategies, it can be demonstrated that, in our case study, temporary contracts do not have much influence on the staff's work experience. Part-time employment has mixed consequences: lower job satisfaction and autonomy but higher eustress, and lower distress and burnout. Outsourcing is accompanied by low job satisfaction, but by high distress and burnout. Downsizing shows significant results for all dimensions and clearly has negative effects on employees.

All in all, we can conclude: if public sector organisations become increasingly flexible, work experience depends on the strategies followed by the organisation. Should the trend to "modernize" organisations by downsizing continue, severe effects can be expected on the employees' side.

As demonstrated, in terms of the tendencies they highlight, the results of our study are often comparable to those of other studies. This could also lead to the assumption that it does not matter that much whether employees of either private or public organisations are affected, nor in which countries the study was carried out. What seems to be more important is which organisational strategy an organisation implements. Yet this is only an assumption, which cannot be proved with the data at hand.

This is partly due to some of our study's limitations: Although the results presented above make sense and are coherent with other study results, the causality of flexible structures and work experience is not determined by our data. Work experience does differ in the groups which we distinguished. However, it could also be influenced by other factors. In general, work experience is a result of a complex person-environment-interaction. It is therefore possible that some of the results describe indirect effects (e.g. maybe outsourcing leads to team problems, which in turn affect work experience).

The results of our study and other empirical data are not easy to compare in detail as in each case different dimensions of work experience are analyzed by using different measures. Also, various kinds of organisations have been included in other studies.

Further to the above, the results of our case study are not representative of all city councils in Germany as, for example, the economic status of city councils in Germany differs a lot from one case to another.

Nevertheless, the study results could be used both by the city council in question for its management policy change and by researchers for further studies.

References

Barzelay, M. and Füchtner, N., "Explaining Public Management Policy Change: Germany in Comparative Perspective", in *Journal of Comparative Policy Analysis: Research and Practice*, Vol. 5, 2003, pp. 7-27.

Benach, J. and Benavides, F. G., *Precarious employment and health-related outcomes in the European Union*, European Foundation for the Improvement of Living and Working Conditions, Luxembourg, Office for Official Publications of the European Communities, 1999.

Bogumil, J., *Modernisierung lokaler Politik*, Baden-Baden, Nomos Verlagsgesellschaft, 2001.

Bommer, M. and Jalajas, D., "The threat of organisational downsizing on the innovative propensity of R&D professionals", in *R&D Management*, Vol. 29, No. 1, 1999, pp. 27-35.

Bond, J. T., Galinsky, E. and Schanberg, J. E., *The 1997 National Study of the Changing Workforce*, New York, Families and Work Institute, 1998.

Davidson, J., "Overcoming resistance to change", in *Public Management*, Vol. 84, No. 11, 2002, pp. 20-23.

Dougherty, D. and Bowman, E. H., "The Effects of Organisational Downsizing on Product Innovation", in *California Management Review*, Vol. 37, 1995, pp. 28-44.

Durant, R. F. and Wilson, L. A., "Public management, TQM, and quality improvement: Toward a contingency strategy", in *Public Administration and Public Policy*, Vol. 90, 2001, pp. 148-170.

European Commission, *New forms of work organisation. Case Studies*, Luxembourg, Office for Official Publications of the European Communities, 1998.

European Commission, *Government support programmes for new forms of work organisation*, Luxembourg, Office for Official Publications of the European Communities, 2000.

European Foundation for the Improvement of Living and Working Conditions, *Quality of Work and Employment in Europe – Issues and Challenges*, Dublin, 2002, EF/02/12/EN.

European Foundation for the Improvement of Living and Working Conditions, *Sectoral profiles of working conditions*, Dublin, 2003, EF/03/08/EN.

Fagan, C., *Gender, employment and working time preferences in Europe*, European Foundation for the Improvement of Living and Working Conditions, Luxembourg, Office for Official Publications of the European Communities, 2001.

Feather, N. T. and Rauter, K. A., "Organisational citizenship behaviours in relation to job status, job insecurity, organisational commitment and identification, job satisfaction and work values", in *Journal of Occupational and Organisational Psychology*, Vol. 77, 2004, pp. 81-94.

Goudswaard, A. and Andries, F., *Employment status and working conditions*, European Foundation for the Improvement of Living and Working Conditions, Luxembourg, Office for Official Publications of the European Communities, 2002.

Hood, C., "A Public Management for All Seasons?", in *Public Administration*, Vol. 1, 1991, pp. 3-19.

Keil, J. M. *et al.*, "Part-time nurses: The effect of work status congruency on job attitudes", in *Applied Psychology: An International Review*, Vol. 49, 2000, pp. 227-236.

Kennedy, J. F. *et al.*, "The Influence of Outsourcing on Job Satisfaction and Turnover Intentions of Technical Managers", in *HR. Human Resource Planning*, Vol. 25, No. 1, 2002, pp. 23-31.

Kivimäki, M. *et al.*, "Sickness Absence and Organisational Downsizing", in R. J. Burke and C. J. Cooper (eds.), *Organisation in crisis*, Oxford, Blackwell, 2000, pp. 78-94.

Letourneux, V., *Precarious employment and working conditions in Europe*, European Foundation for the Improvement of Living and Working Conditions, Luxembourg, Office for Official Publications of the European Communities, 1997.

Lilja, R., *Working time preferences at different phases of Life*, European Foundation for the Improvement of Living and Working Conditions, Luxembourg, Office for Official Publications of the European Communities, 2001.

Littler, C. R., "Comparing the Downsizing Experiences of Three Countries: A Restructuring Circle?", in R. J. Burke and C. J. Cooper (eds.), *Organisation in crisis*, Oxford, Blackwell, 2000, pp. 58-77.

Moscovici, S., *Social Representations*, New York, New York University Press, 2001.

Nelson, A., Cooper, C. L. and Jackson, P. R., "Uncertainty Amidst Change: The Impact of Privatisation on Employee Job Satisfaction and Well-Being", in *Journal of Occupational and Organisational Psychology*, Vol. 68, 1995, pp. 57-71.

Osborne, D. and Gaebler, T., "Reinventing Government. How the Entrepreneurial Spirit is Transforming the Public Sector", Reading, MA *et al.*, Addison-Wesley, 1992.

Parker, S. K. *et al.*, "Effect of temporary contracts on perceived work characteristics and job strain: A longitudinal study", in *Personnel Psychology*, Vol. 55, 2002, pp. 689-790.

Platt, S., *Employment and health: A literature review*, European Foundation for the Improvement of Living and Working Conditions, Luxembourg, Office for Official Publications of the European Communities, 1997.

Thorsteinson, T. J., "Job attitudes of part-time vs. full-time workers: A meta-analytic review", in *Journal of Occupational and Organisational Psychology*, Vol. 76, 2003, pp. 151-177.

Van Dyne, L. and Ang, S., "Organisational citizenship behavior of contingent workers in Singapore", in *Academy of Management Journal*, Briarcliff Manor: Dec. 1998, Vol. 41, No. 6, 1998, pp. 692-704.

Postface

Donna KESSELMAN

Labour and Employment in a Globalising World: Autonomy, collectives and political dilemmas develops the transversal concept of *globalising* as a comparative analytical tool. Contrary to the alleged era of post-nationalism prematurely decreed, in academic circles notably – see introduction by Christian Azaïs – this collection of essays provides insight into the complex and often conflicting realities of labour and employment market globalisation. It advances a South-North paradigm, yet one which challenges the pertinence of borders as its central problematical scheme. For instance, the South's incomplete welfare state intertwines with – is not distinct from – deregulating and increasingly "casualised" labour and employment markets in the North through delocalisation. In lieu of static transpositions of phenomena formerly characteristic of southern labour markets, the globalis*ing* process incorporates trends of "standardisation and differentiation which tend to converge". They become a single process when grasped in political terms, as labour and employment market interactions which a society's institutions and relations must accommodate: globalisation places, in particular, *glocal* pressures – from outside and below – upon national governments (introduction and Giraud's article).

What tends to standardize is the patent, while unequal, deconstruction of social and political frameworks set up to regulate work and institute rights. The 20th century Welfare State ideal was an axis of comparison which gave rise to various model theories and remains a reference in policy-making and research. Differentiation occurs as these institutions wither and transform. While rooted in interlocking, turbulent historical circumstance, their distinct constructions already reflected national traditions in government and labour relations, as well as cultural tints, both between and within continents, South and North. In face of globalising market pressures, these deeper-going identity traits tend to re-surface as vectors of countervailing powers, thereby revealing globalisation's contradictions and limits.

Thus the cases and concepts presented here demonstrate how financial globalisation, thought to be detached from the productive economy when perceived through the lens of redistribution but specifically targeting labour in attempts to externalize it's crisis, only accelerated underlying processes already underway. The financial collapse also demonstrated to what extent our worldview and social theory are distorted by the "hegemony" of capitalist logic and ideology such as management workplace discourse, in particular flexibility (Henning).

One generation of globalisation, then, has elicited public and institutional reactivity and left its mark upon, but not done away with, the national state. As policy and mediators restructure and renew to adapt to these evolving and conflicting pressures *Labour and Employment in a Globalising World: Autonomy, collectives and political dilemmas* sheds light upon a fundamental dimension of politics: how global market forces enter into more direct conflict with working people's daily plight in the workplace and beyond, with their historical experience and democratic bonds. Thus the interest of this book's focus on of lower-levels of mediation, emerging mesa and local, para-institutional and associative structures which are closer emanations of the what can be paraphrased as the roots of national resistance to globalisation. Its pluridisciplinary and multi-faced understanding of globalisation, based upon ground research in ten countries from South to North, as its contextualisation of labour and employment markets within political globalisation, are opposed by the authors to the reductionist economic construct of neo-liberalism – inseparable from its political agenda.

Two main political threads of standardisation and differentiation, woven within a single and converging – *globalising* – labour and employment market, are pulled here. The second, to be dealt with below, places autonomy at work within political perspective. The other interprets globalisation through the challenges it entails for the structures of representative democracy in terms of decision-making and policy implementation. The political space occupied by legislative statute and public interventionism have had to accommodate emerging regulatory paradigms, in order to carry out its governing mandate.

The Brazilian government introduced employment flexibilisation in line with neo-liberal injunctions for free trade, privatisation and market deregulation. However, historical features highlighted here show how policies of accelerated industrialisation and urbanisation towards an export-economy aggravated an already fragile labour market and crisis-ridden public sector, incapable of ensuring balanced development. "The Federal state, which had been a beacon for previous cycles in the Brazilian economy, has practically disappeared from the scene, making the private sector the prime mover in this new scenario" including relocation of companies from region to region. Economic and industrial policy decisions – and potentially labour rights – have been mediated by social partner consensus-making, granting a major role to multinational actors. This creates a new "sphere for negotiation" with government, "redefining Brazil's underdevelopment, which is now globalized" (Carleial).

The freeing-up of labour market legislation, combined with a loosening of regulatory enforcement in Brazil are common traits in most countries, at a time when increasingly casualised and precarious populations need more effective mechanisms of redistribution. As governments search for alternative protections which extend beyond the common law employment relationship – the welfare state's key redistribution instrument, the void is being filled by privatising constructions such as partnerships through the empowerment of decentralized actors, which is a feature of the globalisation era.

Thus what is true in Brazil is also true in France, though the standardising trend of decentralisation is differentially experienced, sending institutional and cultural shockwaves through its centralized social state. In response to multinational employer challenges for individualised, localised and autonomised employment relationships and the European Union Lisbon Process for a "knowledge economy", industrial dynamics, economic and social governance have been encouraged at the meso, notably regional level, in territorialized industrial zones, *poles de compétitivité*. The logic of equal treatment by national public service institutions is being transformed. Rather than reified territorial alternatives, government has incited differentiation by encouraging competition between "horizontal differentiations of localized blocks": moving, "amorphous", more or less lasting configurations of clusters of activities and/or firm networks. The territory as a "new social bargaining place" both opens up and closes off labour market opportunities, while leaving space for large corporations to exercise decisive control, given their investment capabilities (Perrat). Proximity networks imply local, contractualised relations and increased competition among workers as an expression of withering labour organisations and collective action.

Switzerland demonstrates how globalising decentralisation impacts a country whose institutions are theoretically suited to such evolutions. Yet globalisation's empowerment of local actors has resulted in interregional inequalities in the implementation of federal legislation explicitly intended to homogenize public norms and labour market practices. Weakening federal authority has allowed local governing styles, including partisan political options, to permeate and so differentiate what had been deemed as basic rights. The influence of meso-level mediators like trade unions also explain these variations which place Swiss cantons along a sort of continuum between unprecedented extremes of advantageous social protections and priority towards social control (Giraud).

The case where state intervention acts most directly as a vector of differentiation is Scandinavia. The hypothesis of converging contradictory trends makes Scandinavia an anti-intuitive case in point: the overall tendency towards decentralisation is taken here to a point of modifying the nature of social protection. In name of front-line decision-making and participation by the actors themselves, civil rights are traded off against obligations placed upon individuals by the state itself. Instead of incorporating variable mitigators, a significant number of municipal governments in Finland, Denmark and Sweden act as vehicles for globalising market individualisation through activation policies and stringent employment terms. This shift whereby personal obligations of disadvantaged job seekers become greater than the rights they can claim has occurred in conjunction with increased state scrutiny over the aid recipients' lives, jeopardising the fundamental right to privacy and equal treatment, without any genuine participation in determining their career paths (Van Aerschot).

This Scandinavian experience provides a transition as it pulls the political thread between national and institutional adjustment to globalising markets and personal responsibility, in relation to the changing role of the state. In all the national cases, from the Brazilian South to the Scandinavian North, at once geographical and social references, state interventionism does not necessarily recede but transforms through mediating configurations and social partnerships, including outside actors at multiple levels of negotiation and decision-making.

Another problematic thread which weaves through globalising labour and employment markets concerns autonomy at work. Heretofore, the trait which characterized all capitalist labour markets was the employment relationship understood in terms of subordination, whatever its common law definition and associated rights in a given country. As frontiers between dependent and independent workers are diluted, and in a parallel manner, between subordination and autonomy. The degree and content of autonomy at work may translate into opportunities for personal fulfilment or merely novel genres of flexibility and submission to market demands. *Labour and Employment in a Globalising World: Autonomy, collectives and political dilemmas* opens its pages to this essential debate. The international and interdisciplinary viewpoints of work autonomy, perceived from the standpoint of national case studies South and North as well as philosophical perspective, demonstrate how what may be a dilemma for the worker as individual takes on broader significance when analysed in political and comparative terms.

Thus autonomy at work in not equivalent to "individualisation": both concepts are complex and are component parts of radically changing workplace organisation which demand workers to assume greater responsibility. The idea is spread that it is compulsory to involve oneself in both the productive ends and their risks, and to privately and permanently ensure their competitiveness, their attractiveness and their ability to adapt to circumstantial and structural changes. But autonomy is a narrower notion with a more positive connotation than workplace performance results. It positions the individual with regards to series of actors, changing temporalities and spatial distinctions between work and non-work representations within evolving strategies of production and management. Conceptual tools must be constructed to clarify the relationship between autonomy, rationalisation and control (Dieuaide). The concept also takes account of subjective dimensions, both experienced by the worker and expected of her/him, like the mobilisation and investment of cognitive and emotional skills. This may prove to be personally rewarding, as when high skilled professionals act in a para-salarial way. In information and communication technologies (ICT) sectors, as telework in Portugal and Brazil, the need for workers' subjective mobilisation constitutes a case of conceded autonomy – autonomy is granted as a "concession" to the workers but, at the same time, it's imposed limits constrain it into an order, comparable to subordination (Rosenfield). The flexible work world applies as well, contrary to common wisdom, to the public sector in Europe. And these flexible "new public management" strategies negatively correlate with work autonomy and job satisfaction in almost all cases (Wüstner 220).

Is autonomy a new, more humanly engulfing form of Taylorist domination in capitalism or a non-Taylorism path towards the rationalisation of tasks? Are we entering a new age, a "Second Modernity" which begs for heightened workplace creativity which allows employees to "feel ownership in organisational outcomes" (Serksnyte-Sappington)? These questions and answers are conceived here in more or less political terms. Viewed from Australia – an exception to the individualising workplace when an ultra-liberal labor law was revised by the current left-wing government – global market trends are rooted in an elite ideological onslaught rather than any genuine shift of popular ideology, worker adherence to market liberalism or their markedly more individualistic attitudes or behaviours (Murray, Peetz).

Hybridisation pulls the thread of work in the opposite direction: how proactive individuals manage their labour market insertion through their own mediation of regulations, mediations and constraints. This personal "make do" approach leads them to combine various kinds of contractual, autonomous or extra-labour market strategies, tending towards "atypical" forms of salaried work. It is an almost universal labour and employment market phenomenon, inherent in so-called incomplete welfare states such as Brazil, but attainting globalising developed countries, as expressed through the introduction of the *parasubordinated* status in

Italy. In this way labour law attempts to eliminate legal *grey zones* which result from difficulties in distinguishing dependent from independent labour (Azaïs). Grey zones also correspond to a void in social protection which is of major political significance: between increasingly hybrid and atypical work situations of individuals and groups, affecting a wide variety of professions, compromise their access to social rights, traditionally linked to the common law employment relationship.

Labour and Employment in a Globalising World: Autonomy, collectives and political dilemmas develops a useful South-North paradigm and also sheds light upon comparative *North to South* dynamics. Worker welfare and regulation is being externalized to private firms in developing countries like Brazil through experiments in corporate social responsibility (CSR), imported by North American multinationals. Corporate welfare initiatives are "vehicles or privileged intermediates in relations between employers, society and the State"; they are incorporated into global business strategies, meant to provide a competitive edge and allegedly corporate accountability. The result is particularly inequitable distribution of benefits due to diverging objectives and perceptions of social responsibility among actors as differentiated as management and consumers, within markets of varying cultures and scales. Most programs are carried out through partnerships with local and regional state agencies which exclude trade unions: can it be claimed that corporate social agendas nevertheless integrate their demands? Indications are that this is not the case (Cappellin).

The book's main claim is that pulling the tread of politics helps weave the articles, each dealing with a singular but interlocking dimension of globalising labour and employment markets, into an emerging research agenda. Do welfare state deconstructions contain reconstructions of public, market-based or hybrid social protections or rather inevitable disparities and precariousness? Much work needs to be done on emerging regulatory paradigms, the varying configurations of social partnerships, associations and alliances engaged in non-classical forms of negotiating (social dialogue, consensus-based consultation). Their development is inseparable from the weakening of labour organisations and the changing relationship between the state, the market and the individual. Our own view introduces a nuance here: can federal and decentralised territorial levels be so strictly opposed within a problematical context which reasserts the centrally of the nation-state, which necessarily emanates from foundations of fundamental political consensus?

In any event, all of these factors participate in recasting the notions of work, employment and rights. This comprehensive approach takes issue with the neo-liberal conception of work as a mere social fallout of the economy. Among the prominent territorially built governance solutions studied here in several countries is the key area of skills acquisition through social-partnership training schemes: a more precise, point by point comparison would be welcome. Also, to what extent do such constructs act as mediations of parliamentary and public mandates or become outsourced decision-making centres? The notion of autonomy at work in globalising markets is a promising domain of investigation especially when linked, as it is here, to the receding common law employment relationship in favour of hybrid work situations and legal grey zones. The political voids corresponding to these grey zones and their repercussions is also a globalising market phenomenon which invites comparative perspective. Finally, in this light, are "the South" and " the North" still viable problematical frames?

As labour and employment markets standardise and differentiate, what other problematical threads can be pulled to strengthen the hypothesis that these trends converge within a single globalising process? Building upon the comparative concepts and tools proposed in this volume will help to answer these queries.

Kolibri 360 GmbH
Ferdinand-Jühlke-Straße 7
99095 Erfurt, Deutschland
produktsicherheit@kolibri360.de